Racism and Migration in Western Europe

Racism and Migration in Western Europe

edited by

JOHN WRENCH AND JOHN SOLOMOS

BERG

Oxford/Providence

First published in 1993 by

Berg Publishers Ltd

Editorial offices:
150 Cowley Road, Oxford, OX4 1JJ, UK
221 Waterman Street, Providence, RI 02906, USA

Library of Congress Cataloging-in-Publication Data
A CIP catalogue for this book is available form the Library of Congress

British Library Cataloguing in Publication Data

Racism and Migration in Western Europe
I. Wrench, John II. Solomos, John 325.4

ISBN 1 85973 007 8

Printed in the United Kingdom by WBC Book Manufacturers,
Bridgend, Mid Glamorgan.

For our parents

Contents

List of Tables   ix

Acknowledgements   x

Part I   Historical and Contemporary Perspectives   1

1   Race and Racism in Contemporary Europe
    John Solomos and John Wrench   3

2   Migrations and Minorities in Europe. Perspectives for the
    1990s: Eleven Hypotheses   *Stephen Castles*   17

3   The Articulation of Racism and Nationalism: Reflections on
    European History   *Robert Miles*   35

Part II   Tendencies and Trends   53

4   Tendencies to Racism in Europe: Does France Represent
    a Unique Case, or is it Representative of a Trend?
    Michel Wieviorka   55

5   The Ideological and Institutional Foundations of Racism in
    the Federal Republic of Germany   *Czarina Wilpert*   67

6   Rights and Racism in a New Country of Immigration:
    The Italian Case   *Ellie Vasta*   83

7   The Thorny Road to Europe: Swedish Immigrant Policy in
    Transition   *Aleksandra Ålund and Carl-Ulrik Schierup*   99

8   Political Participation and Civil Rights in Scandinavia
    Tomas Hammar   115

9   Migrant Women, Racism and the Dutch Labour Market
    Helma Lutz   129

10   The Politics of Marginal Inclusion: Racism in an
     Organisational Context   *Philomena Essed*   143

Contents

11 The Politics and Processes of Racial Discrimination in
Britain *John Wrench and John Solomos* 157

Part III Issues and Debates 177

12 Denying Racism: Elite Discourse and Racism
Teun A. van Dijk 179

13 Difference, Diversity, Differentiation: Processes of
Racialisation and Gender *Avtar Brah* 195

14 The Ideological Representation of Migrant Workers in
Europe: A Matter of Racialisation? *Jan Rath* 215

15 Unravelling Racialised Relations in the United States of
America and the United States of Europe *Stephen Small* 233

16 Research and Policy Issues in a European Perspective
Cathie Lloyd 251

Bibliography 265

Notes on Contributors 288

Index 290

List of Tables

Table 8.1 Persons elected to the municipal councils, 1979–1988   121

Table 8.2 Participation (per cent) in five local elections and in
one referendum in Sweden, 1976–1988   123

Table 9.1 Registered unemployment: difference in sex, absolute
numbers and percentage of the working population of
the group   142

Acknowledgements

One of the main lessons we have learned while working on this book is that recent debates about immigration, race and ethnicity in European societies are the outcome of complex historical and political processes. It is therefore difficult to make easy generalisations about the nature of contemporary developments or indeed to explain them. There is a need for greater dialogue between scholars and researchers if we are to make sense of the developments that are currently going on around us. This book is intended as a contribution to this process. It grew out of a conference on 'Racism and Migration in Europe in the 1990s', held in September 1991 and organised jointly by the Centre for Research in Ethnic Relations, University of Warwick, and the Public Policy Centre of the Department of Politics and Sociology, Birkbeck College, University of London. We would like to thank the Commission for Racial Equality, the Friedrich Ebert Foundation, the Anglo-German Foundation for the Study of Industrial Society, the Centre for Research in Ethnic Relations, and the Department of Politics and Sociology, Birkbeck College, who made the conference possible through their financial support.

Apart from the contributors, we would like to acknowledge the support of the other participants who gave so much to making the conference and this volume a success. We would also like to acknowledge the support of Rachel King of the Centre for Research in Ethnic Relations for her assistance in organising the conference, and for keeping us going when all seemed lost. Rose Goodwin prepared the manuscript for publication with her usual efficiency and good humour. Joanne Winning kindly helped with sorting out the bibliography. Terry Mayer provided invaluable administrative and moral support and endeavoured to sort out all the editorial problems that arise when editing a book of this kind. Our editors at Berg dealt with this project efficiently and in a supportive manner. We hope that all the people who helped us make this book possible will find that it helps us to understand at least some of the changes that are going on around us at the present time, so as to be better able to deal with the threats ahead.

JOHN WRENCH, University of Warwick
JOHN SOLOMOS, Birkbeck College

PART I

Historical and Contemporary Perspectives

Race and Racism in Contemporary Europe

John Solomos and John Wrench

Contemporary European society is in a period of rapid transformation and change. The pace and nature of change in eastern Europe since 1989 has emphasised the contingent and contradictory nature of existing social and political institutions. At the same time political and economic changes in western Europe have highlighted the need to rethink conventional ideas about the dynamics of political action and mobilisation. Given this context it has become clear that it is simply not possible to address key aspects of contemporary politics within the limits of national boundaries. Key political, economic and social issues are increasingly shaped by events and actions in 'Europe' as a whole.

Perhaps there is no more clear example of this than the subject matter of this volume, namely the changing face of immigration and racism in contemporary European societies. During the past few years this is an issue which has received widespread coverage in the media, with numerous features in the popular and serious press and programmes on television addressing key aspects of this question. At the same time an ever growing number of academic studies are addressing the need to understand both the historical background and the dynamics of contemporary developments (Hammar 1985; Layton-Henry 1990; Lloyd this volume). Writers such as Etienne Balibar have argued forcefully that we are witnessing the development of what one may call a 'European racism' that is likely to have a major impact on the political and social configuration of European societies over the next period (Balibar 1991). From a different but connected perspective, Robert Miles has argued that in the current environment

This volume grew out of a conference on 'Racism and Migration in Europe in the 1990s', held during 20–22 September 1992. It was jointly organised by the Centre for Research in Ethnic Relations, University of Warwick, and the Public Policy Centre of the Department of Politics and Sociology, Birkbeck College. The conference brought together approximately 70 speakers and participants from all over Europe, and first drafts of these and other papers were discussed by the participants.

the construction of a 'European identity' inevitably involves a pattern of the exclusion of 'the other', whether they be 'migrants', 'foreigners' or 'blacks' (Miles, this volume; see also Bovenkerk et al 1990).

In many societies in contemporary Europe, questions about migration and the position of minorities are amongst the most hotly contested areas of social and political debate. Developments in Britain, France and Germany over the past decade have highlighted the volatility of this phenomenon and the ease with which it can lead to violent conflict. During this same period there has been mounting evidence of growing racism and hostility to migrants, with neo-fascist and right-wing political parties using immigration as an issue on which they could attract support (Husbands 1991; Balibar 1991). There have also been numerous forms of policy and political intervention to deal with the social and economic position of minority communities (Castles, this volume).

In the present socio-political environment there seems no doubt then that the questions of immigration and racism are becoming key issues on the political agenda of a number of European societies, and the signs are that they will continue to be so for some time to come. Two immediate conjunctural factors are often singled out as helping to shape recent developments. First, it is argued that developments in eastern Europe and the former Soviet Union have helped to create 'fears' about the likelihood of mass immigration from the former communist states in countries as diverse as Germany, Italy and Austria. This is indeed an issue that is touched upon at a number of points in this volume, though it is not easy to draw any clear conclusions about future patterns of migration or to predict the nature of the political responses that are likely to arise (R. Cohen, 1991). Second, it is argued that the question of immigration from north Africa has become a key political issue in France and other societies. It is argued that political instability and demographic changes are likely to lead to pressures to migrate in the North African region as a whole and that this is likely to have a major impact on countries such as France and Italy.

But do such developments, in and of themselves, help us to make sense of the virulence and power of racist social and political movements? Do they help us to understand the complex debates that are going on at the present time about the position of those migrant communities that have been settled for decades in societies such as the ones we look at in this volume? What can best be done to develop policies to tackle the root causes of racism in contemporary Europe?

These are some of the key questions that the chapters in this volume address. Arising as it does from a working conference that brought together some of the main researchers working on these issues in different European societies, it can be seen as an attempt to examine this important dimension of contemporary European society, which draws together the findings of researchers working in a variety of analytical perspectives and examining specific socio-historical situations.

While it is clearly impossible in one volume to cover all dimensions of this issue, we have sought to remedy the general dearth of knowledge about this issue by providing a critical analysis of the situation in a number of key European societies. We would have liked to include more material on the emerging situation in eastern Europe and recent developments in southern Europe, and this is something which we hope other researchers will begin to address more fully. Indeed, there are signs that some are already beginning to do so (R. Cohen 1991). But taken together we believe that the chapters in this volume provide the basis for serious debate about the current situation and the prospects for the future.

In the rest of this introductory chapter we want to address some of the themes which are central to the volume as a whole by examining the historical and contemporary political trends that have led to the present situation. In the process of looking at these issues we shall also attempt to highlight questions which need to be placed on the political and research agendas of those concerned with the role and impact of racism and migration in the present political environment (see also Lloyd, this volume).

The Politics of Immigration

Debates about immigration and racism in Britain and other European societies have taken place within particular contexts of social, political and economic change which have influenced the ways in which such issues have been perceived. It is not possible to draw a direct comparison, for example, between the situation in France and Britain. The discussion in Britain about 'race' and 'race relations' is not to be found in other European societies (Bovenkerk et al. 1990; Lloyd 1991). Indeed, as a number of authors in this volume argue, there is a need to be aware of the complex processes of migration and settlement that have shaped the situation in various national political contexts.

Bearing in mind the need not to lose sight of the relevance of national political differences, it is still the case that over the past decade there are a number of trends that have had an impact on a European–wide basis. From a broader perspective the period since the 1980s has seen the emergence of:

1. New patterns of migration and settlement which have had an impact on Europe as well as other parts of the world. These new processes of migration have emphasised, according to writers such as Stephen Castles, the fact that 'the world is entering a new phase of mass population movements, in which migration to Europe and the situation of ethnic minorities in Europe can only be fully understood in a global context' (Castles, this volume).
2. A growing number of refugees and asylum seekers who have been displaced by a combination of political instability, economic and natural disasters and the threat of genocide. The extent of such displacement has helped to put the question of refugees and asylum seekers high on the political agenda of many countries in Europe and elsewhere.

These transformations have taken place at a time of uncertainty and confusion over the economic and political orientation of the 'new Europe'. Questions are being asked about what it is that we mean when we talk about the construction of a new 'European identity', and the interplay with established national and ethnic boundaries.

It is perhaps not surprising therefore that in this environment the position of ethnic and racial minorities who are already within Europe is intimately tied to the overarching issue of the politics of immigration. Rapid processes of transformation experienced by a number of societies over the past two decades, particularly in relation to the economic and social infrastructure, have provided a fertile ground for extreme right-wing parties and movements to target ethnic and racial minorities as 'enemies within' who are ultimately 'outsiders' or 'foreigners'. In Britain this has led, for example, to the racialisation of issues such as employment, housing, education and law and order (Solomos 1989). In other European societies, where the targets are not necessarily 'racialised', there is still a tendency for minorities that are defined by ethnic, cultural or religious attributes to become the target of attack from both the fringes and the mainstream of political life (Brubaker 1990).

What is also clear, however, is that this process has moved public and political debate beyond the question of immigration *per se*, with the focus moving towards the identification and resolution of specific social problems perceived as linked to ethnicity and 'race'. But the link with the immigration question is maintained at another level, because it is the size of the minority populations, whether in the schools or the unemployed queue, which is identified as the source of the problem.

Such developments have fuelled the growth of political movements that uphold racist and anti-immigrant political platforms. In this environment it seems quite clear that the issue of immigration policy cannot be seen separately from a broader set of policy agendas about the social, economic and political position of migrant communities. This is evident from recent debates about immigration in a number of west European societies, and it has long been evident in the development of public policies about the position of ethnic minority communities in British society. Indeed what is becoming even more clear is that as the migratory process has matured and new migrations have developed, policies have to address an increasing number of areas and to deal with ever more complex situations.

The question of the social and cultural implications of past and future migration is of course quite broad. But the chapters in this volume address at least some of the key questions. Among the most important are the following: What social and political initiatives are necessary to deal with the position of established minorities and migrant communities in a European context? What kind of policies could be developed to deal with the short- and long-term consequences of new patterns of immigration and settlement in the 1990s and beyond? What measures can be taken to counter racism and to develop a greater awareness of the value of a multi-ethnic society?

These are important questions and they have to be discussed in the context of contemporary debates about the future of immigration. But more importantly, however, they have to be seen in the broader frame of the changing political responses to minorities in the present political environment.

Racism in Contemporary Europe

The current resurgence of racist and extreme nationalist movements in a number of European societies is perhaps the most widely commented upon aspect of public and media debate about the 'new Europe'. While this phenomenon has not as yet become a major issue in British society, it is clear that a variety of political and social movements in both western Europe and the ex-communist societies are mobilising support with the help of symbols and ideologies which reflect a resurgence of both old-style and new forms of racism.

Racism is taking on new forms in the present political environment, and there is widespread confusion about the boundaries of national identity, and the role of cultural, religious and linguistic differences. It is important therefore that policy debate in this field does not ignore the issue of racism in its various forms.

As Robert Miles acutely observes in his contribution to this volume, it is important to move beyond descriptive accounts of racism to an explanation of the forms that racism actually takes on in contemporary societies. Indeed, he points out that perhaps what is novel about contemporary forms of racism is not the proliferation of racist social movements but an intensification of ideological and political struggle around the expression of a racism that often claims not to be a racism (see also Miles 1989).

What other recent studies show, however, is that there is no easy model that we can use to explain the power and role of new types of racism in contemporary Europe and elsewhere (see Miles 1989; Goldberg 1990). We need to be aware that simplistic notions of racism, or notions derived from one specific socio-historical context, cannot be used to explain the growing role of racist ideologies and movements in the 'new Europe'. Part of the problem is that the role of the Front National in France and similar movements in Belgium, Germany, Austria and elsewhere needs to be contextualised against the background of developments in particular national political settings *and* trends in European societies more generally. Researchers have generally not been good at combining these two levels of analysis and ensuring that they explain as well as describe the development of new forms of racism.

But perhaps the most glaring absence is the lack of serious debate about the best ways to tackle the growth of racism and the articulation of appropriate anti-racist initiatives. This is certainly a difficult aspect of policy in this field, as we can see by the confused and conflicting accounts of anti-racism that are found in current political debates in Britain (Donald and Rattansi 1992). But in the present political context it is impossible to ignore the urgency of measures to tackle the growth of racism, and the need to develop initiatives to promote an image of Europe which challenges the narrowness of the visions articulated by racist movements and parties.

Racism and the Underclass Debate

One of the points of reference in debates about racism is the situation in the United States of America. As Stephen Small argues in this volume, there are some interesting similarities as well as differences when we begin to compare the situation in the USA and Europe closely. One example, which has gained increasing relevance in the aftermath of the political debates about the 1992 Los Angeles riots, is the question of the 'underclass'.

In the USA references in public debate and the media to the 'underclass' have become so commonplace that 'the concept has virtually become a household term within the past five years alone' (Heisler 1991: 455). The concept, first used by Myrdal (1962), has come to signify a segment of people at the bottom of or beneath the class structure, permanently removed from the labour market, with no power or stake in the economic system. More specifically, in the USA the term has come to represent the black urban poor.

The underclass debate has recently been discussed in the UK and broader European context (Rex 1987; Policy Studies Institute 1992). In particular this has been stimulated by recent economic and social developments in Europe: economic stagnation and recession, deindustrialisation, high unemployment, welfare state contraction and new ethnically and racially distinct migrant populations (Heisler 1991: 457). However, Heisler is not convinced that the concept of underclass is transferable to immigrants in advanced industrial European countries, even though they do occupy low socio-economic positions. For one thing, European immigrants come from a tradition of above-average participation in the labour market, albeit in inferior employment, and they are not completely disconnected from mainstream social institutions, often creating their own social and political organisations. Welfare dependency is not the norm, and they are not generally characterised by 'hopelessness' (Heisler 1991: 470–1). It is true that the isolation and alienation of second- and third-generation descendants of migrants in Europe have been increasing, particularly with the growth in unemployment. Heisler sees ethnic minority youth in the UK as particularly disaffected and marginalised, yet she also points out that youth disaffection and marginalisation have been high overall in the UK (Heisler 1991: 474–5). The rioting and violent unrest on white working-class housing estates in Britain in the early 1990s shows that alienated and disaffected youth are not only found in black communities.

Heisler concludes: 'Whether the emergence of an underclass is a strictly American phenomenon or an emergent characteristic shared by all advanced industrial societies is an empirical question that can only be fully addressed by systematic comparative research' (1991: 475). Similarly the question of the extent to which ethnic minority descendants of post-war migrants in Europe will figure in such a concept is still open. Nevertheless, even if the concept of underclass is not yet transferable to Europe, the academic and political debates surrounding the concept certainly are, and parallels to these are also found in the European context in debates on ethnic minorities and migrants.

In the USA there have been contrasting lines of explanation regarding the emergence of a black underclass and the related social policies. Three major ideological positions are described by Weir (1993) as follows:

1. An emphasis on racial discrimination as the main cause. The underclass is seen as a result of the abandonment of the liberal agenda of the 1960s. Racial barriers permeate society, and discrimination is making the situation worse. Vigorous equal opportunities action is needed, with compensatory economic programmes aimed at blacks.

2. An emphasis on class aspects of black disadvantage. Writers such as W. J. Wilson (1987) have argued that the emergence of the underclass is largely due to structural changes in the US economy, with the shift from manufacturing to a service economy, and the re-location of industry away form black urban areas. 'Race' is not the fundamental cause; black Americans have suffered because of the timing of their migration to the north, the skills they brought with them, and the place they occupy in the labour market. It is past discrimination, not current discrimination, which is the major factor. The recommendation is for polices to reorganise the economic structure in general, rather than 'race-specific' policies.

3. An emphasis on behavioural explanations and the characteristics within the poor themselves. Ghetto blacks are seen as refusing jobs because welfare is available; in refusing low-income employment they are responsible for their own economic difficulties. No special status is accorded to the concept of race – policies that treat blacks differently are seen as the cause of current problems. The latest manifestation of this position came after the 1992 Los Angeles riots when the White House Press Secretary located the root causes of inner city problems in Government programmes of the 1960s and 1970s (*Washington Post*, 6 May 1992). Some writers argue for a *laissez faire* position by government; others argue that policies are needed to change the behaviour which resulted in their location under the underclass, such as strict workfare to inculcate improved norms and behaviour (Weir 1993).

This last position of 'blaming the victims' is not restricted to right-wing commentators. Similar stances are also found more generally amongst liberal academics and policy-makers. For example, Lutz in this volume describes the developing official view in the Netherlands that ethnic minorities exhibit high rates of unemployment because they have in the past been treated by the government as a 'care' category and have become dependent on public money, with the implicit assumption that they are abusing the social security system. At a broader level Miles shows how political discourses often involve a denial of racism and its relevance for contemporary European societies (Miles, this volume).

Gould (1991) explains how the denial of racism can be related to egalitarian values predominant in a society:

> ...in an individualistic and egalitarian society where hierarchically ordered racial barriers are no longer visible, the failure of blacks to achieve the same level of success as their white counterparts is readily interpreted as a factual indication of the inferiority of those with black skins.....Thus it is clear how racist misperceptions may be generated within egalitarian values (Gould 1991: 107).

In this denial of racism, a particular group which does not achieve success may be perceived to be deficient. In European countries there may be similar, though qualitatively different, phenomena operating. A good example of how this process may work is to be found in van Dijk's account, in this volume, of the 'denial of racism' in the Netherlands. The ethnic or racial inequalities implied by discrimination or racism would be inconsistent with official ideologies of liberal democracies, and thus instead of recognising such 'imperfections', it is more expedient to deny them or explain them away as a characteristic of the victims, or as a temporary phenomenon of transition for new immigrants. Furthermore, he argues, that as long as the existence of racism is denied, it also denies the need for anti-racist and anti-discrimination legislation.

While the debate on the 'underclass' in the United States has a particular history which may not easily be reproduced in the European context, it is perhaps of some significance that such notions are also beginning to be used in the European context in order to describe the position of migrant communities.

Citizenship and Multiculturalism

Perhaps the key issue in recent debates about migrant workers is the complex question of 'citizenship rights' and how these should be reconceptualised in the context of the 'new Europe'. Some important elements of this debate are discussions about:

1. the political rights of minorities, including the issue of representation in both local and national politics;
2. minority religious and cultural rights, and their role in the context of a society which is becoming more diverse;

3. the role of legislative interventions to protect the rights of minorities and develop extensive notions of citizenship and democracy in the 'new Europe'.

There are clearly at this stage quite divergent perspectives about how best to deal with all of these concerns. There is a wealth of discussion about what kind of measures are necessary to tackle the inequalities and exclusions which confront minority groups. At the same time there is clear evidence that existing initiatives are severely limited in their impact. A number of commentators have pointed to the limitations of legislation and public policy interventions in bringing about a major improvement in the socio-political position of minorities (Hammar 1985; Layton-Henry 1990).

This raises a number of questions. First, what kind of policies could tackle discrimination more effectively? Second, what links could be made between policies on immigration and policies on social and economic issues? What kind of positive social policy agenda can be developed to deal with the position of both established communities and new migrants in the 1990s and beyond?

There are no easy answers to these questions, and the experience of the past two decades indicates that any set of policies will by no means achieve unanimous support in society as a whole. But perhaps a starting point for future policy agendas is the recognition that there is a need for a co-ordinated public policy to deal with various social, political and cultural aspects of the position of ethnic minorities. In the past, policy initiatives have been at best *ad hoc* and piecemeal. This is partly because although public policy has been committed for some time to the pursuit of equal opportunity and multiculturalism, there is no clear political and social consensus in society about what this means, either ideologically or in practice. There is little agreement, for example, about what public policies need to be developed to deal with discrimination in such areas as education, social services and employment. Additionally, as recent debates about anti-racism seem to indicate, there is also a denial that racial and ethnic inequality is an integral feature of contemporary European societies or that racism is an important issue.

Whatever the merits of such arguments it seems clear that there is still much confusion about the objectives of public policy. Because of the *ad hoc* nature of policy development in this field it is difficult to talk of national strategies or European-wide strategies to deal with the changing economic and social dynamics which we face today. Perhaps more fundamentally, there is also confusion about the links between:

1. anti-discrimination legislation and its role in creating greater opportunities and providing remedies for ethnic minorities and new migrants;
2. multicultural and anti-racist initiatives which address the situation in areas such as employment, education, social services and housing;
3. national policies and initiatives developed by European-wide institutions and bodies in response to specific issues.

This lack of co-ordination needs to be overcome if the oft-repeated call for more effective policies in this field is going to become reality. The process of change is not likely to be easy. The very plurality of categories used in current debates would seem to indicate that the objectives pursued are by no means clear and are in fact essentially contested notions. In particular, researchers and practitioners do not concur on what they mean by such terms as equality of opportunity and anti-discrimination or what they consider as evidence of a move towards the stated goals of policies. Some argue that the development of equal opportunity policies is the outcome of a process of political negotiation, pressure group politics and bureaucratic policy-making. Others, however, emphasise the need to look beyond the stated objectives and public political negotiations and explore the ways in which deeply entrenched processes of discrimination may be resistant to legal and political interventions while inegalitarian social relations structure society as a whole.

Following on from the discussion of social policy perspectives it is important to note that policy debate in Britain, unlike other European societies, has often not looked seriously at the issue of political and citizenship rights of migrants and their descendants. This is partly because it is widely assumed that such issues are not as relevant in this country. But it is also clear that ethnic minorities in Britain and elsewhere are questioning whether they are fully included in and represented through political institutions. It is not surprising, therefore, that an important concern in recent years has been with the issue of citizenship and the rights of minorities in British society. This is partly because there is a growing awareness of the gap between formal citizenship and the *de facto* restriction of the economic and social rights of minorities as a result of discrimination, economic restructuring and the decline of the welfare state.

Recent controversies about the Rushdie affair and a number of other controversial cases across Europe have highlighted the increased prominence of these issues in current political debates. The growing public interest about the role of fundamentalism among sections of the Muslim communities in various countries has given a new life to debates about the issue of cultural differences and processes of integration.

The full impact of the debate on multiculturalism on both the British and the wider European context is not as yet clear, but it seems likely that it will have an influence on debates about such issues as 'multiculturalism' and 'anti-racism'. In the context of national debates about the position of ethnic minority communities the impact is already evident. In Britain, for example, there are already signs that the Rushdie affair has given a new impetus to debates about issues such as immigration, integration and public order. The hostile media coverage of the events surrounding the political mobilisations around the Rushdie affair also served to reinforce the view that minorities who do not share the dominant political values of British society pose a threat to social stability and cohesion. Some commentators have argued that as a result of the Rushdie affair more attention needed to be given to the divergent political paths seemingly adopted by sections of the Afro-Caribbean and Asian communities.

Such developments are not simply limited to Britain. There have been similar events and trends in France, Germany, Holland, Scandinavia and other countries as the various chapters in this volume show.

Conceptual Themes and Arguments

The substantive chapters of this volume are organised into three distinct but interrelated parts. It may be useful to say something here about the rationale and content of each part, though it is beyond the scope of this chapter to provide an overview of all the complex themes which are touched upon by the various authors. Nevertheless, it is important to attempt to situate the contribution of particular authors within the broader framework of the volume as a whole.

Part I brings together a number of contributions which address in one way or another the issue of the historical and contemporary trends which have shaped the present conjuncture. The chapters by Stephen Castles and Robert Miles, in particular, attempt from rather different points of departure to question some of the commonsense assumptions that are made about the processes of migration and growing racism which are the subject of so much debate. Both Castles and Miles suggest that researchers must rethink in quite a fundamental way existing accounts of migration and the role of racism.

The chapters in Part II take a somewhat different perspective, by exploring trends and developments in particular societies, namely France, Germany, Italy, Sweden, Holland and the United Kingdom. In all of these chapters there are accounts particularly of recent trends and developments and a conscious attempt to think through the implications of trends in particular societies. A good example of this is the attempt by Michel Wieviorka to use recent developments in France as a basis for a more general rethinking of the origins of contemporary forms of racism. Another interesting case is the study by Ellie Vasta of the upsurge of racism in Italy, a society which has not traditionally been viewed as a country of immigration. This suggests the importance of broadening our horizon and looking beyond the boundaries of northern Europe for a rounded analysis of migration and racism.

The final part of the book extends the coverage further by focusing in on key issues and debates. While the issues covered are by no means exhaustive, the papers by Teun van Dijk and Avtar Brah look at current debates about the political and civil rights of migrants and minorities and the role of racism and ethnic diversity in contemporary Europe. Jan Rath's chapter explores the ways in which minorities are constructed and asks the question of what are the most appropriate concepts to use in analysing this process. This ties up with the earlier discussion in Miles and Brah about the appropriateness of categories such as 'race' and 'ethnicity' to describe the position of migrant workers in rather different social and political positions.

The final two chapters, by Stephen Small and Cathie Lloyd, cover a broader range of issues. Small provides an interesting comparison of recent trends in Europe and the United States, and in so doing he is able to draw on a wealth of research from America that has some relevance to recent developments in Europe. Lloyd's paper takes up the question of the kinds of research and policy issues that are likely to confront us over the next decade or so. In so doing, she suggests avenues for comparative research that may well lead to a better understanding of the current situation and allow us to analyse future trends.

Conclusion

This volume will, we hope, shed some light on the reasons why immigration and racism are such controversial phenomena in contemporary Europe. The various chapters bring out the complex variety of political debates and ideas about these issues, and the need for us to understand better the similarities and differences between national political cultures and traditions. They also provide substantive information on the changing dynamics of racism and about how to understand and challenge the specific racisms which have developed in different societies. The authors in this volume do not hold to one monolithic view of this issue, and many of their ideas may be seen as controversial by some. But their ideas will, we hope, challenge many widely held assumptions and suggest avenues for further analysis and debate.

We also hope that the book will add to the debate about the kind of policy initiatives that are needed to improve the social and political rights of migrants and established minority communities. What policies can provide a more positive framework of action in the future? How can we tackle the resurgence of racism that is so evident across Europe today? These are some of the questions that are tackled in the substantive chapters of this volume, and in thinking about the development of alternative policies it is vital that we see that in practice there is a close relationship between policies on migration and settlement and wider initiatives about the social position of new and established ethnic minority communities.

It is clear that racism is likely to remain an important aspect of contemporary social relations, and that it will be manifested in a variety of forms. We hope that this volume will be of some relevance to those who are interested in challenging racist ideologies and practices and in ensuring that the protection of the rights of minorities becomes more than a pious hope.

–2–

Migrations and Minorities in Europe. Perspectives for the 1990s: Eleven Hypotheses

Stephen Castles

The aim of this chapter is to look at global patterns of migration and ethnic minority formation, and to relate these to other major political, economic and cultural trends in this post-Cold War world. The significance of these developments for migrants and minorities in western Europe will be examined, in particular with regard to migration policies, citizenship, racism and identity. Finally, I will discuss some consequences, firstly for social scientists, secondly for the anti-racist movement. In view of the general and provisional nature of these considerations, I will put them in the form of eleven hypotheses, which I will try to explain and justify.

1 The world is entering a new phase of mass population movements, in which migration to Europe and the situation of ethnic minorities in Europe can be fully understood only in a global context.

At the beginning of the 1980s, there was a widespread belief that mass migrations to western Europe had, for the time being, ended, allowing a stabilisation of immigrant populations. The stopping of labour migration to most countries following the 'oil shock' of 1973–4, and the gradual completion of processes of family reunion (despite attempts by some governments to prevent them), seemed to provide conditions under which the new ethnic minorities could settle and form their own communities. Stabilisation facilitated gradual improvement in the socio-economic situation and the civil and political rights of immigrants. This was the context for debates on pluralism, multicultural policies and measures against discrimination and racism.

The situation changed dramatically in the late 1980s, with a rapid increase of migrations to north America[1], Australia and western Europe. There was also growth in migrations concerning the countries of the south (SOPEMI 1990), including rural–urban movements within less developed countries (LDCs), migrations between various LDCs, from LDCs to newly industrialising countries (NICs) and between LDCs and oil countries. The 'new migrations' were new in areas of origin and destination, with more and more countries participating: for instance, southern Europe, which had experienced mass emigration until the early 1970s, now became an area of immigration from Africa and Asia. The migrations were new with regard to the characteristics of migrants: for instance the increasing participation of women workers, and an emerging polarisation of skills with both unskilled and very highly qualified personnel participating. They were new with regard to forms of migration: former 'guestworker' countries now became the destinations of family migration and refugee movements, while new 'guestworker systems' developed in the oil countries. The overwhelming trend was towards spontaneous movements – uncontrolled though not necessarily unwanted – by governments and employers, and often taking the form of illegal or refugee movements.

At present there are estimated to be eighty million migrants (that is, people living permanently or for long periods outside their countries of origin) – the equivalent of 1.7 per cent of world population. Thirty million of these are said to be in 'irregular situations' and fifteen million are refugees or asylum seekers (IOM, 1990). The number of asylum seekers coming to European OECD countries per year increased from 65,000 in 1983 to 289,000 in 1989 (SOPEMI 1991: 122). the main increase was at the end of the decade, mainly because of movements from eastern Europe. However, entries of workers and of family members of previous migrants also rose sharply in the late 1980s.

2 Previous distinctions between types of migrations are becoming increasingly meaningless. This is undermining government policies.

Migration policies have been premised on the belief that movements could be divided up into neat categories, such as economic migration, family reunion, refugees and illegals. Economic migrants in turn were subdivided into unskilled labour, highly skilled employees and business migrants; while refugees were separated into 'Convention refugees' and

---

1. In the case of the USA, the growth got underway following the new Immigration Act of 1965, which repealed the restrictive and racist measures which virtually stopped mass immigration from the early 1920s.

asylum seekers. Another distinction regarded as highly significant has been between temporary migrants (usually workers) and permanent settlers. Such categories have been central to a variety of migration systems, including the Australian immigration programme, the US Preference System, the German 'guestworker' programme and the United Nations High Commission for Refugees (UNHCR) framework.

Today these distinctions are collapsing. Migratory chains, once established, continue, even when the original policies on which they were based are changed or reversed. For example, when the German federal government decided in 1973 to stop labour migration and to encourage return migration, the main migratory chain – that from Turkey – continued to develop, initially in the form of family reunion, then through refugee entries (Blaschke 1990). Similarly, what appears as entrepreneurial migration, may in fact be a form of permanent family movement, as in the case of some south-east Asian migration to Australia, Canada and the USA.

The classic case for the erosion of neat categories is that of asylum seekers. The overwhelming majority of these do not fall under the criteria of individual persecution of the UN Convention definition, even though they are forced to leave their countries by war, famine, economic pressure, ethnic persecution or ecological catastrophe (Ministry of Labour, Sweden 1990). For the year 1990, the UN High Commission for Refugees estimated resettlement needs at just 150,000, and called on governments to be less generous to asylum seekers who did not meet UNHCR criteria, because giving them support might divert efforts from 'real' refugees (UNHCR 1989: 2). The huge gap between the UNHCR figure, and the world's fifteen million refugees and asylum seekers casts doubt on the viability of the Convention definition, and points to the pressing need for new international policies.

The overall effect is a general breakdown in regulation of migration and settlement by governments or supranational bodies. As the OECD has pointed out, policies to contain migratory flows are becoming 'difficult to implement' and there is a growth in illegal movements to Europe as well as to other regions (SOPEMI 1990). Certainly there are no comprehensive joint European policies on migration and refugees. However, where there are moves towards such policies – such as through the Schengen and Trevi agreements – the emphasis is on restriction and exclusion rather than on rational and humane immigration policies, or on providing more effective support to refugees.

3 The growing disparities between economic, social and demographic conditions in south and north (and east and west) provide the context for future mass migrations.

In the 1990s, ninety to a hundred million people will be added to world population every year. By 2025, world population is expected almost to double to 8.5 billion people. While the industrialised regions are projected to grow relatively little from 1.2 billion people in 1990 to 1.35 billion in 2025, the LDCs will increase from 4 billion to 7.15 billion (IOM 1990). This will lead to a vast increase in demand for jobs: the total labour force of the LDCs is projected to grow by 733 million between 1990 and 2010. This is more than the total current labour force of the industrialised countries – 586 million in 1990. The LDCs need to create thirty-six million new jobs each year in the 1990s – a target which seems quite unattainable in the light of past performance (Golini, Gosano and Heins 1990). Population growth in LDCs is linked with rural–urban migration and rapid urbanisation. In 1970, there were only twenty cities in the world with more than five million inhabitants. By 2000, there are expected to be forty-four – and most of them will be in LDCs. The largest cities will be Mexico City and São Paulo with twenty-four million people each. Other huge cities in LDCs will include Calcutta (sixteen million), Bombay (fifteen million), Teheran (fourteen million) and Jakarta (thirteen million). Poor housing, lack of infrastructure and high unemployment are likely to make these cities unattractive places in which to live.

These demographic and social factors will create enormous pressures for south-north migration (Zolberg 1989). In terms of the push-pull models which were used to explain migrations in the past, one could argue the *pull* factors were the main explanatory factor during the mass labour migrations to western Europe from 1945 to about 1973: migrant workers came either because they were recruited or because they had a justified expectation that they would find a job (Castles and Kosack, 1973: 25–8). During recessions, labour migration declined. In the 1980s, this changed: the *push* factors became dominant and people came mainly because the conditions of life were intolerable in the area of origin. Even unemployment and a marginal existence in the north became preferable to staying in the south. Such movements are likely to continue whatever the labour market situation and the policies of governments in the north. However, push-pull theories – generally based on simplistic human capital theories – have only a limited explanatory value. It is necessary to look beyond individual movements and their immediate causes, to understand the fundamental processes

4 Economic, social and demographic disparities alone do not cause migration. Rather, the movements are an expression of the interdependence between sending and receiving areas within the political economy of the world market. Once movements start, they often lead to chains of

migration, which continue even when the initial causes or policies have changed.

It has long been obvious that it is not people from the very poorest countries, nor the most impoverished people within a given area, who are most likely to migrate. Migration requires resources, both of finance and of cultural capital. People do not simply decide as individuals to move to another country to maximise their life chances. Most migration is based on existing economic and social links, connected with colonialism, international trade and investment, or previous migratory movements. For example the US Bracero Program of the 1940s started a long-term migratory movement from Mexico to the USA, just as the German 'guestworker' programme led to a permanent chain of Turkish migration. Research by Sassen (1988) has shown the strong connections between investment, trade and migration; increasing mobility of capital in the contemporary world economy is a principal determinant of labour mobility. International migration is a collective phenomenon which arises as part of a social relationship between the less developed and more developed parts of a single global economic system (Portes and Böröcz 1989).

Understanding these links has important consequences. Many people believe that economic development of the countries of the south will reduce emigration. The left has long called for 'development aid instead of migration', while the neo-liberal slogan has been 'trade in place of migration'. Today we must understand that economic development, at least in the short and medium term, will lead to increased emigration from the poorer countries (see Tapinos 1990). This is because the development process – i.e. bringing less developed areas into the world economy – leads to such severe disruption of existing societal structures that previous ways of living become unviable, and migration appears as the only solution. In general terms, the process has the following stages:

increased links between less developed and developed countries through colonialism, trade, aid and foreign investment;
rural development (the 'Green Revolution') leads to displacement of poorer farmers and to rural–urban migration;
rapid growth of large cities with poor social conditions and insufficient employment opportunities;
improved education but few jobs for graduates, leading to the 'brain drain';
cultural influence of the developed countries through mass media;
tourism and commodification of cultural products;
better transport and communications;
temporary labour migrations;

permanent movements to developed countries;
establishment of links between migrant communities in immigration countries and areas of origin, strengthening the cultural influence of developed countries, and sustaining migratory chains.

A good example of the way this process has worked for a successful newly industrialising country is Korea, where the rapid industrialisation which has made the country one of Asia's 'four tigers' has been accompanied by large-scale migration, mainly to the USA (Sassen 1988: chapter 4). However, this relationship between industrialisation and emigration should hardly surprise us, when we remember that Britain's industrial revolution in the eighteenth and nineteenth centuries was marked by mass overseas emigration of proletarianised farmers and artisans.

The current upsurge in south-north migration is essentially a reflection of the economic, social and cultural crisis in many countries of Asia, Africa and Latin America, caused by the post-colonial mode of incorporation into the world capitalist economy. The end of the Cold War adds a new political dimension: as long as there was a Second World which provided an alternative development model, the concept of the Third World had a political significance as a possible non-capitalist way to modernisation. The rise of OPEC and the NICs had already eroded the economic usefulness of the concept of the Third World. Now the political value has been lost too: there is no other way but the capitalist one. Since millions of people have already experienced the dislocation, destitution and injustice brought about by capitalist development, they are left with no hope of realisation of human dignity and rights in their own countries. Migration to the north now appears as the only way out. At the same time the end of the Soviet empire means an enormous additional potential for migration to the rich countries of western Europe and north America. In both economic and cultural terms, east-west migration is likely to compete with south-north movements, making the situation even more complex.

5 The new types of migration correspond with the restructuring of the economies and labour markets of the developed countries in the last twenty years.

The ending of organised recruitment of manual workers by industrialised countries in the early 1970s was not a mere conjunctural phenomenon, but rather a reaction to a fundamental restructuring of the labour process. The last two decades have been marked by:

the 'new international division of labour', i.e. increased capital export from developed countries and establishment of manufacturing industries in the south;

the micro-electronic revolution;

erosion of traditional skilled manual occupations;

growth in the services sector, with demand for both highly skilled and low-skilled workers;

increased significance of informal sectors in developed countries;

casualisation of employment, growth in part-time work, increasingly insecure conditions of employment;

increased differentiation of labour forces on the basis of gender, age and ethnicity, through mechanisms which push many women, young people and members of minorities into casual or informal-sector work;

considerable international mobility of highly skilled workers.

Taking these tendencies together, we can speak of a new polarisation of the labour forces of highly developed countries: the old blue-collar skilled working class has shrunk, while both the highly skilled work-force and the unskilled, casualised workforce have grown. Social inequality and insecurity have been exacerbated by the decline of the welfare state. The labour movement has lost much of its power and its innovative capacity, in line with the erosion of its former social basis.

Ethnic minorities and new migrants have played varying parts in these developments. Labour market policies which give preference to nationals have contributed to very high unemployment rates for former 'guestworkers' and helped cushion the effects of restructuring for local workers. The highly exploited work of migrant women in the clothing industry has partly counteracted the trend to relocation of this type of workplace to LDCs (Phizacklea 1990). The emergence of ethnic small business as a strategy for coping with racism and unemployment has played an important part in urban renewal and in economic change (Waldinger, Aldrich and Ward 1990; Light and Bonacich 1988; Blaschke 1990). Temporary (and often illegal) foreign workers from Poland play a significant role in the German building industry, while undocumented African workers pick the fruit and vegetables of most southern European countries. In the NICs, the labour of women rural–urban migrants is central to the development of the electronics industry, while attempts at industrialisation in OPEC countries have been largely based on migrant labour, both highly skilled and manual. A new political economy of migrant and ethnic minority labour is emerging.

6 State policies towards migrants and minorities have become increasingly complex and contradictory, as governments have sought to address a variety of irreconcilable goals, such as:

provision of labour supplies;
differentiation and control of migrant workers;
immigration control and repatriation;
management of urban problems;
reduction of welfare expenditure;
maintenance of public order;
integration of minorities into social and political institutions;
construction of national identity and maintenance of the nation state.

As the migratory process has matured and new migrations have developed, policies have had to address an increasing number of areas, and to deal with ever more complicated situations. State responses have almost invariably been piecemeal and *ad hoc*, without any long-term, coherent strategies. This applies particularly where governments, for political reasons, have been unwilling to admit the reality of long-term settlement and continued immigration (e.g. in Germany, which according to the main political parties is still 'not a country of immigration'). To some extent the above list of goals is chronological: the emphasis was on labour supply and control of migrant workers in the 1950s and 1960s; on immigration control and repatriation in the 1970s; on management of the urban crisis and on cutting welfare in the late 1970s and early 1980s; and on public order, the long-term position of minorities and – again – on immigration control in the late 1980s and early 1990s.

The overlap of these policy goals leads to major contradictions. Here are a few examples:

exclusionary policies which deny rights and citizenship prevent integration into political institutions and exacerbate public order problems;
immigration control and repatriation threaten the situation of existing ethnic minorities by criminalising later segments of migratory chains;
policies which lead to employment of undocumented workers provide cheap labour for certain economic sectors, but also undermine general labour market polices, split the labour force and help cause racism;[2]
crisis management strategies based on blaming the 'enemy within' contribute to racist violence and threaten public order;
attempts to stabilise national identity through the strengthening of ethnic boundaries lead to increased racism and push minorities into separatism and fundamentalism.

2. Or, as Balibar puts it, 'The modern state ... opens the door to 'clandestine' circulation of the foreign labour force, and at the same time represses it' (Balibar 1991: 16).

To make matters even more complicated, it is becoming difficult to identify clearly the state, both because of the unclear division of responsibilities in the migration area between national and supranational authorities, and because of still contested and unfinished reordering of the division between public and private in social policies. What state is responsible for migration policies: the individual states of European countries, the European Community as an embryonic all-European state, or even the superstate of the north, responsible for imposing the 'new world order' on the south? Balibar (1991: 17) concludes that there is no 'law-governed state' in Europe and that this leads to a 'collective sense of identity panic'. This contributes to the psychological insecurity which helps to cause informal racism, as well as providing the political space for populist racist movements.

7 Racism in western European societies has two sets of causes. The first concerns ideologies and practices going back to the construction of nation states and to colonialism. The second set derives from current processes of social, economic and political change. The increased salience of racism and the shift in its targets over the last twenty years reflects the rapid pace of change in living and working conditions, the dissolution of the cultural forms and organisational structures of the working class, and the weakness and ambivalence of the state.

Racism has been a significant factor in European societies for centuries (see, for example, Miles 1989; Cohen and Bains 1988; Gilroy 1987). Its manifold roots lie in the ideologies of white superiority which underpinned colonialism, in processes of ethnic exclusion as part of the development of nation states, in chauvinist nationalist ideologies linked to intra-European conflict, and in attitudes and practices towards immigrant minorities. Western European countries have long-established cultures of racism, which lead to a predisposition to 'racialise' immigrants and ethnic minorities, i.e. to categorise alleged differences between them and the majority group in either biological or cultural terms, which are seen as 'natural' and hence immutable (compare Brah, Miles in this volume).

This predisposition may be seen as constant, but it is clear that racism as an empirical reality changes over time, with regard to its targets, its forms of expression and its intensity. For practical politics, it is crucial to understand and explain these variations. There is considerable evidence of increasing intensity of racism of all kinds – institutional practices, vilification, discrimination, harassment, violence – in most western European countries since the early 1970s (European Parliament 1985; Castles, Booth and Wallace 1984: chapter 7). The recent outbreaks of racist violence in Germany, the strength of the extreme right in France and the emergence of new racisms in southern Europe all point to a new strength of racist ideologies. Racism appears to be taking on a new character which is threatening not only to ethnic minorities but to democratic structures in general. The background to this trend lies in:

the end of European colonialism;
the decline of older industrial areas, the end of full employment (both as
    a reality and as a policy aim) and the erosion of the welfare state;
the social and urban crisis in many parts of western Europe
the economic ascendancy of some former colonies or semi-colonies,
    particularly in the Middle East and Asia;
mass migration and establishment of new ethnic minorities in European
    cities.

In the early 1970s, racism appeared to have the same character towards immigrant workers in all the labour-importing countries in western Europe, and did not depend primarily on phenotypical factors (skin colour, features etc.) or origins (non-European as opposed to European periphery). For example, there were strong similarities in attitudes and behaviour towards Italian workers in Switzerland and black workers in Britain (Castles and Kosack 1973). By the late 1980s, there appeared to be a much higher degree of social acceptance of intra-European migrants, which contrasted with strongly exclusionary attitudes towards immigrants from the south and minorities who were phenotypically different. This change can be attributed to a number of factors: the end of migration from the European periphery; the absorption of some former European migrant groups into citizenship or secure resident status; the decline of individual European nationalisms due to European integration; and the tentative emergence of a 'European consciousness'.

The danger is that this 'European consciousness' will be constructed in exclusionary and discriminatory terms, based on the perceived threat of being swamped by the 'desperate masses' from the south. Indeed, it is possible that it might turn into a much narrower western European nationalism, owing to fears of east-west migration. An example for the ambivalence of the situation was the reaction of Italians to the so-called 'Albanian invasion' of August 1989 (see Vasta in this volume). On the one hand, there were calls for admitting the several thousand spontaneous migrants, on the grounds that 'after all they are Europeans too' and desperately in need of help. On the other hand, it was pointed out that letting in one group would encourage further waves and, furthermore, that it would be hard to justify excluding equally desperate people from Africa, except on openly racist grounds. In the end, the reaction of the Italian state was uncharacteristically draconian and repressive: mass expulsion using military means.

A further differentiation is currently emerging: Muslim immigrants are becoming the main targets of racist discourses. This is partly because Muslims form the largest non-European minorities in France, Germany, Britain and Belgium. Anti-Muslim attitudes are also based on historical conflicts between Christian and Muslim peoples in the Mediterranean region. A further link is with international affairs: in the early 1970s, the recession was blamed on the 'oil sheiks', while the Islamic revolution in Iran and more recently the Gulf War have led to fears of a challenge to western dominance. Public debates on the 'population explosion' of the Maghreb increase the perception of an imminent invasion. Thus Muslim minorities appear threatening partly because they are linked to strong external forces, which appear to question the hegemony of the north, and partly because they have a visible and self-confident cultural presence. The Rushdie affair took on major significance because it linked all these factors. At the same time, such discourses present an ideological opportunity to the extreme right: by playing on such fears and linking them to historical traditions, it can take on a new pan-European character, and break out of its old ultra-nationalist ghetto.

The current increase in racism, and the changes in its form and character, are closely linked to the processes of rapid economic, social and political change affecting the population of western European countries in the last three decades. Their main impact has been felt by the urban working class, which has seen its economic and social conditions severely eroded. Immigrants and new minorities have become the visible symbol of this erosion and hence the target for resentment. Thus as Balibar (1988a: 289–302) points out, racism is not so much a result of the crisis as one form of its *expression*. Racism should not be analysed as a working-class phenomenon, but rather as one product of the dissolution of working-class culture and political organisation (Balibar 1988b: 272–88). As popular cultures have been pushed aside by multinational cultural industries, the power to deal with change and to absorb new influences has been lost. As the membership of unions and working-class parties has declined, the ideological and organisational basis for an effective response to the attack on living standards has been lost. The decline of the labour movement creates the social space for racism, which is a central aspect of a movement based on communal (or 'white ethnic') identity (compare Wieviorka 1991 and in this volume).

8 The constitution of new minorities, with distinct cultures, identities and institutions, is an irreversible process, which questions existing notions of national identity and citizenship.

The transformation of immigrant groups into new ethnic minorities[3] is not inevitable. In a non-racist society immigrants could become equal members of civil society while maintaining their own cultures and identities as much as they wished. But the experience of discrimination and racism in western European countries forced immigrants to constitute their own communities and to define their group boundaries in cultural terms. In turn, community formation has reinforced fears of separatism and 'ethnic enclaves' on the part of sections of the majority population, leading to reinforcement of exclusionary practices and racism. Ethnic minority cultures – even when they take on traditionalist forms – have the vital task of self-protection (in both material and psychological terms) against a hostile environment.

Today, the reversal of racist and exclusionary policies would no longer be sufficient to bring about the cultural and political integration of minorities, in the sense of eliminating the need for some degree of organisational and cultural autonomy.[4] Ethnic minorities are now firmly established so that western European countries have no choice but to accept some form of cultural pluralism for the foreseeable future. Policies based on political and cultural assimilation (the French model) or on exclusionary definitions of nationality (the German model) (see Brubaker 1990b) can no longer serve as effective forms of integration of the nation state.

9 Western European countries of immigration are being forced to examine the relationship between ethnic diversity, national identity and citizenship. Multicultural models appear to offer their best solution, but there are substantial obstacles to their realisation.

The varying ways in which the 'imagined community' of the nation state has been constructed in western European countries in the past are losing their viability. The presence of new ethnic minorities is only one facet of the challenge. Others include:

European integration and the emergence of a European consciousness. On the positive side this means overcoming old chauvinisms; on the

3. For the purposes of the present paper, ethnic minorities may be seen as social groups which are the result of both other-definition and self-definition. On the one hand their boundaries are defined by dominant social groups according to perceived phenotypical or cultural characteristics, which leads to the imposition of specific economic, social or legal situations. On the other hand, their members generally share a self-definition or ethnic identity based on ideas of common origins, history, culture, experience and values. The relative importance of other- and self-definition varies according to the group and its situation.

4. Anyway, it is questionable whether this can ever happen in the first few generations of a migratory process even under the best possible conditions. It is also questionable whether such cultural homogenisation is desirable. These are issues which will not be pursued here.

negative side it means erecting boundaries towards the rest of the world: the 'fortress Europe' model.[5]

The development of a commodified global culture, borne by transnational capital and the mass media, which challenges national cultures.

Emergence of regional movements, often based on the rediscovered ethnic cultures of historical minorities within nation states.

The emergence of a right-wing, populist nationalism as a reaction to the failure of modernity to keep its promise of material prosperity to substantial sections of the population.

The only viable solution appears to lie in an approach to identity and citizenship similar to the multicultural models which have emerged in Australia and Canada. These are countries which have consciously used immigration as part of the process of nation-building, and have in the long run been forced to revise their concepts of national identity and their institutional structures to take account of the growing cultural diversity of their populations. These models are not without their problems (see Castles, Cope, Kalantzis and Morrissey 1990) but they have been fairly successful in managing ethnic diversity and maintaining good community relations. Western European countries did not aim to change their demographic and cultural composition through immigration, but that has in fact happened, and the current debate on national identity and citizenship must take account of this, by moving away from monocultural myths.

Certainly there is a debate on multicultural models in Europe. Sweden has gone some way to applying them, though with considerable difficulties (Ålund and Schierup 1991 and in this volume). The Netherlands minorities policy has similarities, though there currently appears to be a shift away from cultural pluralism, and more emphasis on labour market and educational measures (Rath, this volume). It is important to look both at the general principles necessary to apply multiculturalism in western Europe, and at specific issues like the social and political rights of permanent settlers, naturalisation policies, citizenship of the second generation and minority cultural rights. The main issue, however, is still that of the political will to move away from outmoded forms of nationalism and the nation state. Major obstacles to the introduction of multicultural policies include:

---

5. An interesting expression of this is the term *extracomunitario* now widely used as a label for immigrants from outside the European Community in Italy. The term has become as pejorative as *Arab* in France or *Ausländer* in Germany. It is a way of homogenising difference in exclusionary terms, whereby the core of difference is non-belonging to a (new) imagined European community.

the conflict between immigration policy, as a form of differential exclusion from the territory and hence society, and citizenship as a way of including people in civil society and the nation state;

the gap between formal citizenship (as a system of civil and political rights) and the de facto restriction of economic and social rights of members of ethnic minorities, particularly due to economic restructuring and the decline of the welfare state;

racism and nationalism.

10 In view of the multifaceted links between the world economy, migratory processes, minority formation and social change, research in this area can no longer be monodisciplinary and national in focus. There is a need for a multidisciplinary and international social science of migration and multicultural societies, combining elements of political economy, sociology, political science, law, demography, anthropology and related disciplines.

In the period of mass labour migration to industrialised countries, the focus of academic research was on the economics of migrant labour, and on the sociology and social psychology of 'immigrant-host relations'. Later, in response to the apparent ending of labour migration and the permanent settlement of immigrant groups, more critical approaches developed, which sited labour migration in the political economy of capitalism, examined the sociology of minority formation and the racialisation of social relations, or looked at the politics of crisis management. It is now clear that labour migration did not end, but has merely changed its form. Indeed, migration and use of 'unfree labour' has always been part of the capitalist system (R. Cohen 1987). It is also clear that minority formation and racialisation are central aspects of social relations at the national and international levels.

What is new is that all these processes are taking place simultaneously and increasingly in many parts of the world. The long-term result seems likely to be the emergence of multicultural societies, leading in turn to new concepts of citizenship and the nation state. The consequence for critical social scientists working on immigration, racism and ethnic relations should be a new awareness of the global scope of the subject of research. Monodisciplinary studies of particular facets are justifiable only within the context of an interdisciplinary framework which provides understanding of the links between the particular and the general, the local and the global. The study of migration and multicultural societies should therefore be understood as a social science in its own right, which is strongly multidisciplinary in its theory and methodology.

11 The increasing volume and changing character of migration, together with the emergence of ethnically heterogeneous societies in Europe makes a re-examination of political positions essential. We need to redefine the meaning of 'international solidarity' with regard to migration policies and the north-south divide, to examine potential contradictions in anti-racist positions, and to work out political agendas which can lead to democratic, multicultural societies.

Labour migration has often been an issue of contention within the labour movement, due to the potential threat it presents to wages, conditions and organisational unity. Policies have ranged from international solidarity through to racist exclusionism. Since 1945, the western European left has generally taken an internationalist and anti-racist line. In the current situation, it seems necessary to re-examine and redefine such positions. A number of dilemmas need to be addressed.

Immigration control is by its nature selective, exclusionary and restrictive. Should we therefore reject all control and demand 'open borders' (as has recently been debated within the German Green Party)? In the present circumstances this could lead to large and chaotic flows, resulting in conflict and racism, giving increased impetus to the extreme right, and probably – in the long run – bringing about even stricter control. On the other hand, there is a realisation by governments and international agencies that immigration control, in its present form, is increasingly ineffective (Purcell 1990; Ministry of Labour, Sweden 1990; SOPEMI 1990).

South-north and east-west migration can present effective individual strategies for survival and improvement in life chances, but it cannot provide general solutions to global disparities. The number of people who could conceivably migrate to the industrialised countries is a drop in the ocean, compared with the number of people facing severe economic and social problems in the LDCs. There is little evidence that migration, under current arrangements, does anything to support development in the areas of origin. Indeed individual movements can hamper development, for example by withdrawing people with desperately needed skills. In the past, the answer to this dilemma was found in the principle 'development in place of migration'. As pointed out above, it is now clear that these are false alternatives: development and industrialisation actually lead to increased migration for a substantial period.

Finally, there seems to be a potential conflict between the ethnic minorities which developed out of the labour migrations between 1950 and the early 1970s, and the new immigrants. The former sometimes see the newcomers as a threat to the gains they are beginning to make, and as a catalyst for increased racism. Again, the actual content of solidarity needs to be discussed in this context.

There are no easy answers to any of these dilemmas. To find solutions it is necessary to perceive migrations and the shift to multicultural societies as a central aspect of contemporary global development. For the left in industrialised countries, that would mean developing and advocating a co-ordinated strategy which simultaneously addresses issues of migration, multiculturalism, foreign and trade policy, and development policy.

Migration

It is necessary to advocate a migration policy that balances international solidarity with social and economic interests in the receiving areas. That means that western European governments and supranational bodies, such as the European Community and the OECD, need to accept that a certain amount of both permanent and temporary migration will take place, and that it is better to plan and administer this, than to drive it underground. I have in mind something like the systems adopted in the USA, Canada and Australia, where regular decisions are made on the numbers to be admitted in the categories of economic migrants, refugees and family reunion. All long-term migrants should have the right to permanent residence and family reunion, although this does not preclude special temporary admission schemes for students and trainees as part of development policies. Entry criteria should be free of discrimination on the basis of ethnicity, country of origin, religion, culture or gender. This need not prevent selectivity on the basis of criteria like education or training (in economic migration categories) and need (in refugee categories).

The demand for a migration policy may seem paradoxical in view of previous remarks on the breakdown of migration control and the erosion of entry categories. Nobody should have the illusion that such a policy can be easily and fully implemented. My argument is that it is better for countries to have policies based on a reasonable amount of immigration, selected according to fair criteria, even if these can only be partially effective, rather than to have unrealistic and discriminatory policies which lead to chaotic, exploitative and conflictual situations.

Multiculturalism

Demands for a fairer immigration system should be accompanied by a struggle for improved rights for immigrants and their descendants. This means working towards policies of multiculturalism. Citizenship for permanent settlers and their children is crucial. Where immigrants do not want to give up their previous nationality, dual citizenship is the answer (see Hammar in this volume). An alternative is some type of quasi-citizenship, that gives essential rights but stops short of naturalisation. Multiculturalism also implies the guarantee of minority cultural and linguistic rights. These include not only the right to individual and collective expression, but also the provision of necessary services, such as translation and interpreting facilities, to guarantee equal access to courts and social services. Educational measures need to be twofold: on the one hand support services to prevent disadvantage for children of different linguistic and cultural backgrounds in the mainstream school, on the other hand support for the maintenance of other languages and cultures. The core of multiculturalism is the demand for full political, economic and social participation of all members of society, whatever their ethnic background. Multicultural policy therefore necessarily includes a range of measures to counter discrimination, to ensure equal opportunities in all areas, and above all to combat racism.

Foreign and trade policy

Measures to reduce the north-south divide, and, in the long term, to reduce the need for migration, are as much issues of foreign and trade policy as of development policy. Stopping arms exports to LDCs could be the biggest single step towards cutting the number of asylum seekers. Trade policies which change the conditions and terms of trade in the favour of the south could make a major contribution. A drastic overhaul of the European Community's Common Agricultural Policy is an example. New attitudes towards social development on the part of the International Monetary Fund, the World Bank and similar agencies would also be important. An emphasis on human rights in all international and trade relations is an important demand.

Development Policy

As pointed out, in the short to medium term, development in the countries of the south will lead to increased emigration. Nonetheless, economic and social development is the only long-term solution to current imbalances, and should therefore be given priority. That means supporting development policies which involve real transfer of resources from north to south. A further demand is to include principles of ecologically sustainable development into all investment projects. Measures to improve health and social security in LDCs are also significant, in view of their long-term demographic consequences. Finally, development and migration policies should be linked, for instance through training schemes for migrants to provide the skills necessary for economic development upon return, or by making investment resources available to returning migrants.

Conclusion

Such proposals sound utopian, in view of the current priorities of the 'new world order'. Even if they were introduced, they would not bring about quick solutions to the increasing problems of migration and racism. Global migration is certain to go on increasing for the foreseeable future, and it will take place under very difficult conditions. Nonetheless, it is important to be able to put forward an alternative long-term perspective, because it gives credibility to the more immediate demands: those for fair and humane immigration policies, and for the recognition of the rights of immigrants and ethnic minorities within multicultural societies.

The Articulation of Racism and Nationalism: Reflections on European History

Robert Miles

Introduction

Throughout the 1960s and the 1970s, British writing on racism evolved largely in isolation from other European work but this solitude is now coming to an end. The 'race relations' paradigm was successfully challenged during the 1980s (Miles 1982) and, as a result, new theoretical approaches have emerged which are more open to a comparative perspective on Europe. Moreover, what appears to be a common, although uneven, political process throughout at least western Europe encourages a common European analysis. For example, in the context of the restructuring of capitalism since the early 1970s, the political crisis in most western European nation states has hinged in part upon a debate about the migrant presence, or rather, about the presence of certain groups of migrants (e.g. Wihtol de Wenden 1988). And, throughout Europe, fascist political organisations have re-emerged from the isolated corners to which they had been confined since 1945 (Cheles, Ferguson and Vaughan 1991).

The new interest in Britain in comparative research on racism in Europe has followed a broadening of the parameters within which racism is analysed. During the 1980s, a number of British writers (who were influenced in different ways by Marxism) concluded that the contemporary expression of racism in Britain could not be adequately explained without taking account of contemporary nationalism (Barker 1981; Miles 1987a,b; Gilroy 1987). Elsewhere in Europe, a similar conclusion has been reached (e.g. Balibar and Wallerstein 1988; Autrata et al. 1989). Interest in the articulation between racism and nationalism signalled movement away from a concern with the narrow question of whether or not racism was a product of (or functional to) capitalism. This concern had structured, directly and indirectly, much of the analysis of racism during the 1960s and 1970s and refracted the more general theoretical problems that arose from the 'base/superstructure' problematic. By posing the problem as one of an articulation, it was suggested that ideologies have ideological and political, as well as economic, determinants.

In Britain, research 'on Europe' is now *de rigeur*. Yet, unfortunately, some of this discussion and research is being conducted without sufficient reflection on the theoretical problems, and the historical complexities and contradictions. This chapter begins by identifying some of these difficulties and proceeds to discuss both modalities of racism and the articulation of racism and nationalism in a European context.

A New, European Racism?

References to a 'new racism' or a 'neo-racism' have become increasingly common in the British literature over the past decade. Indeed, the idea of a new racism has become a constituent element of a new radical orthodoxy. At the beginning of the 1980s, Barker claimed to have found a new racism in the discourse of right-wing politicians during the 1970s. He noted that references to 'race' and biological inferiority had given way to an argument that it was natural for people to wish to live amongst 'their own kind' and to express hostility to the presence of culturally different populations who had 'their own countries' in which to live (Barker 1981: 21–2). This new racism, Barker continued, had displaced the 'old racism' (characterised by its depiction of hierarchical 'race' typologies) (1981: 4).

More recently, in an analysis of the implications of the introduction of the Single European Act, Sivanandan (1988) has also identified a new racism. This variant is additionally described as a 'European racism', a 'pan-European racism' and a 'Eurocentric racism' which, he argues, is 'emerging from the interstices of the old "ethnocentric" racism' (1988). This concept of a new and European racism has structured an analysis of the contemporary expression of racism in the European Community in which different national racisms are presented as cohering into a new, unitary pan-European racism (Sivanandan 1991: v–vi; Webber 1991).

Balibar also claims to have identified the emergence of a 'modern racism' (1991: 15) or a 'European racism' (1991: 6). For Balibar this is 'not just a variant of the earlier racisms' but rather 'a *new* configuration' (1991: 11). What is new about it is that it is 'never simply a *"relation-*

ship to the Other" based on a perversion of cultural or sociological difference; it is a relationship to the Other *mediated by the intervention of the state* ... it is a *conflictual relationship to the state which is "lived" distortedly and "projected" as a relationship to the Other*' (Balibar 1991: 15). By implication, preceding or 'old' modes of racism were 'simply' discourses of difference which represented the Other as a mythological and negatively evaluated essence. Balibar's new racism is therefore new because it '"reflects" the originality of the social structure and the relationships of force that are being constituted in Europe at the end of twentieth century' (1991: 11).

What are we to deduce from these similar arguments? The most sympathetic conclusion is that the new racism comes in three different forms. But this is perhaps too generous. A more critical assessment would note that the three writers disagree about its nature and origins. According to Barker, the new racism is very different from the 'old' (and untypical) racism of the nineteenth century. But if the racism of the nineteenth century was a historical aberration, there is a presumption that the new racism entails a return to a form of racism that is historically typical and that existed prior to the nineteenth century. Barker fails to identify the characteristics of this racism. Indeed, his analysis is devoid of any extensive historical content (cf. Miles 1989: 62–6).

For Sivanandan, the new racism is emerging out of an older 'ethnocentric' racism. But, because he too does not specify the respective characteristics of these different forms, the sense in which the new, European racism is new is unclear. Indeed, when viewed in the light of his earlier writing, the new racism seems remarkably similar to the old. The objects of this new racism are 'the migrants, refugees and asylum-seekers displaced from their own countries by the depredations of international capital', as 'Third World immigrants', as 'blacks' (1988: 8–9), categories that have remained the object of his analysis of racism since the 1970s (e.g. Sivanandan, 1982). In this analysis, the only thing that seems to be new is that it is the same old story reproduced in all the nation states of the European Community.

Balibar's new racism represents not a continuity but a break with the past: it is a post-modern racism in all but name, a new modality 'reflecting' the novelty of the totality of contemporary relations of domination. One aspect of this uniqueness is, for Balibar, the intervention of the state. But is this mediation of the state in the identification of the Other an original, distinctive feature of the current relations of domination? Elsewhere, Balibar refers to Nazism, colonialism and slavery as three formations where racism has played a major ideological and political role in structuring social relations (1988a: 56–9). And, in all three *historical* formations, the state was a central mediator of the relationship between the dominator and the dominated, was the ensemble of institutions that ordered and legitimated social relations in accordance with racist discourses (e.g. Miles 1987c; Burleigh and Wippermann 1991). Stated more abruptly, it is mistaken to suggest that the active presence of the state has become an original feature of contemporary social relations, including those structured by racism, in Europe only as the twentieth century draws to an end.

Given these contrasts between the different conceptions of the new racism, it is difficult to conclude that each is correct. And even if it is resolved that each may contain an element of truth, it is impossible to determine wherein it lies without unravelling the contradictions. In part, this is because the quality of novelty embodied in the concept of new racism presumes an account of another, earlier instance of racism, an old racism, by which the qualities of newness might be measured. In other words, historical analysis is a necessary precondition of the concept of new racism. And if the new racism is additionally described as a specifically, even uniquely, European phenomenon, then that history must be, in part, a European history.

In this context, I have two reservations about the notion of a new, European racism. First, there are good reasons to characterise the old racism of the nineteenth century as a European racism, even though the economic and political context of the period was different in a number of respects. Within nineteenth-century Europe, those who contributed to the science of 'race' were aware of, and often very knowledgeable about, the work of members of the 'community of scholars' in other countries (Miles 1989: 34). Given that investigations conducted and conclusions drawn in one country were a stimulus to, and legitimation of, developments in another, there is a sense in which evolution of the scientific, biological racism of the nineteenth century within Europe can be described as a European racism. That is to say, there is nothing new about an imagination of Europe and its antinomies as sites for racialised populations and identities: what is new is the determinants and content of that imagination.

Furthermore, the evolution of this scientific racism was shaped by the wider context in which it evolved. European ideas of the Other beyond Europe were influenced by colonialism, and by the end of the nineteenth century, all of the nation states of north-west Europe had a colonial history, although for some (e.g. France, the Netherlands) that history was more extensive than for others (e.g. Germany). One small measure of this collective participation is found in the fact that those directly involved in colonialism often referred to themselves, and were often referred to by those who were the object of that practice, as 'Europeans'.

Second, I have reservations about the holistic and totalising character that is often attributed to the notion of a European racism. There is a body of work which links the origin of racism with certain core values and precepts that accompanied the emergence of Europe as a material and political force within the evolving world system in the sixteenth and seventeenth centuries (e.g. Balibar 1988a: 80). The European Enlightenment is the subject of this argument. Goldberg, for example, argues that 'The coherence of the racist project, then, is a *function* of the preconceptual elements that have structured racist dispositions' (1990a: 301; my emphasis). These elements include classification, order, gradation, hierarchy etc., and they 'generate the concepts and categories in terms of which racism is expressed and comprehended' (Goldberg 1990a: 301). Some writers have traced the foundations of this rationalism to an older Greek philosophy (e.g. Delacampagne 1983), thereby further extending the genealogy of racism.

This argument can be interpreted to mean that European culture is, *by its very nature*, racist. If this is indeed the claim, then the charge of essentialism would be valid. But let us consider the argument more carefully. It is true that, without science, there could not have been a scientific racism. It is equally true that the rationally planned mass murder of Jews, gypsies, homosexuals and communists in concentration camps was a *function* of the invention of poisonous gases such as cyanide. These are elemental and simplistic truths. But their analytical significance hangs on the meaning of *function*. Does the invention of cyanide *explain*, for example, the fascist attempt to solve for eternity the 'Jewish question'? There are other means of effecting mass murder, and, more significantly, why did the 'Jewish question' become a central political issue in fascist Germany? The fact of the invention of poison gas does not provide any kind of answer to these questions.

Similarly, the evolution of attempts to find order in the world, to identify hierarchies etc. does not explain why so many practitioners of science transformed the idea of 'race' in order to assert the existence of a fixed, biological hierarchy of different types of human being. The principle of classification, even of hierarchy, did not lead inevitably to the formulation of racist discourses. The simplicity of the claim that these preconceptual factors 'define in a general way the expression of those agents ... who speak and act in terms of racist discourse' (Goldberg 1990a: 301) does not grasp the multidimensionality and the contradictory character and consequences of the Enlightenment. Thus, while it is true that certain forms of racism were grounded in the principles of the new humanistic paradigm, those principles do not in themselves *explain* those racisms.

The Enlightenment contained many different ideological currents, and the manner in which they were utilised was not determined by the ideas themselves but by the interests of the different collectivities that sought to utilise them. Moreover, it is significant that there has been a consistent questioning of scientific racism as it evolved within Europe. This critique may have been irresolute throughout the eighteenth and nineteenth centuries but its existence requires explanation. The scientific critiques of typologies of 'race' which became increasingly hegemonic during the 1920s and 1930s (Barkan 1992) have parallels in the scientific and philosophical writing of the eighteenth century. The principle of underlying systems of fixed and discrete classification was criticised soon after it was formulated. The critics advanced the alternative principle of continuity, and claimed that the supposedly fixed boundaries between types of human being were socially constituted rather than created by nature (Gates 1990: 320–3).

In other words, if the Enlightenment bequeathed to us racism, it also bequeathed a basis for the critique of racism that was grounded in the same preconceptual terrain set in place by the transformation in 'ways of seeing'. Hence, it is relevant that it was to scientists that UNESCO turned when seeking to discredit the ideas of scientific racism that had been employed by fascism in the 1930s and 1940s (Montagu 1972). And, as I have shown elsewhere (1989: 36–7), the ideas and arguments that these scientists employed had precursors in the product of scientific practice in the late nineteenth and early twentieth centuries. My mistake lay in a failure to trace the full genesis of this scientific anti-racism.

In arguing that racism and anti-racism (or rather, certain instances of racism and anti-racism) are both rooted in the European Enlightenment, one is perhaps confirming that they both reproduce the same logic, but with reverse meanings and evaluations (in the manner of a mirror image), with the result that each requires and legitimates the other (cf. Taguieff 1988, 1990). There are real difficulties here which require careful consideration. But, in order to avoid a retreat to relativism, one can argue that the principles of the Enlightenment constructed a terrain on which a contradiction (between racism and anti-racism) was formulated: and the existence of *contradiction* opens the door to the possibility of negation rather than a mirror reproduction in the manner of a circle that always returns to its point of departure. Thus, if we are to prioritise the analysis of a European racism, we should approach this analysis with the presupposition that its evolution was a contested and contradictory process rather than unilinear and unquestioned.

Third, the distinction between 'old' and 'new' racism, in itself, presumes a unilinear evolution: by definition, it periodises different forms of racism as characterising successively different conjunctures. In the absence of supporting historical evidence, it is more valid to conceptualise the distinction as a difference of form and content rather than as chronological. In this way, one leaves open the question of which modalities of racism were dominant in different conjunctures. For example, Taguieff has expressed Barker's distinction between an old and a new racism analytically by referring to a *racisme différentialiste* and a *racisme inégalitariste* (1988: 321–3), thereby avoiding the implication that the contemporary racism is *by definition* a new or 'post-modern' phenomenon.

While there are difficulties with the concept of a new, European racism, it is true that contemporary expressions of racism in Europe (or rather, certain of them) are different in certain respects from those of preceding periods. Certain racisms have been transformed, but the nature of this transformation has not yet been adequately described and explained. Too often, analyses of the contemporary situation are devoid of any historical perspective: the present is compared with an imaginary past. In order to recover that past, a comparative, historical analysis of the evolution of racism and antiracism within Europe is needed urgently.

Typologies of Racism

The possibility of such an analysis is enhanced by theorising the concept of racism in such a way that it does not designate a singular, unchanging essence. The fact that the recent British discussion conceives of an old and a new racism presumes that we can talk of distinct *racisms*, each of which can be located in a distinct space and time. For one of the important analytical advances of the 1980s was the creation of the concept of *racisms*. This resulted from a critique of the assumption or claim that the object of the concept of racism was a single, static complex of beliefs and negative evaluations. Rather, so the counter-argument goes, we should understand the concept to refer to a range of historically specific instances of racism, each of which embodies contradictions and is in a constant flux (Hall 1980; CCCS 1982; Goldberg 1990b).

While the concept of racisms represents an important analytical advance, the promise so far exceeds the product. This is in part because the problematic character of the anterior concept of racism is too quickly marginalised as an 'academic' question. Analysis commonly commences with an *ad hoc* identification of the defining characteristics of racism which are derived from an empiricist depiction of a contemporary discourse. For example, much of the recent British literature assumes (and sometimes argues) that the only or the most important racism is that which has 'black' people as its object. The outcome is often an exclusive conception of racism which is blind to, or cannot permit the existence of, other modalities of racism. Indeed, a number of writers in the USA and Europe have proposed definitions of the concept of racism which preclude any 'non-black' population from being its object (e.g. Wellman 1977: 76; van Dijk 1991: 26–7; Essed 1991: 39).

This theoretical closure is highly problematic (Miles 1989: 54–61). It is also analytically unnecessary if one takes seriously Hall's reference to racisms being 'historically-specific' (1980: 336). This conception prioritises historical analysis and presumes the possibility of tracing continuities (and discontinuities) in the expression of different modalities of racism through historical time and space. But the notion of racisms does not abolish the concept of racism: rather, it requires us to be even more clear about its object. We need to have at least a preliminary definition of what it is that different racisms have in common to warrant designation as instances of the same genus of phenomenon, as *racisms*. Only then do we have a facility to periodise and select from history in such a way as to identify historically-specific racisms. Furthermore, the suggestion that there are different racisms does not by itself identify the dimensions and analytical categories by which a typology of racisms can be constituted. How are we to categorise these different racisms? Should racisms be differentiated by their object, by their structure or by the historical conjuncture in which they appear or are reproduced? Or by some combination of these different dimensions? In sum, the concept of racisms presumes a prior programme of conceptual analysis.

Within the recent British discussion, few contributors have extended their analysis beyond that single contemporary modality of racism which is usually analysed as having 'black' people as its unique object (but see Holmes 1988, 1991; Kay and Miles 1992). Those who have questioned this conception have constructed relatively circumscribed typologies which tend to be organised by reference to the object of racism and by historical conjuncture (Miles 1982; P. Cohen 1988). Cohen's work exposes the silence in most recent British discussions about anti-Jewish racism and hence demonstrates the need for a comprehensive analysis of the interrelationship between historical and contemporary racisms. Without it, British researchers will be ill-prepared to contribute to the analysis of racisms throughout Europe. Anti-Jewish racism is a central dimension of the histories of the evolution of the nation state in, for example, France, Germany and the Netherlands (Mosse 1978; Geiss 1988), while the escalating expression of nationalism in central and eastern Europe since the collapse of communism often draws upon the same modality of racism (Ascherson 1990; *Independent* 3 July 1991). Recent events in Britain reinforce the importance of the analytical challenge. Anti-Jewish racism has remained a central strand of neo-fascist political ideology since 1945 (Billig 1978) and there has been a recent escalation of violence directed towards Jewish communities in Britain (*Independent* 10 June 1990, 25 August 1991).

Much more attention has been devoted to specifying analytical distinctions between modalities of racism within the recent French discussion (e.g. Memmi 1982; Taguieff 1988; Balibar 1988a). Balibar's distinctions and historical typology (1988a: 56–65) are useful, if not yet systematic, reflections: they map out a series of analytical distinctions which can be employed when extending the existing historical research. Balibar acknowledges (correctly) their abstract quality and he would probably agree that their analytical power and utility remain to be assessed in the course of a historical analysis of different racisms in and of Europe. In contributing to that task, it is valuable to explore his distinction between racisms of the *interior* and racisms of the exterior (Miles 1991).

Interior and Exterior Racisms

The dichotomy implies the existence of a boundary. Use of the category 'Europe' offers a first approximation of the location of that boundary: the edge of Europe marks the distinction between interior and exterior. But the object of the category itself remains to be defined. Its contemporary usage does not define a geographical entity abstracted from social relations.

Its contemporary referent is an ensemble of nation states, whose social relations are structured by the capitalist mode of production and which are spatially located on the west and centre of a continental land mass. This ensemble includes some of the most economically and politically powerful nation states within the capitalist world system. But, a thousand years ago, Europe in this sense did not exist (Tilly 1990: 38–46, cf. Abu-Lughod 1989: 13; Pomian 1990: 36–41). This territorial space was then connected by no more than a loose network of trading cities, manors and monasteries, and the majority of the population were peasants engaged in localised agricultural production. There was no centralised political unit, and its southern edge was part of the Muslim world.

Thus, when referring to the *interior* of Europe, I am alluding to the transformation within this territorial space of feudal social relations into the structure of capitalist nation states that first approximated its current form only during the nineteenth century. This transformation was effected in part by the establishment of multiple relations with territories exterior to Europe: with the evolution of the world capitalist system, the interior and exterior of Europe therefore became a totality, but a totality structured by a hierarchy of economic and political power.

Accounts and explanations of racism within many European countries have highlighted the contemporary significance of the exterior. In particular, the *colonial paradigm of racism* asserts that colonialism was legitimated by racism, with the result that European images of colonised populations had a racist content. Thus, when colonised people migrated after 1945 to their respective 'Mother Countries' in Europe (including Britain, the Netherlands and France) to provide labour power, this racist imagery was reproduced and reworked to comprehend this supposedly novel presence within the nation states of Europe (e.g. Memmi 1990). This paradigm is closely related to the *labour migration paradigm* which has also been employed to explain contemporary racisms in Europe (e.g. Castles et al. 1984). Both trace a continuity from the exploitation of labour in the colonial conjuncture during the seventeenth, eighteenth and nineteenth centuries to the exploitation of labour of colonial and/or peripheral origin at the centre of the world capitalist system during the second half of the twentieth century.

Certain contemporary expressions of racism in Europe are partially explained by these two paradigms, but not all of them. Neither do they explain all historical modalities of racism. This is demonstrated by the silence within analyses grounded in a political economy of labour migration about that form of racism which has Jews as its object. Put another way, there is no necessary connection between the expression of racism and the migration of exterior, colonised populations as sources of labour power: there are certain modalities of racism which signify *interior*, rather than *exterior*, populations as their object (e.g. the Jews, the gypsies, etc.). The explanation for these other historically-specific racisms must be sought elsewhere. Certain of them can be explained by an analysis of the evolution of economic and political relations within the interior of Europe.

Racisms of the Interior: the Articulation of Nationalism and Racism

The history of the construction of the interior of Europe is a history of the inter-relationship between the emergence of the capitalist mode of production and the creation of a system of nation states. These nation states are the product of specific practices and strategies, of a process of *nationalisation* which, when measured against the legitimating ideology of nationalism, is incomplete and ongoing. It is this political process that should be analysed in its association with the development of the capitalist mode of production if we are to comprehend the origin and development of certain of the interior modalities of racism within Europe.

A comment on the meaning of *nationalisation* is necessary because of its connotations, at least in Britain, of bringing certain sectors of (inefficient) production under the control of the state. This is not the meaning employed here. Following Nairn (1988: 281) and Balibar (1988b: 122–6, see also Noiriel 1991: 84–93), I use the concept to refer to (since the late eighteenth century) the increasingly conscious and organised attempt by the state in Europe to create and reproduce a certain cultural homogeneity and a sense of commonality amongst the class- and gender-differentiated population within the territory over which it claims sovereignty. The resulting imagination of community is sustained, in turn, by the constant reference to, and the reality of, other 'nations' beyond the boundary of 'our own'.

Since the seventeenth century, the territorial spaces within which separate feudal classes have organised themselves in Europe (and which they have not only defended but also sought to expand in the struggle to sustain the extraction of an economic surplus) were slowly enlarged and reorganised by the centralising power of the state increasingly under the control of distinct bourgeoisies. As a central dimension of this process, the boundaries of nations were constructed and defended. From the end of the eighteenth century, Europe's cultural patchwork was reconstructed in accordance with the precepts of the ideology of nationalism which increasingly served as an agent of legitimation during the nineteenth century. By the middle of the nineteenth century, the multiplicity of languages, of local and regional identities, of distinct 'ways of life' (evident in diet, dress, religious belief etc.) in Europe were the subject of this cultural reorganisation which sought consciously to bring reality into line with ideology. This was often a formidable task: for example, in France in 1789, 50 per cent of the population did not speak French at all while, at the time of Italian unification in 1860, only 2.5 per cent of the population used Italian for everyday purposes (Hobsbawm 1990: 60). They were also often a formidable obstacle, a foundation for resistance to these forces of change.

But the impetus for transformation was not only political. The nationalisation impulse was grounded in the development of the capitalist mode of production: peasants were also being turned into nationalised proletarians throughout Europe (e.g. Weber 1977). The extension of commodity production within these nationalised boundaries was accompanied by a rural–urban migration, by the growth of towns and factory production, and by the commodification of agricultural production. These transformations had their own disintegrative effect upon local and regional cultural forms. But, by its very nature, it was an uneven transformation within and between different nation states (cf. Noiriel 1990: 33–71): industrial commodity production was centralised in certain locations and proceeded at different speeds. While by the middle of the nineteenth century, few rural areas remained uninfluenced by the transformation, cultural heterogeneity was far from having been eliminated within each nation state.

The nationalisation project sought to construct a national identity and a national culture within each nation state in Europe. The concept of *internal colonialism* (e.g. Hechter 1975) has a utility in describing this process of cultural transformation. Culturally distinct modes of existence and reproduction were erased or reconstituted in different forms following the migration of a large proportion of the rural peasantry and proletariat to the growing towns and cities. Languages were marginalised or eliminated by the introduction of state compulsory education which sought to instil a knowledge of the nationalised language. And the extension of the franchise required the participation of an increasing proportion of the population (but still not a majority until women were deemed to be full citizens) in a nationalised political system which further reinforced the idea of the nation as a political unit in which each individual had a direct interest.

The history of nation state formation in Europe is a history of a multiplicity of *interior* processes, including those of *racialisation* and *civilisation*. The concept of *racialisation* is now widely used in British analysis and does not warrant any extended discussion here (for a definition, see Miles 1989: 73–7). The concept of *civilisation* is routinely employed in analyses of that modality of racism that was articulated in European colonies in the nineteenth century (a racism that claimed that it was the 'white man's burden' to civilise the 'backward races' of Africa and Asia), but this usage commonly ignores the fact that the origin of the process to which it refers lies *within* Europe. The civilisation process was initiated by certain European, feudal aristocracies who sought to 'refine' their own behaviour (Elias 1978). A code of manners which stipulated the way in which daily life should be conducted was devised and revised, laying down the criteria to be met if a person wished to be accepted as civilised. The notion of a civilised person presumed and identified its opposite, whose existence provided a measure of achievement as well as a reminder of the dangers that awaited those who failed in the struggle to civilise themselves: the civilised Self and the uncivilised Other constituted an inseparable dialectic.

The emergence of the capitalist mode of production provided a new context within which the process of civilisation was sustained. The initiative passed to the rising bourgeoisie which (unlike the feudal aristocracies) sought to civilise not only itself but also the subordinate classes that it dominated, the rural peasantry and the expanding urbanised working class. Within Europe, civilisation thereby became synonymous with nationalisation. In the interstices of this articulation, a modality of racism was often expressed (Miles 1991, 1993): the 'backwardness' and 'insularity' of rural peasants, and the 'savagery' of the urbanised working class were often interpreted as biological attributes which obstructed their incorporation as 'races' into membership of the nation (e.g. Chevalier 1973; Jones 1976; Weber 1977; Womack 1989).

But the bourgeois ruling classes of the European nation states, several of which were created only during the nineteenth century, not only often racialised the classes that they exploited. They also racialised themselves in the course of constructing myths of their own origin *qua national* as well as *bourgeois* classes. And they had plenty of myths upon which to draw. Amongst the many racialised discourses produced in Europe during the eighteenth and nineteenth centuries, there was one which conceived the population of Europe as composed of different 'races'. It became commonplace for members of the bourgeoisie in each nation state to identify themselves with a particular imagined line of racialised descent on this genealogical map, often using it additionally to identify the criterion of membership of the nation, to specify the common 'we'. As a result, each nation was imagined to have a 'racial' character, composition and history. In these discourses of descent and membership, 'race' and 'nation' often became indistinguishable categories (e.g. Barzun 1938, 1966).

Formally, there was a contradiction between those discourses which represented the working class as 'urban savages', and hence as a 'race apart' and in need of civilisation, and those which represented the bourgeoisie as having a 'racial history and character' which typified the 'nation' as a whole. The former racialised discourse excluded the working class whereas the latter included it. But formal logic was not the important criterion in determining the political utility of these different discourses. Rather, their utility depended upon the often conflicting interests and strategies of different fractions of the ruling class. Moreover, the ideology of nationalism was available for pirating (Anderson 1991: 67): as a result, there were different nationalisms constituted not only from above but also from below.

During the last three decades of the nineteenth century up until the end of the First World War, the nationalisation process became partially autonomous as well as directly initiated by the state. Political movements developed within Europe which advocated a modality of nationalism which idealised cultural and 'racial' homogeneity as the foundation of the nation and so constructed an internal racialised Other (Miles 1989: 115–16; Hobsbawm 1990: 102, 105–8, 117–21). Drawing upon the prevalent scientific discourse of 'race', as well as much older negative religious imagery (Mosse 1978), sections of the *petite bourgeoisie* and the emergent 'middle class' complained that there were 'racially impure' elements within 'their' nation. This specific articulation of racism and nationalism identified Jews as the primary source of 'pollution'. The dynamic underlying this modality of racism, at least in the cases of France and Germany, had little to do with the signification of a recently arrived migrant population as a unwanted intrusion.

So, within the nation states of Europe, certain modalities of racism were organised and expressed from the eighteenth century onwards as a constituent element of the nationalisation process. But the project of nationalisation was never completed: cultural homogeneity within each national boundary within Europe was never achieved. The central class division between bourgeoisie and proletariat was expressed in part in the maintenance and reproduction of certain kinds of cultural expression which were only ever partially transcended by nationalisation. Moreover, the continued existence (although to varying degrees) of a peasantry and a rural proletariat in European nation states sustained a rural and regional cultural differentiation. Additionally, the prior growth of territorially specific cultural identities, expressed in a particular language and/or way of life, were often sufficiently strong as to be able successfully to resist, at least in part, the nationalisation attempted by the centralised state. In certain instances, these populations were incorporated into the nation-state on specific and privileged terms, as in the example of Scotland (Nairn 1981).

Successful resistance ensured the retention of the cultural 'raw materials' which have, since the late nineteenth century, become the subject for (but not the 'cause' of) political movements for 'national liberation' within a number of nation states in Europe. Examples include, in the case of France, Brittany and Corsica; in the case of Spain, Catalonia and the Basque region; and, in the case of the United Kingdom, Northern Ireland, Scotland and Wales (e.g. Foster 1980; McDonald 1989; Watson 1990). For many of those involved in these political struggles, the often repeated claim that decolonisation has been completed cannot be true: there are places in the interior of Europe where the idea of a post-colonial Europe is difficult to equate with the realities of material disadvantage, cultural difference and the discriminatory exercise of state power.

Is there an articulation between nationalism and racism evident in these instances of incomplete nationalisation and resistance, and if so, what are its parameters? Few writers on racism have posed such a question, and even fewer have attempted to answer it. I cite a single example to demonstrate only that the question is worth asking. The colonisation of Ireland by the English state has been accompanied by a long history of legitimation in which different representations of the Irish have been articulated. By the middle of the sixteenth century, the English ruling

class typified the Irish as savage and wild, although these attributed negative characteristics were paralleled by others which were more positively evaluated (Quinn 1966: 26, 32–3). This discourse of savagery and
civilisation was later racialised (Miles, 1982).

For example, seeking to explain the greater advance of capitalist
industrialisation in Ulster (the larger part of which was to become
Northern Ireland when the Irish Free State was constituted in 1922)
compared to the rest of Ireland, a letter writer claimed in the penultimate
decade of the nineteenth century in a Belfast newspaper:

> Ulster is not in my opinion, in feeling and sentiment with the rest of Ireland.
> There is much more Scotch and English blood in Ulster amongst all classes
> of society. There is certainly a larger preponderance of a race who are self
> reliant, industrious and aspiring, and who do not sit down to whine and
> blame their rulers, when their laziness, their thriftlessness and their want of
> enterprise make them poor ... (cited in Patterson 1980: 21)

Remove the reference to Ulster, and one could easily conclude that this
was written by an English or Scottish coloniser about Africa: in both
instances economic 'backwardness' was explained by attributing the
colonised 'race' with a set of negatively evaluated attributes while
'progress' resulted from the qualities of the superior 'race' of the
colonisers (Miles 1982: 95–120).

Thus, a form of racism was one strand in the domination and
exploitation of Ulster in particular and Ireland more generally, a form
which articulated with a religious differentiation between Protestantism
and Catholicism which had deeper roots in European history. It is worth
investigating the other instances of internal, separatist nationalism in
order to identify the influence (if any) of a racism expressed by the
'colonising' state and sections of those classes which identified themselves with that political and economic project which sought to overcome the 'backwardness' of the peripheries.

There is another sense in which the nationalisation projects of the
nineteenth century were (and are) incomplete. In so far as nationalisation idealised the notion of a unity of a culturally and/or biologically
homogeneous population, the continued existence of people possessing
(or thought to possess) those characteristics beyond the national boundary constituted (and constitutes) the potential for either an extension of
the boundary to include them or a migration into the nation state. There
are, for example, many hundreds of thousands of people living in central
and eastern Europe who can claim that they are German by cultural and
biological descent: such people migrated in large numbers into the Federal Republic of Germany during the 1980s (Räthzel 1991). In such circumstances, there is considerable potential for a renewed articulation of

nationalism and racism in the context of a struggle about the criteria used to define who 'belongs' to the nation.

Conclusion

There are three conclusions. First, the process of nationalisation has been integral to the development of capitalism in Europe and has resulted in different national histories, each with its own specificity. These histories are characterised by different articulations between nationalism and racism, and therefore by the presence of different interior and exterior racisms (and their articulation). While their common elements can be captured by typologies which, for example, distinguish between 'anti-black' racism and anti-Jewish racism, the strength of the nationalisation process should alert us to the importance of nationally-specific determinants of their genealogy and trajectory, and of their articulation with other ideologies and processes. The distinct legal definitions of 'belonging' in each nation state in Europe testify to this (Brubaker 1990a). The notion of a European racism, by its very nature, tends to suppress these distinctions. More seriously, a concept of European racism that treats all these national histories as identical instances of a singular historical evolution imposes a tidy homogeneity that negates these specificities (cf. Bovenkerk, Miles and Verbunt 1991).

Second, the contrast between the continued reproduction of the racisms that implicitly or explicitly refer to the national frontier in order to map the frontier between an internal Self and Other and the transnationalism of the emergent European racism is not located in the originality of the latter and the antiquity of the former. The scientific and colonial racisms of the nineteenth century were already European racisms. The contrast lies in the character of the structural context in which these racisms were and are expressed. The national racisms of the nineteenth and early twentieth centuries were articulated in a context of intense economic and political conflict between capitalist nation states within Europe. Hence, in the case of Britain, people believed to be of German origin, along with their property, were attacked during the First World War, and a similar fate befell people of Italian origin during the Second World War, violence that was preceded and legitimated by discourses that were in part racist and that were encouraged by the state (Holmes 1988: 97–9, 193–4; Panayi 1991).

The key novel element is not (as Balibar puts it) the mediation of the state between Self and Other but rather (as he also acknowledges) *the partial transmutation of the nation state* as a result of the creation of supranational economic and political structures within Europe, the underlying determinant of which is the desire to create a political space to facilitate the growth of units of capital which can remain competitive with those based elsewhere in the world economic system (Miles 1992). The national political unit remains a powerful reality, as does each state, but the movement towards a form of economic and political union within the European Community ensures that a multitude of economic and political issues, which individual states have in the course of the twentieth century each had to deal with in accordance with perceived national interests, are now increasingly being dealt with in accordance with perceived collective interests. Thus, the boundary of 'our' economic and political field has been extended, necessitating an extension of the boundary of the 'imagined community' beyond that of each nation state to Europe (and hence the *renewal* and *reconstruction* of the *idea* of Europe). At the edge of that recently extended boundary, there are 'new' and 'old' Others who can be presented as a threat to 'our' interests as Europeans, especially where material inequalities and political conflict sustain the potential for migration into Europe. Moreover, and herein lies a central contradiction, representatives of those 'old' Others are now permanently resident within the supranational entity of the European Community: in the structure of social relations, they are Europeans too, even if their Europeanness is denied ideologically and thereby becomes a site of struggle.

Third, and especially since the collapse of communism, the complex interrelationship between the incompleteness of nationalisation within Europe and the contemporary form of the process of Europeanisation constitutes a context favourable to the expression of racism irrespective of immigration. Both separatist nationalisms, and the revived nationalisms of the extant nation states of central and eastern Europe (including Germany since unification), induce debate about the criteria of belonging to the nation, augmenting the possibility that racist definitions might be employed. Separatist nationalisms commonly seek to reverse a historical 'injustice': the building of supranational European institutions provides a new context in which to seek independence from 'national oppression', a political struggle that necessarily requires a debate about the parameters of the 'we' who have been suppressed and that reconstitutes the history of the events and struggles by which the nation is socially defined. The history of contemporary nationalist political movements in the United Kingdom, France and Spain should therefore be analysed to assess the extent to which they have been constituted by racism and the extent to which they construct racialised myths of origin and destiny (e.g. Conversi 1990).

In the case of the nation states restructured by the collapse of communism, while new migrant populations can become the focus of debate about the criteria of belonging, the presence of internal cultural minorities can also be signified as the internal Other. These contemporary significations can draw upon commonsense memories of former identifications of these same minorities as some form of 'racial intrusion'. For this reason, an understanding of the history of earlier interior racisms is necessary in order to comprehend how such a historical legacy can be reworked in a new structural context. The imagined quality of Europeanness can constitute a transnational definition of Self to which the nationalised Self is imagined to belong: that is, it can be imagined as an extension of the nationalised genealogy in order to reinforce the alienness of the internal Other who has always belonged elsewhere.

PART II

Tendencies and Trends

Tendencies to Racism in Europe: Does France Represent a Unique Case, or is it Representative of a Trend?

Michel Wieviorka

For many foreign, and even French observers, the main characteristic of contemporary racism in France is a political phenomenon: the rise of the Front National (FN). For the ten years following its creation in 1972, the FN was nothing more than a very small group, a 'groupuscule'. But since the elections of 1983 in the city of Dreux (see Gaspard 1990), when it obtained 16.7 per cent of the votes, the FN has appeared as a real political force, a party with widespread networks and a constituency that makes it as powerful, or more so, than the French Communist Party.

There are now a considerable number of serious political and sociological analyses of the Front National which help to explain the reasons why France is a unique country in Europe where the extreme right has extensive political coverage (see Mayer and Perrineau 1989; Orfali 1990; Tristan 1987). But we must not mistake and deduce from this political reality that France is also a unique case from the point of view of racism. The FN should not be reduced to this single dimension. It brings together many other social and political meanings besides racism. It appeals to a more populist than frankly racist electorate. Similarly, all that is racist in France should not be attributed to it.

Even among the French extreme right, racism is not the monopoly of the FN. There are many small extreme right groups, such as Troisième Voie, which is nationalist-revolutionary, the Oeuvre Française, the Parti Nationaliste Français (PNF), the Parti Nationaliste Français et Européen (PNFE), which are more classically nationalist, and many others (see Bourseiller 1991). The ideology changes considerably from one group to another, but racism and antisemitism are common features. They may have connections with the Front National, but are usually jealous of their independence. Networks originating amongst these groups and in the Front National exert an intellectual influence, for instance the so-called 'revisionists', who deny the genocide of the Jews or the existence of the gas chambers. Even if most of them are extreme right-oriented, the main forms of racist violence during the past decade cannot be imputed to the FN, but to skinheads, to soldiers renewing with the principle of 'ratonnades', as was the case in Carcassonne in 1990, to individuals, or to small groups such as the PNFE, which was responsible for several terrorist attacks on migrant workers' hostels in the south-east of France in 1989.

Furthermore, it is also clear that racism is not restricted to the extreme right. This is particularly the case if one considers the main issue of discrimination. There is a real paradox in France: discrimination in housing and employment is very well known, and almost not studied. Everybody knows that it constitutes a major expression of racism, but it is very difficult to prove, and it is often ambiguous (see Commission Nationale Consultative des Droits de l'Homme 1991). A recent action can illustrate this last remark: in 1991, the President of a public housing institution, the SCIC, was condemned for racism because of his policy of refusing to allocate flats to foreign people as such, which is unlawful. But his policy was based on the idea of cleverly allocating the apartments, in order to avoid ethnic concentrations which could lead to racist troubles and tensions. Among the witnesses were some of the main antiracist leaders, including Harlem Desir, for the defence.

But the main aspect of racism in contemporary France is neither the small extreme right groups, nor the murderous violence, nor even the various forms of discrimination, but the extension to a popular level of a renewed set of racist discourse and practice that started during the 1970s, but became really visible in the mid-eighties. It is this pressure (along with electoral abstention) which sustains the Front National. Even if the Front National did not exist, or were to disappear, this pressure would exist, and be quite impressive.

Forms of Racism in France

There is a discourse at popular level which permeates French society, and includes in its various expressions two different kinds of proposals. On the one hand, this popular discourse is directly racist. The racism here is first of all hostile to foreigners, most of whom come from Turkey, Haiti and Black Africa. The racism is limited as far as Indo-Chinese people are concerned. It can aim at French citizens, from the Caribbean for instance, or gypsies, and to the numerous migrants who are, or who have become, French citizens. One of the main racist stereotypes today is based on the idea of cultural difference: the migrants, from this point of view, will never be assimilated – or rather 'integrated' which is the word that French people generally use. It is argued that there is something deeply distinct in the culture of migrants that will never be reduced to the dominant culture of France. Being irreducible, the difference is then not only cultural, it is also natural, inherent in racial attributes. The difference is often claimed to be easily stated, to appear in daily life for those, at least, who live among migrants: migrants are presented as noisy and dirty; their children are accused of being unbearable, disrespectful to people and the law, and when grown up, of being delinquents and drug addicts and dealers.

For many French people, there is a kind of inversion. Formerly, the present migrants were colonized people. Then they were unskilled workers. Today, they behave like invaders, or like a ruling group, and this image of a reversal of history leads to the idea that the real racists are not the French but the migrants, that there is an anti-French racism and that the French are the victims. This idea is all the more widespread as many French people are convinced that migrants are much cleverer at getting public welfare, that they pervert the whole system of the welfare state, which has not been created, for instance, for unemployed people with two or three wives and eight or ten children. Migrants are accused of becoming rich thanks to public welfare.

The second kind of argument, in popular discourse, is not directly racist, and deals with elements other than migrants, such as the state, social institutions and the political system. If migrants are the source of so many problems, it says, it is because the police and the justice system are failing and powerless. It is because the school system is no longer able to educate children. It is because the family, as an institution, does not transmit fundamental values any more. In this perspective, people complain of the great distance of politicians, who live far from real life and people, have no idea of the real problems, have ceased to be representative of new demands, and even more, are suspected sometimes of preferring migrants to the local French *'de souche'* (from old stock).

This discourse, that articulates direct racism with populist criticisms of the state, of the political class or of the institutions, varies in 'subtlety' and 'blatancy', depending on the social groups considered. It is not only a set of prejudices. It also leads to practical effects, or accompanies or underlies racist action (see Wieviorka 1992).

Racist action may be political, and not confined to voting. For instance, political pressure can be exerted on local authorities to prevent the opening of a mosque or a decision on a programme of public housing targeted at poor and migrant people. At a local level, this pressure may be constant and effective by means of joint letters sent to the mayor, interventions by firms and others in the local press. It is not difficult for a mayor to let his constituency know that he understands clearly this kind of demand.

Action may also be external to the political system. For instance, it may be explicitly intended to create or reinforce a form of segregation. Parents will stop sending their children to sporting or cultural meetings in so-called 'Maisons pour tous' or 'Centres Sociaux' as soon as the person in charge has an Arab name, or if young migrants participate in these meetings. Very real and solid walls are built by the inhabitants of a neighbourhood to ensure that the inhabitants of the nearby neighbourhoods do not cross their territory, bringing all the troubles that the poor and migrants are supposed to bring. Sometimes people get ready for violence. They buy guns, as individuals, and explain to their neighbours that they would not hesitate to use them in case of emergency. In many cases people speak of creating a private local police – a militia – though usually they do not implement this idea.

There are also links between popular racist discourse and the racism that can be observed in some institutions. For instance, there is a racism specific to the French police, but this racism is not radically different from the more general French racism. Education is also an important issue because it is increasingly becoming a field for both social and ethnic segregation: if you have the means, you will arrange not to send your children to the neighbouring state school if it has a high percentage of migrants. Instead, through a political network, you either send them to a 'good' state school, or pay for a private one.

To understand recent developments, which we have very rapidly summarized, it is necessary to introduce two different and complementary perspectives. The first one presents the general conditions that have enabled the renewal and growth of racism in the 1980s; the second one gives a precise image of the different processes that converge in the same racist hatred. But before examining these two perspectives, we must take into account the concepts of race relations and communities.

Race Relations and Communities

If racism has been strengthened in France during the last fifteen years, is it because migrants have become more numerous, and less and less able to integrate into the French society? This idea is rather popular, even among some social scientists who do not really distinguish between a sociology of migrant people, and a sociology of racism. But this idea is not plausible. Migrants are victims of racism, they are not its cause, they cannot explain it. In many situations, you do not have any migrants, but there is strong racism. In other places we know that it is possible to meet with antisemitism without Jews. Not only can racism not be explained by the people it aims at, but the notion of 'race relations' seems to be inadequate, at least in the French case. This notion suggests that racism is a product, or an element of real, practical relations between groups that define themselves in terms of race. In France, the notion of 'race relations' is not used, and if we want to retain the image of groups and relations, we can only speak in terms of culture, and in terms of religion or of what we call in France 'communities' (*communautés*).

But these images are often misleading. For instance, during the Gulf crisis, many journalists expected the Islamic or Arab 'communities' to start riots and anti-French violence, and nothing occurred. Similarly, when Salman Rushdie was condemned to death by the religious and political authorities in Iran, the only demonstrations against him in France were very weak – a few hundred demonstrators, most of them recently arrived in France from Pakistan, and not at all representative of the so-called 'communities' of migrants. There is some reality in the notion of 'communities', but we must realise that the 'communities' are also a social product, that they are built through political and social processes, through social exclusion, police violence and political ignorance. Similarly in the summer of 1991 important events shed light on the dramatic experience of the 'Harkis'. In the 1950s, these people, who were Muslim and lived in Algeria, had chosen the French camp, and fought with the French army against the FLN. In the 1960s, they had to settle in France. But nothing was done for them, they lived in very poor conditions and were socially excluded. Thirty years later, they appeared as a community, and even an ethnic community, whereas their definition, at the outset, was an administrative one. They were 'supplétifs' – supplementary soldiers in the French army.

More generally, I would say that racism contributes to produce 'race relations', or intercultural relations, much more than it is produced by them.

Processes of Change and Racism

Over the past twenty or twenty-five years, France has experienced a considerable change, which defines the general conditions of the rise of racism. Let us emphasize four aspects of this change.

The first and main one is the decline of classical industrial society and, consequently, the exhaustion of its central actor, the working-class movement. The end of the working-class movement does not mean the end of trade unions, but a vanishing ability to bring universal values into social conflicts. In the past, struggles starting from work and production could go beyond corporatist or limited interests, and unite different actors who were in other struggles.

The working-class movement has never been more powerful than when it was able to speak in the name of skilled and unskilled workers, of female as well as male workers, of white and coloured people. When it vanishes or weakens, many projects and hopes, even those far from the shop-floor disappear, or become artificial, in the neighbourhoods, in universities, in political parties, in various firms. Some actors, who could find in it a reference, the highest meaning for their own action, look for other references, other meanings, and will sometimes find them in ethnicity, nation, identity, roots and, in some more extreme cases, in race (Wieviorka 1991).

A second aspect of social change in France deals with French national consciousness. In the past, France could identify itself with a universal nation. As a colonialist power, for instance, the aim was to bring to colonized people progress, science, education, reason. The idea was that France was the only nation that could really do so. Even decolonisation, under General de Gaulle, was characterised by this conception, the idea being that a universal nation like France had to play a leading role in the self-determination of other nations. Today, this image of greatness, linked to universal values, has weakened. In some cases, French national consciousness becomes a provincialism, or a retraction which becomes a dark, populist, xenophobic nationalism.

A third important aspect of social change in France is the crisis of the republican state which originated in the revolution, the Empire and the Third Republic. At the end of the nineteenth century, the cultural centralisation of the country had not yet been achieved. At that time, important changes occurred, through conscription (the recruitment of young men for the army) and also through the state school system, which became free and compulsory. The welfare state really developed at that time, but also the dissociation between religion and politics, with the unique formula of '*laïcité*' or secularism.

But today, this republican state is in crisis. The welfare state is not able to deal with extensive and structural unemployment – approximately 10 per cent of the active population. The model of a strict separation between church and state, or of a secular society which had never been perfectly achieved, has been challenged, as was revealed with the scandal around the Islamic hejab or headscarf in 1989. The republican school is losing its capacity for integration.

The last important aspect is cultural change. In the recent past, in France, effort, deferred gratification and saving were central positive values, and at the same time there was some trust in collective and political action. Since the beginning of the 1980s, it has become possible to speak of a social vacuum and to emphasise tendencies to individualism, narcissism, self-reflection and overvaluation of private and family life.

These tendencies are not incompatible with the quest for non-social identities, religious or nationalist feelings. Some authors have insisted on the strengthening of this individualism, which means a behaviour of *homo oeconomicus*, and gives considerable importance to the market. Others have shown that this evolution could also mean a greater subjectivity, and have spoken of the return – the return of the subject, the return of the actor (see Renaut 1989; Touraine 1984). But it is true that individualism has been more visible than subjectivity, and that tendencies to refer to communities, roots and non-social identities have been stronger than efforts to participate in the birth of new forms of collective action.

So, there has been in France, since the end of the sixties, a considerable change with two major consequences. One is the dualisation of French society. In the industrial past, people were defined by their position in the same social system. They were dominant or dominated, exploited or exploiters. Nowadays, people are defined by their participation: they are either *inside* the social system, or *outside* it.

A second consequence is an ethnic revival that concerns very different populations. At the beginning of the 1970s a wave of regionalism began but did not really last, with Basques, Alsatians and Corsican, Breton and Occitanist movements. On the other hand, transformations among the French Jews are still in process. They started at the same time, breaking with the time-honoured tradition dating back to the Enlightenment and the Revolution, when being a Jew was significant only in private life. The Jewish revival has two aspects. One is defensive, defined by action against antisemitism, and this aspect appeared in strength at the time of terrorist attacks on synagogues in the rue Copernic (October 1980) and the rue des Rosiers (August 1982), with large demonstrations in the streets, or later, after the profanation of Jewish tombs in Carpentras (May 1990). The other aspect is more offensive, and also more diversified. It defines the space in which Jews try to assert their religious, political, ethical and cultural identity, or their relationships with the state of Israel.

These first expressions of an ethnic revival did not arouse attention in France, even if they were sometimes violent. They were rooted, even if mythically, in the domestic history of the country. Everything changed when, at the beginning of the 1980s, the growth of Islam came to public attention. Ethnicity, then, was perceived as a danger coming from abroad, an invasion. Previously, migrants were defined as workers. Suddenly, they appeared as Muslims. There has been a clear exaggeration in the images of these populations, in the description of their communities, in the threat of fanaticism, fundamentalism or Islamic terrorism. The counterpart of these images, and of the beginning of ethnicisation, has been the resurgence of a defensive form of nationalism, which is grist to the mill of the Front National.

Racism as a Process

Contemporary forms of racism correspond to various processes which have been produced by profound social change. We can distinguish four main processes.

The first is constituted by the various forms of behaviour which consolidate segregation when it has been gained or acquired in fact. It occurs in pleasant neighbourhoods, in gentrified parts of the inner city, in some suburbs where there are few migrants, where there is no threat of 'invasion'. In such areas, racism has two functions. On the one hand, it maintains a gap between the people who live inside the area, and the people who live outside it. It forbids any connection, and resists, for instance, the efforts made by social workers or teachers to create some communication between people living in the two different areas. On the other hand, racism helps maintain the inferiority of the few migrants who live in the neighbourhood, by discriminating against them in terms, for instance, of housing, jobs and even school. The case of Marseilles is a good illustration of this first type of racism, which is very obvious in the 'quartiers sud' of the town. Racism of this type is a mixture of fear and affirmation of social status, and is much more intense among people who are not really stable in their status and fear downward social mobility.

A second kind of process is the exact opposite of the previous one. It happens in areas where 'poor whites' have been forced to stay, and to live among migrants. These French people are as poor as the migrants. They have a deep feeling of injustice. They do not understand the reasons why they stay in poverty and underemployment. They are exasperated, and they can really explode and express a strong but unstable racism, which brings a racial distance to replace the social distance which is missing between the migrants of the neighbourhood and these poor French people.

A third process is represented by the phenomenon of loss of social status due to the dualisation of French society. Many people, among the middle classes, and even among the working class, have lost social status and their job, being obliged to live in poor or declining neighbourhoods. The greater the loss, the more radical is the racism, especially when a decline in status increasingly means living among migrants who appear as the symbol of one's failure, and become its cause through the classical process of scapegoating.

A final pattern corresponds to situations where a way of life disappears, where solidarity networks, traditions and community relationships begin to break up. This phenomenon is particularly impressive in a neighbourhood, or even a whole town built during the industrial era and as a function of industry, in which the more dynamic people have not left but industry is over and workshops closed. In old neighbourhoods of the inner city, but also in recently urbanised suburbs, with housing having been built during the 1950s or the 1960s, the youngest and well off people, even among the working classes, have left, and the people that came in were poorer and poorer, and increasingly migrants. The oldest inhabitants, those who could not leave, sometimes resign or adapt themselves to the new situation. But sometimes, they are exasperated because of the migrants, but also by the state and the political system that has abandoned them. These people are among the most radical racists we met during our field research, maybe because they are living the end of their own traditions, a true solitude, the loss of previous social and cultural networks, and at the same time suspect, not without reason, that the migrants opposite are able to develop their own powerful networks and solidarity, their religion etc. (Wieviorka 1990).

France in European Perspective

Starting from the perspective which takes into account the profound social change in contemporary France, and the various logics of racism which this facilitates, it is possible to sketch a comparative approach between France and other western European countries. If one compares political expressions of racism, there are clear differences. The British National Front, for instance, never got the support that the French Front National has obtained. While a new political extreme right resembles these parties ideologically in Italy, this is not the old Movimento Sociale Italiano (MSI), but regional organisations, such as the Lega Lombarda. But political differences should be analysed in political terms, and not with the idea that they express differences of nature and intensity in racism. For instance, one can argue that the long presence, in the United Kingdom, of a vigorous right-wing government with Mrs Thatcher at its head, restricted the political space for the extreme right, while in France, the decomposition of the classical right exerted the opposite effect. One can also explain the Italian phenomenon of extreme right regionalism as being connected with the structural weakness of the state and the nation.

All these political differences do not necessarily mean that the same overall change has occurred in all countries, and that contemporary racism originates in fact from the same developments. But we should be aware of broad trends which can help us to understand the emergence of racism in societies such as France. In fact, a similar line crosses all western European countries whatever their differences. This line is defined by the decline of classical industrial society and the exhaustion of the working-class movement. For several countries, this means the end of an era when migrant people were considered as workers and were victims of a racism that was characterised by contempt and treated them as inferiors. It also means, whether there are migrants or not, that there is a dislocation of traditional relationships, dualisation, considerable downward mobility, and ethnic or nationalist revivals that induce tendencies to racism everywhere. These tendencies are mainly differentialist, i.e. they call for their victims to be expelled, or at least segregated, much more than inferiorised. They consider that there is no room in the society for the migrants. They do not stress contempt, but instead hatred, fear and obsession of being invaded. The problem, in this new racism, is not to give a place, the lowest one, to the migrants, but to rid the country of those people who belong to different cultures and cannot be integrated, not because of the society, but because of themselves.

The sources of racism, from this perspective, are not so different from one country to another. Nor is its content. The new racism described by Martin Barker (1981), for instance, is very close to what we can observe in France. This is the essential point. Then, the differences that can be observed should be analysed in terms of historical backgrounds and specific political and administrative cultures. For instance, such countries as the United Kingdom, the Netherlands, Belgium and France have a heavy colonial past, and in these countries migrations were due to the historical ties resulting from this past, and not only as a direct function of the economic demands from industry. In these countries, the institutional treatment of migrant people facilitated the transformation of their situation when they no longer corresponded to economic needs. Then the exasperation and fear for instance of 'poor whites', downwardly socially mobile or excluded, were more easily directed towards migrants as scapegoats.

By contrast, though countries like Spain, Italy or Portugal also have a colonial past, they were also the point of departure of important migrations, much more than a point of arrival for people coming from former colonies. Racism there is not so strong, or takes very different expressions. For instance in Italy, the main phenomenon until recently has been a deep contempt in the north against the people from the south, the *'terroni'* (people that have the black colour of earth). The political and administrative culture is sometimes a break with classical racism, which treats migrants as inferiors, and a move to the new racism, that treats them as radically different. In Germany, for instance, considerable racism has developed aimed at Turkish people. But these people are defined as workers, they are economically included and politically excluded, having for instance nearly no chance of acceding one day to German citizenship for themselves or their children. In this situation, Turkish people, even if they are perceived as different, do not appear as a threat, a potential invasion, and the racism is less 'new', as Barker says, less cultural or differentialist, as French social scientists say, than in other countries.

Other differences could be pointed out, for instance between countries with a pluralist political system, opened to various ethnic communities, and countries such as France, which are far from this model. But the main point is that all these differences should not conceal the deep unity of racism in Europe: in spite of its diversity, the phenomenon is the fruit of the move from an industrial society to a post-industrial one. The question then becomes: if racism was invented with the industrial era, and renewed with its decline, will it be a central figure of evil in the post-industrial era?

–5–

Ideological and Institutional Foundations of Racism in the Federal Republic of Germany

Czarina Wilpert

The concept of racism in post-war Germany has been complicated by the weight and stigma of the past. Race as a legitimate basis for scientific categorisation and hierarchisation of peoples has been discredited, and with it the concept of racism. Racism is identified with genocide. This is the past. It is a horrid, an unfathomable, non-repeatable mistake. The concept of racism has been ignored within mainstream academic discourse and has had no place within university curricula, nor has it been on the agenda for social scientific research.[1]

Only with the advent of unification do we find the concept of racism beginning to enter the public debate. Official discourse never speaks of racism. *Ausländerfeindlichkeit* (xenophobia or hostility towards foreigners) is at issue, as a study commissioned by the federal Ministry of Labour (1991) formulates, but, in this case, primarily, in the former east German Democratic Republic. This study found that over two thirds of the foreigners interviewed in the east had been insulted by Germans, 20 per cent more than once physically attacked, and 40 per cent discriminated against in shops. This seemed to substantiate beliefs that hostility toward foreigners (Ausländerfeindlichkeit) is greater in the east than in the west (although the latter has not been systematically studied) (Gaserow 1991). Clearly it took the increasing visibility of public acts of racial violence in the east to motivate such a study. Although racial violence existed in the west before the Berlin wall fell, it was unlikely to be categorised as such and received little public

---

1. Obviously, an exception are the numerous works committed to the study of anti-semitism in its historical, political, and social psychological dimensions, such as the work being conducted at the Zentrum für Antisemitismus Forschung in the Technische Universität Berlin. A few colleagues have been steadfast in their focus on other forms of contemporary racism (or *Ausländerfeindlichkeit*) in west German society since the middle of the 1980s, but have received little recognition within academia.

notice. Since the Federal Republic of Germany has no anti-discrimination legislation and lacks a well and widely organised civil rights movement, no central or systematic documentation on racist and discriminatory behaviour existed.

Pro and Con: The Significance of Racism in Post-War Germany

In the meantime several other studies have been conducted. Comparing findings from studies in east and west, the first indications were that east Germans were more willing to express openly their fears and animosities towards foreigners and ethnic minorities than west Germans, who perceive themselves as more tolerant. A study conducted by members of the Youth Institute in Leipzig in 1990 (Friedrich et al. 1991) found that 30 per cent of young adults supported the call for the expulsion of foreigners, although less than 1 per cent of foreigners reside in the eastern states today and over half of the interviewees had never had contact with foreigners. Another study (Funke 1991) which compared the attitudes of youth in east and west found that 40 per cent of all young adults in the east could be considered to be xenophobic, while *only* one fourth of young persons in the west could be considered anti-foreign. In the east one fourth of the respondents even went so far as to give vocal support to racist activities against foreigners.

Later studies confirm the higher per capita frequency of racial violence in the east than in the west. A recent report conducted for the Bundnis'90/Greens in the state of Sachsen-Anhalt found that the likelihood to be a victim of violence from the radical right was thirty times greater in that state than in the west German state of North Rhein-Westphalia (Löblich 1992). On the other hand, the data collection procedures are certainly very unreliable and the registration criteria appears to differ from one police agency to the other. The Berlin bureau of police claim that they do not register statistical data about victims (Antwort des Senats, Kleine Anfrage Nr.1511: 6 January 1992).

Shortly following the unification process a sentiment grew among west German intellectuals that the concept of racism might well be applied to behaviour in the east. ('Before the east opened ... we in the west were truly a multicultural society', commented a west Berlin sociologist who counts herself as belonging to the left.) West Germany has clearly felt the weight of its past and blatant racist attitudes and ideologies have been stigmatised. Democratisation had worked. And if there was the slightest impression of a slip of the tongue by prominent politicians, 'the eyes of the world were upon Germany'.[2] At the same time, liberal-thinking west Germans generally believed that foreigners were better off in Germany than immigrants in most other places, such as racist France and England, and certainly better than in their own less enlightened home countries. The comfort and prosperity of the welfare state seemed to conceal the significance of ideological and institutional discrimination of foreigners. Racism was ignored as a concept pertinent to contemporary German society. Today feelings have changed; more and more Germans are concerned about racial violence and the political racism potential of the radical right.

While racial violence in the east may belong to what some social psychologists currently term blatant as opposed to subtle racism (Pettigrew and Meertens 1991), there is a danger that the focus on the east disguises the existing racist ideologies and their anchoring in the institutions of German society west and east. On the one hand, the upsurge of attacks against foreigners and homes for asylum seekers in the east lend credence to the belief that this behaviour results from a lifetime shaped by a corrupt dualistic communist regime. On the other hand, racial violence continues to erupt in the west as well. There is good reason to believe that the ideology which feeds this behaviour may be perceived by some in the east as fundamental to west German society, as indicated by the dominant political discourse in the west.[3]

As we know, the skinheads – those who have received the most publicity for their violence, first came to life in the west. Their existence in the east even before the Wall fell might be interpreted as one of the first identifications with western forms of protest.[4] The usual interpretation in the West is, however, that racial violence and its toleration in the east is possible because of a xenophobic consensus created by forty years of socialization in a corrupt dualistic totalitarian system (which denied any responsibilty for the Nazi past) and the currently experienced socio-economic insecurity. This is no doubt a plausible argument, and many may find it convincing when seen in the context of the rising nationalism throughout eastern Europe.

Nonetheless, these events and their publicity should not veil the existence of racist ideologies and behaviour in the west. It could be that factors central to west German society may assume a new importance in the

2. Jenninger affair

3. Cf. discussion of the evolution of policies toward foreigners in the west in Wilpert 1983 and 1991.

4. An expert on the development of right-wing extremism in the east during the last decade (Seidel-Pielen 1991) claims that extremist groups had contact with right-wing movements in the west before the fall of the Wall. With the opening of the Wall the elite of the west German right made its way into the east to help in propagating their ideologies.

context of unification. My primary argument is that institutions upon which the west German Federal Republic was founded are supported by a dominant ideology which distributes rights according to ethnic origins and these have implications for racist beliefs and behaviour. The main objective of this chapter is to establish the relationship between institutions and ideologies in west German society and to illustrate the legitimacy this conveys to everday racist ideologies and behaviour. It is not within the scope of this chapter to explain comprehensively why certain forms of racial violence have emerged in the context of unification. At the same time I believe that the arguments presented provide a basic rationale behind these activities.

The focus of this chapter will be on the west and not the east, although I will return to reflect on the situation in the east and some implications of the unification process as I conclude. To develop this argument it is necessary to sort out some suppositions about the role of ideologies and institutions in contemporary Germany.

Ethnic Nationalism, Migration and Racist Ideologies

The constitution and legislation of the Federal Republic of Germany are based on a historical tradition and belief that the modern German state is legitimately founded on one culture, one nation (*Volk* in the sense of *ethnos*) and a biological principle of descent. Germany is a nation state. The government, ruling parties, politicians and intellectual elite do not consider themselves to be in any way nationalistic. Nationalistic ideologies, along with pan-Aryan ideologies, lost their legitimacy in the post-Nazi Federal Republic. Thus, how can one propose that racist ideologies be tied to the new Federal Republic state and its institutions? Ultimately this poses the question as to whether the ethnic nation state itself provides a basis for institutional racism and thus legitimacy to racist ideologies.

Central to this issue is Germany's definition of rights to citizenship and its language of migratory phenomena. The semantics of migratory phenomena derive from the German concept of citizenship and rights to membership. It is the primordial ethnic quality of origins and the institutions which define the criteria for membership rights and equal treatment which links processes of international migration, ethnic nationalism and the integration of immigrant groups to the legitimation of racist ideologies. The terminology commonly employed in Germany defines persons newly entering the country first according to ethnic categories, and then according to social categories. Together, these reveal an extreme diversity of legal rights, access to membership and contradictory levels of meaning.[5] The terms 'immigrant' and 'immigration' have no official status. These legal/institutional distinctions are based on underlying beliefs about who qualifies to belong and who does not. The criteria for categorisation of eligibilty are grounded in ethnicity and linked to Germany's past. These semantics conceal the duality of German migration policy, although the German state proclaims officially that it cannot be defined as a country of immigration.

In the perspective I am pursuing, racist ideologies are defined as constructing the collective other, members of certain social groups, as inherently inferior by reason of their origins, which may or may not be defined in a biological/genetic (phenotypical or genotypical) sense. Cultural, ethnic or religious criteria may assume a phenotypical quality and also be applied. It is important that the criteria identify these as inherently inferior and inalterable characteristics of the collective. Racist ideologies, moreover, assert an active effort at social subordination, exclusion or avoidance of the identified groups (See 1986). In the ethnically defined nation the ideology of ethnic nationalism constructs a myth of communal belonging and creates a collective identity which claims that only those so defined belong for ethnic (natural/kinship, i.e. primordial) reasons. This ideology threatens to become racist because it supplies, especially in the context of a parallel process of migration and settlement of foreigners and ethnic Germans, the logic for social institutions which set boundaries and systematically discriminate against others because of their unchangeable ethnic origins.

In the German case these institutions may be considered racist in the sense that two different sets of criteria are applied in policies toward migrants. Neither policy is considered to be an immigration policy (Germany not being a country of immigration). The first is the policy for *Volksdeutsche (Aussiedler)* which is hewed out of responsibility for Germany's Nazi past. This policy applies to non-territorial ethnic Germans who were resident before 8 May 1945 in what had been defined by annexation as the territory of the Third Reich on 31 December 1937. The second is the 'guestworker' recruitment policy. This applies to persons from recruitment countries who are members of collectives meant to return and in principle have no *right* to membership in German society. Contrary to its official proclamation, the Federal Republic of Ger-

---

5. The ethnic Germans from the east are *Aussiedler*. *Vertriebene* were those Germans expelled from eastern Europe after the War. The recruited foreign workers were the *Gastarbeiter*; today they are *ausländische Arbeitnehmer*. They and their families are sometimes euphemistically referred to as *ausländische Mitbürger*. *Asylanten, wirtschafts Asylanten*, are the asylum seekers or those seeking asylum for economic reasons. *Flüchtlinge* are legitimate refugees.

many has been a country of immigration/migration since its inception. Since the 1950s there have been two types of migrants: *Volksdeutsche* (ethnic Germans from the east) and foreign workers and their families. Semantics do not permit, however, that either group be considered immigrants.

The Historical Roots of the Rights to Membership: The German Communities in Eastern Europe

The issue that the Federal Republic's adherence to a 'volkisch' (ethnic) national identity, rooted in language, culture and history, as being fundamentally contradictory to the notion of a republic was only recently raised (with little political success) by a prominent political scientist (Oberndörfer 1987). This interpretation points out the link between the historical dream of achieving the political unity of all peoples of German language and culture which ended in 1945 to the identity of the new republic for Germans. Having presented Oberndörfer's arguments in other places (Wilpert 1991) here I would like only to emphasise the contradiction he indicates in the federal consitution which at one time speaks in its first three articles of the rights of all persons, but later of rights for Germans only.

According to article 116 a German citizen is either a person who *de jure* holds German citizenship, a spouse or descendant of persons who were settled in the German Reich on 31 December 1937, as well as refugees or deportees with German '*Volkszugehörigkeit*' (ethnicity).[6]

It is this last clause which enabled nearly twelve million refugees from the former Reich in the east as well as the former Austrian Sudetenland, and '*Volksdeutschen*' from east, south-east Europe and the Soviet Union to be integrated into the new Federal Republic. And it is this phrase in the constitution which permitted about 12,000 Saxon and Swabian Germans a year to leave Romania, where they first settled in the twelfth (Saxons) to seventeenth (Swabians) century, and automatically enter the citizenship of the Federal Republic of Germany (McArthur 1976; Verdery 1985).

The national socialist ideology and its perpetuation had disastrous implications for the German peoples on the other side of the border.

---

6. *Aussiedler* are German citizens or *Volkszugehörige* (ethnic Germans) who were resident before the 8 May 1945 in the boundaries of territory of the German Reich from 31 December 1937, and left that teritory after the completion of the expulsion of Germans. (This covers Poland, the Soviet Union, Czechoslovakia, Hungary, Romania, Yugoslavia, Danzig, the Baltic states, Bulgaria, Albania and China.)

Hitler's Germany engaged these communities not only in a political and world view, but their identification with and annexation to Nazi Germany resulted in revenge on them as *Volksdeutsche*, which led them to be punished in their centuries-old homelands as allies of Hitler's fatherland (Weber-Kellermann 1978: 100). Thus, there are unresolved historical issues which directly influence the perception of the legitimacy of racist ideologies in the present.

The political decision to commit the new German Republic to the ethnic German allies of national socialism as a sort of reparation may be logical. The injustice is, however, that the exclusive ethnic definition of the state does not permit a similar commitment to ensure rights to membership to other collectives who were sought out to work in the Federal Republic, where many have settled, despite thirty-five and more years of residence.[7]

The Ideological Implications of Ethnic Descent

This injustice in access to rights and priviliges not only segments German society into who is desirable and who is not, but it also has a number of other important implications. The return to proof of Germanic kin for access to German society creates several dilemmas. It re-establishes the use of criteria similar to those employed within the Nazi system. And because of the ravaging effects of the war, one of the most commonly held proofs is membership of an ancestor in the NS or NDSP. East Europeans who want to be recognised as ethnic Germans (*Aussiedler*) often have no other source of proof than the membership of their father or grandfather in a Nazi organisation (Magen 1990: 40–1). Persons of this category are in a sense more privileged than those whose parents had nothing to do with these organisations. Inadvertently or not, this process could be considered a form of positive compensation for identification with the Nazi movement.

The following example well illustrates the continued effectiveness of the definitions of kinship and race as established by the Nuremberg laws of the national socialist government for establishing rights to citizenship in Germany today. It is a case of a Romanian Jew, recently examined by courts in Berlin, who claimed German language and culture and wanted to be recognised as a German with rights to German citizenship which ethnic Germans from eastern Europe receive. To win the case he had to

7. This does not mean that exceptions do not exist: an individual non-ethnic German may apply for citizenship and it may be granted to him/her. But, this is not his/her right as it is for a Volksdeutsch. It is the exception in the logic of a non-immigration country.

prove that his ancestors were not only culturally German, but also demonstrate that they saw themselves as being German (*Bekenntnis-deutsche*). This requires a consciousness of national belonging. According to paragraph 6 of the German constitution, to be recognised as an ethnic German, indicators are needed of ancestors giving witness to their Germanness. The court judgement of 27 September 1991 – of the constitutional court (OVG 7 B 36.90) – was as follows:

> Affirmation from the military commisariat of the city of Constanta, where the claimant's father was assigned to forced labour (*Zwangsarbeit*) in different places *in years between 1941 and 1944* has substantiated doubt of the German ethnicity (*Volkszugehörigkeit*) of the father of the claimant. According to information from the Jewish Museum in Tel Aviv that all male Jews in Constanta were assigned forced labour during this time, one can assume that the father of the claimant was at least at that time considered to be a member of the Jewish ethnic group. (Scheidges 1992: 3).

This simply states that a Jewish forced labourer cannot claim Germanness, since in Romania at that time special laws were in force based on the Nuremberg laws to define Jewishness. Formally this was stipulated to be on the basis of race; the proof, however, relied on the identification of the religous affiliation of ancestors. This meant that if a person denied their Jewishness, the religious membership of one of the grandparents would be decisive, and any contrary argument would not be accepted. As a professor of law commenting on the above case remarks, the claimant could present his ancestors as Germans in practically all aspects, language, culture and education, but a Jew can never prove membership in the SS, the most common proof to be recognized as an *Aussiedler* (Azzola, in: Schiedges 1992). Here we see how the racist rationale, central to the system which Hitler exploited remains a major principle for determining access to privileged rights within German society.

Obviously extermination or persecution of a specific ethnic group is not in any way a part of this ideology today. Nonetheless, this rationale supplies the logic for access to membership and provides legitimacy for racist ideologies and institutional discrimination toward the collective of foreign workers and their descendants, who are not recognized as having accumulated similar rights within German society.

Institutional Racism and its Underlying Ideology

On the one hand, apprehension about the uses of the term 'racism' within Germany is understandable, especially if it is assumed that all forms of racism have similar roots and effects. On the other hand, many unclarities remain in the minds of people in Germany about the causes of the special form assumed by German racism primarily articulated as the Aryan ideology which finally led to the extermination of Jews, gypsies and others defined as undesirables. Clearly the racism articulated and experienced in national socialism is much more explicit than the racist ideology originating in ethnic nationalism. This exclusive right to an ethnic nation state is considered normal, as xenophobia – the fear of foreigners – is considered to be normal.

This is not to say that there exists only one dominant norm of primary solidarity with ethnic Germans. Even before the Berlin Wall fell apprehension arose about the rising numbers of ethnic Germans entering from the east. Chancellor Kohl felt pressed to remind the German people that 'We shouldn't forget that *Aussiedler* are Germans, Germans in fact, that more than us had to suffer and still suffer, as a result of the Second World War' (König, 1989).[8]

There exist as well important ideologies which may be contradictory to the above and are grounded in a commitment to universal values which are also the basis for other institiutions of the state (such as the judicial system).

That is although citizenship based on ethnicity remains central to the functioning of all organs of the German federal state, adherence to universal values of justice towards all persons irrespective of orgins is also a dominant value. At the same time institutional racism is a reality which, among others, discriminates against the children of the former Guestworkers from birth onwards.[9]

Considering that 55,000 foreign children were born yearly in the west, about 1.2 million in the last two decades or more without German citizenship, the result is that a foreign passport in German urban areas may define which classes these children may attend, which school sports clubs they may join. Moreover a Turk as a non-EC foreigner may

8. Here one might want to counter: Why then solidarity primarily with ethnic Germans? What about the Jews and the gypsies in the east who had to suffer as a result of the Second World War?

9. The enactment of the new foreign law (*Ausländergesetz* 90, April 1990) has created a loophole in this tradition, since it has agreed that the children of foreigners under certain conditions may have a right to citizenship. It is no longer necessary that members of the nuclear family take on German citizenship together. Foreigners who have been legally resident in Germany for at least fifteen years can according to para. 86 (AuslG 90) apply for citizenship under less stringent conditions, until 31 December 1995. For the second and third generation, naturalisation can be considered a regular right (*Regelanspruch*). The regulations have been partially relaxed. The conditions are that individual members of the second and third generation must make their applications for citizenship between their sixteenth and twentythird years of age, have no criminal record, must have been resident eight years previously in Germany and attended a German school for six years. Moreover, they must (as a rule) give up their previous citizenship. These conditons remain an exception and do not challenge the principle of *jus sanguinis* upon which rights to membership are defined.

not travel within the EC as freely (without a visa) as his German class-mates. When he/she reaches maturity new problems begin. He or she may have difficulties if s/he wants to bring his/her partner from the country of origin, or in finding accommodation. While I am writing this paper the most recent case is that of a twenty-year-old Turkish young man born in Berlin, married to a Turkish woman resident here with a permit to stay who may be expelled because he returned to Turkey with his parents during adolescence and is now treated like any other mar-riage partner of a foreign resident brought from abroad. Generally, these regulations are not perceived as institutional racism, but instead as a normal consequence of an ethnic nation state.

The fact that it has not been possible to change through legislation the institutionalization of inequality based on ethnic origins can only mean that this ideology which supports institutional racism is evidently still considered to be too sacred to be revoked. Thus, it continues to dominate within the west German political system.

Dominant and Everyday Ideologies

I have focused primarily on the ethnic-national ideology which is domi-nant in so far as it is linked to the authority of the political system. Dis-tinctions are usually made between dominant ideologies and everyday ideologies which individuals adopt to make sense out of everyday expe-riences or conflicts in social relations (Billig, Condor, Edwards, Gane, Middleton and Radley 1988). There is, however, a link between the two. The social psychology of racist attitudes and behaviour indicates the role which dominant ideologies play in the articulation of everyday racist ideologies and behaviour. Since racism is not simply a question of xenophobia or prejudice, but implies a justification for discriminatory treatment of the collective other, ideologies which can be linked to authorities and societal institutions provide this needed legitimacy. Gramsci (1971: 376) links popular to dominant ideologies, expressing this as the strength of historically 'organic ideas', referring to the influ-ence of the intelligentsia who play a particular role in clarifying ambi-guity. The intelligentsia 'help create and sustain institutional order, organise social sentiment, direct and set social priorities'. In the German case the dominant ideology is tied to the historical institutions of the state as well as foreign worker, refugee or alien policies.

Since there is not only one dominant ideology, conflicting ideologies operate side by side, so far, without necessarily enabling one to trans-form or obliterate the other. We can assume, however, that the most powerful are those ideologies which are institutionally anchored in the constitution and regulatory organs of a society.

Manifest expressions of a racist ideology are not possible among the leadership of the post-war German state. In fact blatant racist statements are a social and political taboo. This taboo has made it difficult to recognise the authoritative legitimacy that the above tradition and system provides for racist ideologies. How else can we explain that the principle of *jus sanguinis* has maintained its sacredness in the current context where there are two types of settlers, the ethnic Germans from the east, and some four and a half million foreigners, the majority of whom have lived over two decades in the country?

A number of intellectuals do not recognise this linkage, or if they do they may argue that the question of *rights* to citizenship is only a formalistic distinction, in itself not significant, because citizenship alone will not settle racism, which we see is also rampant in other countries with different nationality laws.[10] This is certainly true. Others attempt to demonstrate that the west German welfare state, the labour market and the bureaucratic educational system operate in a truly democratic fashion, rewarding achievement and permitting upward mobility.[11] Both positions, moreover, ignore the legitimating effect, the authority, which ideologies embedded in institutions have on the differential treatment of foreigners and the racist beliefs of individual and collective actors in society. This perspective confuses the assumed relatively good status of foreigners in Germany, in comparison to, for instance, the higher unemployment or greater social conflict among immigrants, blacks and ethnic minorities in some of the other European countries, with the prevalence of the concepts of tolerance and lack of discrimination in Germany. Is it not more likely that the ideology of ethnic exclusiveness embodied in institutional discrimination against non-German settlers supplies legitimacy for more blatant and visible racism in periods of crisis and social change?

Blatant and Subtle Racism and Dominant Norms

The apprehensive response of contemporary (west) Germans to the use of the concept of racism relates very well to what has been described as subtle racism. In a comparative study of racism and xenophobia conduct-

10. The argument is also used, that 'they (especially the Turks) don't want citizenship anyway', implying that the problem – equality – resides in the attitudes of the foreigners.

11. Studies which pursue this line of argumentation have serious methodological problems, since no consideration is given to those foreigners who have returned or who have fallen out of the social security system.

ed in 1988 in four European community countries, the concept of subtle racism was developed (Pettigrew and Meertens 1991). They argue that the western European countries have developed a norm against blatant racism and have partially accepted and internalized this norm, but not deeply enough to prevent the indirect expression of anti-minority attitudes. My interpretation is that in the German case this results from two sets of contradictory dominant norms. Racist ideologies are unacceptable, but institutions which regulate access to rights based on ethnic origins may be justified historically as obligations to the past, as a tradition, as the necessity and normality of cultural homogeneity.

Unification and German Identity – Eastern Germany: which Norms and which Dominant Ideologies?

The relationship between institutional processes and dominant, as well as everyday, ideologies has to have a somewhat different history in the east. This is much more difficult to appraise. What follows are some speculative remarks. At present the dominant ideologies are unclear. Some social scientists might describe the current period as one of normlessness. There is very likely a greater discrepancy between the newly initiated legal institutions (west German) and traditional practice, as well as between dominant ideologies and these institutions. It would seem that a different system of norm-building predominated in the post-war period than that which was generally articulated in the west. It is very likely, however, that both in east and west there were major discrepancies between the authoritative norms formulated by the state and controlled by the superpowers and the subjective perceptions of certain segments of the population. Here only some hypotheses can be presented.

Referring to the argument presented at the start of this chapter about racism in the east, the first signs of rightist youth subcultures emerged in the late 1970s, and in the 1980s these began to organise themselves politically. This period became one of increasing political rigidity, and one way to protest was modelled on the skinheads in the west. Going a bit further, one might argue that Germans socialised in the former GDR identified before as well as during the process of unification with a west German identity as perceived from behind the Wall without socialisation within the complex 'post-modern' society of the west. A west German identity stripped of its complexities and contradictary ideologies became the overwhelming source of identification, and with it perhaps the adoption of beliefs about what was thought to be distorting German identity – unwanted foreigners, especially 'lowly' Turks[12] and asylum seekers.

Assuming that this identification with the west was common at least among certain sections of the population,[13] the professed policy of the federal government of not being a country of immigration and its discourse on foreign workers and asylum seekers would give this further legitimacy. This discourse was institutionalised in the unification treaty, where it was agreed that upon enactment, 20 per cent of all asylum seekers would be channelled into the communities of the east. The arrival of busloads of foreigners into unprepared rural and suburban areas of the east has had dramatic consequences.

The first asylum candidates to arrive in the east were met with violence and vandalism. Moreover, foreigners and black Germans born in the east experience an unleashing of aggression that many, despite latently experienced discrimination, would never have previously expected to this extent. Currently, hardly a day goes by without the reporting of some violence by Germans toward foreigners, such as the recent attacks on Poles by neo-Nazis, rowdies and skinheads at the initiation of visa-free entry. Brutal racial violence has led to the death or near-death of black Africans, Vietnamese, Pakistanis and Turks in the east and the west. The ruthless violence of groups of young men towards persons perceived as phenotypically or otherwise different continues (*Tagesspiegel*, 15 April 1992). Repeatedly observed is the passivity of the onlookers and the ineffectiveness of the police.

According to the federal Crime Bureau, there were 2,300 racially motivated crimes (325 crimes of arson and 188 attacks against persons; the rest were categorised either as vandalism or racial propaganda) in all of Germany in 1991 (Siegler 1992). There is good reason to doubt, however, whether these figures reflect the reality, which is probably higher, since many cases are not even reported, or if recorded, not categorised as racial incidents by the local police.[14] There appears to be no official record as yet of the number of persons who were killed as a result of this violence. Until recently there was no special documentation system for pursuing

12. In the first social distance scales which required ranking of nationalities, Turks were ranked consistently as the nationality considered most often as least sympathetic (Bundesministerium für Arbeit und Sozial Ordnung, 1990). Not resident in the east, they assumed a ranking comparable to their position among their west German counterparts.

13. An interesting indicator of orientation towards the west is the similar trend in the naming children. Despite post-war Germany's separation into two non-communicating societies, the same names for new-born children became fashionable from year to year on both sides of the Wall.

14. Cf. note 2

crimes of racial violence, although this is now in the process of being
established within the federal Crime Agency (Bundeskriminalamt).

Political Racism in a New Germany?

In mid-1992 there were new events which suggested perhaps some new
dimensions to racist ideologies and their political organisation. The success (April 1992) of the Republican Party in the state-wide elections in
Baden Württemberg (11.4 per cent) and the Deutsche Volksunion (German People's Party) in the state of Schleswig-Holstein (6.4 per cent)
and in the September 1991 elections in the city of Bremerhaven (DVU
10.26 per cent), all suggest that blatant ideologies are becoming more
attractive and politically acceptable in the west. The major parties which
centred their campaigns on the asylum issue had hoped to keep their
hold on the far right by articulating the need to stop the flow. As the
Minister of the Interior (Seiters) expresses it, Germany cannot afford to
continue to be a haven for the economic refugees of the world. The
Republicans retorted that those in power could not solve this issue: as
Schlierer (who is expected to replace Schonhüber as head of the party)
claims, 'My neighbours are seething, they have become more radical
than we, they are ready to go out with a shotgun after the asylum seekers' (Malzahn 1992: 5). The Republican Party programme addresses
Germany as a multi-criminal society filled with foreigners, 'Italian
mafiosi, Polish car thieves, Yugoslav pimps, Romanian house thieves,
Arab terrorists and Turkish drug dealers' (Willier 1992: 3). This hierarchy is not far removed from ratings on the social distance scales applied
in east and west. The west, it appears, is also entering a new phase, one
where more blatant ideologies may find their articulation and response
among the electorate. Here, it might be asked how these factors, which
are constitutive to the post-war situation, relate to unification and German national identity.

Unfortunately, this brings us beyond the scope of this chapter. Others
might ask why the issue of anti-semitism was not addressed. Anti-semitism, as opposed to hostility toward foreigners, remains heavily stigmatised. As Ostow (1990) formulates it,

> In today's Germany Jews of both West and East Germany have a function.
> They still serve as middlemen —no longer economic but rather political mid-
> dlemen... By their very existence they symbolize and demonstrate the break
> of the respective German states with the Nazi past, and they serve as links to
> Western countries. (Ostow 1990: 285)

Both states, each in their way, actively adhered to what has been termed philosemitic policies (Bergmann 1990). Racism in Germany today is not articulated primarily in terms of anti-semitism. Recent opinion surveys indicate that anti-semitism is expressed by about 13 per cent of the population, less in the east (4 per cent) than in the west (16 per cent) (*Der Spiegel* 1992: 47). It is generally believed that today's anti-semitism is related to Germany's problems of national identity and coming to terms with its past (secondary) anti-semitism (Bergmann 1990: 164). On the one hand, anti-semitic discourse has been successfully banned from public debate. On the other hand, some research using projective tests finds that the 'Jew' who sets out to remind Germans of their guilt for the Holocaust awakens sentiments of aggression and rejection (Bergmann 1990: 165). This research concludes that, to the extent that national pride begins to demand that an end be put to reshuffling the past and that normalisation begin, the danger of a secondary anti-semitism will mount. Will unification increase this likelihood?

There are many issues which need further study. There is certainly a need for more thorough analysis of the special form of racism which is believed to have been nourished in the socialist German Democratic Republic and has only now become so apparent. Certainly socialisation into a totalitarian system, the resulting dogmatic education, the denial of responsiblity for fascism, the discrediting of humanitarian concepts such as international solidarity, as well as their sense of relative deprivation *vis-à-vis* their better-off brothers in the west, could be expected to augment the sense of self-pity, injustice and envy. The primary concern in this paper, however, has been with the west and the ideology of ethnic nationalism which has had far-reaching effects for institutional racism, and which serves as a source of ideological justification for racist behaviour – east and west. Unification may have, subsequently, refuelled the belief in an ethnic nation state, the legitimacy of a Germany for Germans.

One of the most remarkable factors in this context, is the fact that a country which opened its arms to hundreds of thousands of ethnic Germans during the disintegration of the east and which was willing to unify and take on responsibility for another seventeen million persons at a record pace did not consider that the unification of Germany might be the opportunity to offer full, unambiguous membership to the 4.5 million foreigners (less than half are Turks and Yugoslavs) who had been over a decade or two working, paying taxes, increasingly born and schooled in the country.[15]

15. Of the rest about 28 per cent come from EC countries, less than 2 per cent each from the non-EC North African countries and one fifth from other parts of the world.

–6–

Rights and Racism in a New Country of Immigration: The Italian Case

Ellie Vasta

Introduction

Since unification Italy has been a country of significant emigration. As such, twenty-five million Italians emigrated between 1876 (when statistics began to be recorded) and 1965, which is roughly equivalent to the whole Italian population of 1861 at the beginning of the Risorgimento (unification). Fifteen million emigrated between 1876 and 1920, many going to the United States and Europe (Cinanni 1968). After the Second World War, between two and three million Italians emigrated, thus making emigration a continuing feature of Italian culture. Almost all Italians have a relative or friend who has migrated within Europe or to other continents. The Italian state has also had first-hand experience in dealing with migrant rights, since it has played an active role in securing social welfare rights for Italians overseas. Through consulates and other channels, the Italian state has also promoted the maintenance of Italian language and culture among Italian immigrant communities.

Over the past ten years, the situation has reversed: Italy has slowly become a country of immigration. As a relatively new phenomenon, the position of immigrants in Italy is constantly evolving and is attracting attention both from within the country and from its EC neighbours. The response to immigration by the Italian state and by the Italian community raises a number of fundamental questions about the adequacy of the response, whether it is racist, and whether Italy wants or needs immigrants at all. It has become clear that despite the growing attitude of a 'fortress Europe' policy among many western European countries, the south–north and east–west flows will continue for some time (see Ålund and Schierup, and Castles in this volume). Given this reality, one question which emerges from the Italian situation is this: has Italy's past experience of being a country of mass emigration made it better able to deal with becoming a country of immigration? Put more specifically, are Italians today denying immigrants basic social rights in the same way that past Italian emigrants were denied rights as foreigners and even as citizens of other lands? The Albanian 'invasion' in 1991 can give us a flavour of and an initial look at the adequacy of the Italian response to the new immigration flows into Italy.

The Albanian Crisis

The first Albanian 'flight' occurred in March 1991, at a time when Albania was in deepening economic and political chaos. Thousands fled to the east coast of Italy, landing in the Puglian region. Italy was taken unawares and was unable to deal adequately with this influx of people. Asylum seekers were distributed to camps around southern Italy. Eventually, the Italian state declared that if these Albanian refugees could find work in Italy, they could stay. Those who did not find work would have to return. As it turned out, few found work. Many were forced to return, lured by assistance of food, clothing and money from the Italian government. Others 'disappeared' into Italy to join the growing ranks of illegal immigrants. After that event, a Minister for Immigration, Margherita Boniver, was appointed, who was, at the time, the only immigration Minister in Europe.

A new wave of Albanians arrived in Bari (on the east coast of Puglia) in early August 1991 and again took the Italian state unawares, especially as Italy was on the verge of 'closing down' for *Ferragosto* (summer vacations). There were various popular explanations for the Albanian flight. One was that there were labour traffickers in Italy and Albania who had organised these flights. Another was that the Albanian government was aware of the flight and allowed it to happen so that the Italians, who had been slow in delivering aid, would begin to take the Albanian ailing economy more seriously. The only verified explanation is that these people were actually starving. Nearly all production and state services had stopped functioning. During this incident, the Immigration Minister kept a low profile compared to her male colleagues, that is, the Minister for Foreign Affairs, De Michelis, the Minister for the Interior, Scotti, and even Cossiga (President of the Republic) himself. Her low profile in the matter raises the important question about what political value has been placed on the Ministry for Immigration, especially since that ministry has an extremely inadequate budget.

The reaction of the authorities, caught unawares, has been described by some observers as opportunistic and transgressing all human rights conventions. Several thousand men, women and children were herded into football stadiums. Food was dropped to them from helicopters. Thousands of heavily armed paramilitary police surrounded the stadiums, using force to contain attempts to break out by the hungry, ragged and increasingly desperate refugees. Finally they were rounded up, given clothing and sent back to Albania in air force planes and ferries with a military escort. President Cossiga flew to Albania and announced a package of food and infrastructure aid, to be implemented by the Italian army. The British and German governments applauded the measures.

Public response in Italy varied. Some politicians, such as La Malfa, leader of the conservative Republican Party, claimed that the Albanian crisis had brought to an end the Martelli law (see below), which he, as well as many Italians in general, saw as too lenient. Many criticised the Martelli law claiming that it was unable to determine the status of refugees and was not able to stop the entry of illegals. On the other hand, the Italian Greens demanded that Italy, together with other EC countries, should absorb the Albanian refugees. Many Italians were in favour of allowing the Albanians to stay on the grounds that they were Europeans. Not only was this a case of reverting to the pre-Martelli legislation regarding refugees,[1] but it also indicated that 'white' Europeans would be preferable to 'black' Africans and Asian migrants. The response was perceived across the political spectrum as either chaotic or inhumane or too lax. Within the government itself there had been contradictory reactions about how the problem could best be dealt with.

Whether both the first and second wave of Albanian refugees could be defined as refugees under the definition of the 1951 United Nations Convention on refugees was not taken into account by the Italian authorities. Certainly, Italy violated the Convention by not allowing the Albanians due process. While on the one hand the Italians wanted to be seen to be doing their humanitarian best, on the other hand they were bending to pressures which had emerged from the Schengen agreement leading to calls for Italy to tighten its immigration controls to the same levels as other EC countries. In order for the Italians to be seen to have toughened up, the Albanians were deported without due process, though at the same time their expulsion was presented with the 'humanitarian' face of an aid package.

1. This position, to allow in only European refugees, had been part of Italian law since 1951 though it had been removed in the so-called Martelli law no. 39/1990 (see *International Journal of Refugee Law* 1990: 279-80).

Types of Immigrants in Italy

There are four broad categories of migrants in Italy:

1. Legal foreign residents;
2. Illegal immigrants;
3. Immigrants who are now regularised;
4. Large waves of refugees such as the Albanians (many of whom have remained illegally) and recent waves of asylum seekers from Yugoslavia.

Official data on immigrants in Italy are inadequate and often contradictory. According to the Italian Ministry for the Interior in 1988 there were 654, 423 legal foreign residents (SOPEMI 1990). By its very nature it is difficult to give figures on illegal immigration. However, some estimates claim the total figure for 1988 was between 150,000 and 250,000, with the majority concentrated in the regions of Lazio, Campania, Sicily and Lombardy (Perduca and Pinto 1991: 122). Of the 115,000 immigrants who regularised during 1987 and 1988, 40 per cent claimed to be in employment and the remainder registered as unemployed (Pugliese 1990: 74)[2]. However, the Ministry for the Interior in 1991 estimates figures for illegals to be around 100,000 (Ministero dell'Interno 1991). According to ISTAT (the Central Statistical Institute) the non-EC presence in Italy at the end of 1989 was 963,000 (SOPEMI 1991: 53). On the other hand, figures for 1991 from the Ministry of the Interior state that the total of all foreigners in Italy was 881,467 (based on figures for temporary residence permits) and that at least 30 per cent of these come from the developed countries such as America, Japan, Australia and EC countries (Ministero dell'Interno 1991).

The majority of immigrants are single men, though some have wives and children with them. This is typical of the Iranians and the Chinese, many of whom have set up their own small businesses (Campani 1989: 6). Some communities consist of mostly women, notably the Filipino (60–70 per cent) and Cape Verdians (90 per cent) (Campani 1989: 4). The majority of these women have obtained work as domestics. There have been two flows of Cape Verdian women. The first consisted of older women, many mothers of families, with little education. The second group consisted mostly of younger, better-educated women. Overall, the Filipino women have a higher education, though the Cape

2. All these figures should be read cautiously simply because data are not collected accurately by administrative and statistical divisions of the Italian state. The figure for regularization may include immigrants who are applying again for residency after their first permit has expired.

Verdians have shown more interest in gaining skills and higher education in Italy (Campani 1989).

Most immigrants come from Third World countries, especially from the following regions: north Africa – Libya, Morocco, Tunisia, Egypt; Horn of Africa – Ethiopia, Somalia; Equatorial north Africa – Ghana, Nigeria, Senegal, Sudan, Ivory Coast; Equatorial south Africa – Zaire, Angola, Uganda; Middle East – Iran, Iraq; Asia – Bangladesh, India, Pakistan, Sri Lanka, Philippines; Latin America – Chile, Peru, Brazil, Colombia. Some come from eastern Europe, mostly Poles. The largest groups of migrants are the Moroccans, Filipinos, Tunisians, Senegalese, Sri Lankans, Ethiopians and Egyptians. Different nationalities are concentrated in different areas. In one study carried out by a doctor, reading the medical register of a Roman out-patient hospital and analysing the records of 2,600 illegals, there were sixty nations represented; and 60 per cent fell in the 20–9 age bracket, while 24 per cent were in the 30–9 age group. The male to female ratio was three to one (Nonis 1989: 342).

Overall, immigrants are concentrated in three main areas of the labour market: self-employed work, which mostly entails travelling saleswork done mostly by the Senegalese and Moroccans;[3] service industries, which include domestic work, catering and tourism carried out by Filipinos and some Asian and African nationals; and unskilled jobs in manufacturing and agriculture (see Campus and Perrone 1990: 193). Although much of the work the illegals engage in is unskilled labour, many of the Iranians and Filipinos have professional qualifications or have medium or high school certificates (Campani 1989: 4–5). There are also many illegals in Italy who are unskilled, such as some Senegalese and Moroccans, who have left their countries owing to unemployment. These illegals are often referred to as 'economic' refugees because they do not fit the UN Convention definition. This problem exists in numerous countries and is a much debated issue (see, for example, Ministry of Labour, Sweden 1990).

The State's Response to Immigration

The state's reaction has been slow but mixed. There are two laws, Act no. 943/1986 and no. 39/1990, which amount to what can be called Italian immigration laws. In brief, Act no. 943 established regulations governing the admission and residence of foreigners and conditions under

---

3. Illegals have become known as the 'Vu Comprà', meaning 'Do you want to Buy?' They are also often referred to as the 'extracommunitari' that is, people from outside the EC.

which they could work. The Act enunciated general principles of equality of treatment and rights with Italian workers, even as regards wage levels. It included statements on establishment of state organisations to help and protect immigrants, rights to bring in families; acceptance of qualifications etc. It also provided for the regularisation of clandestine workers (Nascimbene 1991).

There were several problems with this Act. One was that it concerned only immigrant workers and ignored refugees and their problems. It related only to employees: small traders and independent workers were excluded. Another problem was that only 14 per cent of estimated illegals (95,000) had regularised by the 1987 deadline. There were several reasons for this. One was that eligibility was difficult to prove and ultimately became discretional (Sciortino 1991a: 92). Secondly, the police were responsible for relevant formalities which deterred illegal immigrants from coming forward. But the fundamental problems were economic ones (Koch 1988: 106). As many illegals knew, regularisation would keep them out of the labour market because employers would take on illegals in preference to regularised immigrants who could demand official pay and conditions. Further, the irregular work situation can often engender complicity between illegals and employers, who are not prepared to forgo the savings they make on labour costs (SOPEMI 1990: 45). For illegals, there was also the fear that regularisation would be used for reasons of law and order, that is, a fear of being charged with minor offences.

As a result of the above problems, and in order to show that Italy was policing the problem adequately and thus appear 'acceptable' to the Schengen partners, Act no. 39 was introduced in 1990 and became known as the Martelli law, after the minister involved with the presentation of the Act. This Act was concerned with six main issues, namely:

1. Entrance: entry was tightened up by making provisions for recording of information at the point of entry. Moroccans, Tunisians, Senegalese, Colombians and Peruvians were singled out as travellers who would have to have entry visas.
2. Residence: three-month tourist visas or two-year work permits were made available.
3. Work: provisions that immigrant workers were eligible to the same pay and working conditions as Italian workers.
4. Refugees: withdrawal of the geographical limitation to Europe only; procedures were to be established for the examination of refugee status including appeal provisions in case of denial.
5. Regularisation: this applied to workers as well as employers. Illegal immigrants, be they in employment, self-employed, professionals, students or unemployed could, within a certain date, register for a two-year residence permit. Provision was made for employers to

declare that they had previously employed illegal immigrants. In addition, sanctions would be imposed on those who employed illegals.
6. Expulsion: regulations established to expel criminals etc. (*Vita Italiana* 1990).

This Act went beyond the previous one, though it too contained many problems. As was to be expected, not many employers of illegal immigrants registered, and it is still unclear how many illegal immigrants regularised in 1990. For those who have obtained documentation, regularisation does have some positive effects (SOPEMI 1990: 82). Regularisation can put to an end to the insecure status of certain categories of immigrant workers, such as the semi-skilled in the service sector. It can also make it possible better to identify the types of employment and sectors of activity that use illegal immigrants so that employers could be sanctioned. Control of illegal employment and sanctions against employers are very hard to implement in Italy since a high proportion of the workforce is employed in the informal sector (according to one source, the proportion is upwards of 25 per cent, Weiss 1988: 219). The Italian informal sector is often aided by state or regional policies and specific institutional arrangements, and is an entrenched part of Italian culture. It would seem racist simply to sanction employers who employ illegal immigrants and not employers who employ nationals illegally, that is, those without proper work documentation for tax and social insurance. Informal work relationships are particularly common in family-owned businesses in the catering and hotels, agriculture and clothing industries. As has occurred in Britain in the fashion industry when faced with severe foreign competition (Phizacklea 1990), the Italian clothing companies, for example, have transferred part of their production to subcontractors who employ outworkers (Weiss 1988: 21), many of whom are illegal immigrants.

By introducing the Martelli law the state believed it had solved the problems (Balbo 1991a). Apart from dropping the geographical limitations of the 1951 Convention, it spelt out the procedures for dealing with refugees, as well as providing definitions of refugee status (Zanchetta 1991: 111–12). However, the Albanian refugees put the Act to the test, in that there was much confusion about what should be done with them. Many claim that the Martelli law has failed, because of these numerous problems with its implementation. On the whole, Italian policies have achieved the opposite of their intentions. Despite the restrictions introduced by the Acts, immigration has continued and has increased, especially around the times of regularisation. The numerous contradictions which occur between the law and its implementation negate the possibility for rational planning of a phenomenon which will not stop with those restrictions (Sciortino 1991a: 93; Balbo 1991b).

Ellie Vasta

The Political, Civil and Social Rights of Immigrants

There are several categories for obtaining Italian citizenship, of which two are relevant to immigrants. The first category relates to naturalisation. The three main criteria in this category are five years of residence, proof of a medium to high income and proof of long-term employment. For many who do apply, the waiting period for a decision can be up to ten years (Zanchetta 1991: 140). Although it is difficult to obtain figures on how many people have applied for and how many have obtained naturalisation, the criteria are stiff enough to disqualify many would-be applicants. A second category refers to children born in Italy of foreign parents. Such children have the right to decide whether they want Italian citizenship at the age of eighteen if their parents had already been resident in Italy for ten years at the time of their birth (Zanchetta 1991: 137). This case would be fairly rare at this stage of the migratory process. This does not go as far as French or Swedish nationality rules which give all children born to foreign parents the right to choose. It is, however, better than the German nationality rule which gives children in this situation no rights at all. Because immigration is a relatively recent phenomenon in Italy, citizenship is not the main issue at present, though, with growing numbers of long-term settlers, it is likely to become significant (see Hammar in this volume). It remains to be seen whether citizenship will become a central issue, as it has in France (Weil 1991: 283).

According to the Human Rights Covenant, foreigners in Italy have freedom of speech, movement, association etc. (Zanchetta 1991). There are, for instance, at least 250 immigrant associations (Tassello 1990: 146). However, immigrants do not have the right to vote or to work in the civil service. Regularised workers who have to pay into the social welfare scheme have the same health service rights as Italians. Further, unemployment benefits are available to regularised migrants who have lost a job, but not to those who are looking for their first job. Those regularised immigrants who continue their social service contributions also have rights to public housing. All foreigners have access to emergency care in public hospitals. According to Italian law, there is a general health provision for foreigners, but in reality there are quite serious obstacles to obtaining these rights (Bentivogli 1990). Health problems amongst immigrants are beginning to cause some concern. The study carried out by Nonis (1989) claims that grave illnesses such as respiritory, gastric, and urinary infections have been acquired, owing to poor conditions in Italy, rather than imported. This corresponds with other studies on the early stages of migration (see for example, Castles and Kosack 1973).

Problems with housing have reached crisis point in some areas. Immigrant seasonal workers recruited to harvest agricultural crops often have no housing provided for them (Ben Jelloun 1991). Although in some regions the local councils do provide public housing for immigrant workers, such as in Bologna (Wrench and Phizacklea 1991), in other regions housing problems of immigrant workers are severe. In Turin, for example, there are many landlords who refuse to rent their apartments to immigrants. Others are exploiting immigrants by turning their apartments into boarding houses, renting out single rooms without kitchen facilities to more people than is hygienically safe.

Policy and practice have varied across regions, and it is at the regional level that most work is being done. For example, in Emilia-Romagna there are programmes for migrant women to learn Italian and for vocational training; frequently there are conferences on multiculturalism and schools organised by the local councils and other groups in cities like Florence and Bologna. It has been interesting to observe that often there are no migrants attending such conferences. The level of migrant representation in the formal and informal structures of the dominant culture is usually a fairly accurate sign of the confidence and strength of migrant groups to challenge the dominant power structures in new countries of immigration. Some regions and local councils have attempted to help immigrants integrate into Italian society, while others have contributed to immigrants' problems. To remedy the unevenness of regional responses to the needs of migrants, the Italian-Razzismo organisation has proposed ten practical projects for the national level (Balbo and Bevilacqua 1991). They include projects on the reception of refugees, centres for immigrant women and help for single mothers, facilitating interpreters, co-ordinating information for professionals working with immigrants.

Racism, National Identity and Citizenship

As in many other countries, racism in Italy is tied up with the issue of national identity and citizenship. Recently, Brubaker (1990b) has provided an interesting contrast between France and Germany about what constitutes nationhood. According to him, the nation in France 'has been conceived in relation to the institutional and territorial frame of the state', that is, nationhood is based on the idea of 'political unity and not on shared culture ... if nationhood is *constituted* by political unity, it is centrally *expressed* in the striving for cultural unity' (Brubaker 1990: 16). In other words, cultural pluralism is anathema to French identity. On the other hand, German nationhood 'was conceived not as the bearer of universal political values, but as an organic cultural linguistic, or racial community'; thus 'nationhood is constituted by ethnocultural unity and expressed in political unity' (Brubaker 1990: 17).

The notion of Italian nationhood has a rather more ambiguous character. To begin to understand it we need to go back in history to the period of unification. Italy was similar to Germany in that both experienced unification in the latter part of the nineteenth century. However, unlike Germany where a strong central state developed, in Italy a profound mistrust for the state emerged, especially in the south where the promised land reforms and relief from grain taxes did not occur. Responses included the development of organised crime and the growth of the informal sector. The regions have retained a strong sense of identity, so much so that it would not be an exaggeration to say that Italian identity is more regional than national.

The strength of regional identity is revealed in several ways. One is through the prejudices and activities of the secessionist groups such as the right-wing Lega Lombarda (Lombard League) and the Lega Autonomista Toscana (Tuscan Autonomist League). One pamphlet produced by the Lega Autonomista Toscana claimed that aid to Albanians in Italy on a per capita basis far exceeds the rate of pensions to elderly Italians. These leagues are becoming popular and strengthening regional identity because of disaffection with the inefficiency of the state. Their growing popularity is shown by recent successes in local and regional elections. The leagues seem to attract the same types of voters as the National Front in France, including disaffected former communists. However, as separatists, they do not aspire to central state power. To some extent the leagues also compete with the more traditional extreme right Movimento Sociale Italiano (MSI).

Another way in which regional identity reveals itself is through the intense discrimination of northerners towards southerners. This form of discrimination has existed at least since the early part of this century and became especially evident when industrial development and public investment became concentrated in the north. As a result, many southerners were compelled to migrate to the industrial north to work during the 1960s, since very little development occurred in the south. There are numerous studies and films which attest to that phenomenon and to the discrimination experienced in the labour market, in the housing market etc. by southerners in the north. In the north, one constantly hears racist remarks about southerners, such as 'southerners are not people who comport themselves as well as us', implying that southerners are not as 'cultured' or 'civilised' as are northerners; and 'Africa begins at Rome', which is a double form of racism against southern Italians and Africans.

The right has clung steadfastly to the ideas of nationalism and national identity. On the other hand, there is a strong left-wing culture in Italy where the political parties of the left have rejected nationalism and racist ideas of national identity as part of the legacy of fascism (Rusconi 1991;

Scoppola 1991: 53), for example, argues that Italy does not have a sense of national identity but that it does have a sense of identity based on a specific form of citizenship, notably based on participation in social movements. He also suggests that in Italy there is a need for democratic maturity which cannot be attained until there is more participation in political life. One deterrent to participation in political life in Italy may be the high level of cynicism Italians have towards the state, and especially towards politicians. The state has contributed to the disactivation of political life, suggests Poggi (1991), which has occurred through several channels. In Italy, as in numerous other countries, one of these is the irresponsibility of the state in not legislating against the semi-monopoly of the television news media, which leads to massive misinformation.

Whatever Italy's national identity, whether nationally weak or regionally strong, it operates in an exclusionary and racist way. The Italian response can be described as racist if we define racism as the process whereby members of social groups categorize members of other groups as different or inferior, on the basis of real or imagined physical or cultural characteristics. The process involves the use of political, social or economic power, and often has the purpose of legitimating exploitation or exclusion of the group so defined. Racism does not depend on the characteristics of the victim, but on historical factors, popular culture, and economic, political and social interests. This contradicts the view held by many Italians that racism, until recently, has not been a part of the structure of Italian society. Balbo, for instance, suggests that there are three phases relating to Italian racism. The first phase, up till 1989 can be described as the pre-racist phase. The second phase, between 1989 and 1991, she describes as 'a not too racist phase'. Balbo claims that from 1991 Italian society can be defined as racist (Balbo 1991a). But the earlier non-racist phases are questionable especially in light of the formal and informal discrimination experienced by southerners in the north where southerners were often constructed as 'racially' inferior to the northerners.

Regarding immigration, there are currently four major arenas of racism, namely the state, the labour market, the media and the community. The state's response has been contradictory. On the one hand, it has attempted to respond in a humanitarian way by developing social policies and by providing regularization. On the other hand, the delivery of these policies has been problematic. For example, the Martelli law proved to be inconsistent with its aims because the state was unable to carry parts of it out. Typically, the bureaucracy collapsed over the issue and local officials were unable to put it into effect (Balbo 1991a). Some Italians and some of the EC governments argue that the Italian state is simply too weak and disorganised to develop a strict policy of regulation of entry and residence (Zanchetta 1991). In a way, Italy is being accused of not being racist enough! Others reply that Italian authorities are especially sensitive to the issue of immigration and immigrants' needs because '(f)or decades the main concern in all bilateral and multi-lateral international bodies had been to protect, strengthen and ensure recognition of the rights and interests of emigrants. That approach (has) shaped (Italy's) behaviour vis-a-vis its new role as a receiving country' (Koch 1988: 195).

Although the Italian state has had some experience in securing social welfare rights for its compatriots overseas, generally the rights have related to the transportability of pensions back to Italy for the aged and the maintenance of the Italian language and culture in the immigrant country. The myriad problems experienced by migrants, in particular issues relating to experience in the labour market, in schooling, in obtaining housing and loans, the co-ordinating of interpreter services, the special needs of women and so on, are not the type of problems that the Italian state has dealt with on behalf of Italians overseas. If anything, it is the Catholic church which has carried out this task in the diaspora.

In fact, the Italian state has developed an ideology of exclusion. Evidence of exclusionary practice occurred with the mishandling of the Albanian crisis, and periodically reports filter through that planeloads of African nationals are being flown back to their home countries. The consequence is an incoherent, inequitable and inefficient policy towards immigrants and refugees. This is especially important in light of the need to respect the human rights of individuals and groups who are fleeing from both economic and political oppression. In Italy, although there is a good body of knowledge developing on the demographics of immigration and on the political economy of immigration,[4] throughout the 1980s there was very little sociological analysis on immigration (Reyneri 1991: 145).[5] There appears to be a distinct lack of study of the relatively progressive policies towards settlers adopted by such countries as Australia, Canada and Sweden. Further, there appears to be very little reference to the experiences and recent analytical debates on the relationship between immigration, social policy and citizenship in those countries where immigration has been a long-standing feature. Reyneri suggests that if too much emphasis is placed on the demographics of immigration and too little on sociological analysis, this can have grave consequences on policy-makers and on public opinion (Reyneri 1991: 146).

4. See for example, Livi Bacci and Veronese 1990; Golini 1988; Pugliese 1990.
5. There are some recent exceptions, for example, Bruni, Pinto and Sciortino 1991; Campani 1989; Chiarello 1990; Gallini 1991; Sciortino 1991a, b.

The position of immigrants in the labour market reveals high levels of racism in Italy. One important point is that the Italian economy has become dependent on cheap, illegal immigrant labour (Kazim 1991), thus providing a breeding ground for formal and informal racism. In terms of the labour market, racism occurs in the following ways:

1. Many Italian employers rely on cheap, illegal labour and go so far as to sack those who have become regularised.
2. Although some unions are 'showing concern' for 'all workers' by introducing policies of non-discrimination, there have been deals between big business and unions which permit immigrant labour to be used instead of native labour at certain times. For example, some unions have negotiated for immigrant workers to do shift work in place of native workers who do not want to do particular shifts. So it becomes clear that immigrant labour is not always competing for Italian workers' jobs (Martiniello 1991: 81). The trade unions, while condemning discrimination against immigrant workers and proclaiming concern for equality of workers regardless of their nationality, 'have not yet drawn up a clear and coherent policy to reduce internal tensions, to reconcile the various interests at stake in the dual labour market or to identify priorities' (Koch 1988: 198).
3. Small businesses in Italy receive major financial concessions. In order to retain their privileges they have to remain small and keep their overheads low. Therefore, small business has relied heavily on the informal labour market by not declaring all their employees (Weiss 1988: 222–4). Italian women have kept that informal sector going, being low-paid and non-unionized. Whether the illegals are pushing women out of that sector is something which still remains unclear, although one suggestion is that Filipino women are pushing Italian women out of the domestic service sector (Koch 1988: 194).

According to Sciortino (1991a), one major peculiarity in Italy regarding the issue of competition for jobs between residents and immigrants is that competition 'occurs not only on the "official" labour market but also – and above all – on the informal labour market. Furthermore, the effects of this competition are intertwined with a secondary competition between the two markets: the size and operation of one of them has repercussions on the other, thus affecting its competitiveness, the actors' inclination to move in or out, as well as the markets' social legitimation' (Sciortino, 1991a: 91). Competition also occurs between migrant groups leading to racialised fractions within certain sectors. For example, a sample of Cape Verdian domestics report that they are receiving a wage 20–30 per cent lower than Filipino women on account of being black (Campani 1989: 11).

The social and political consequences of being forced into the clandestine role means that often immigrants become labelled as deviants on account of 'precarious living conditions, contingent and unprotected work areas that are often contiguous to organised crime-controlled sectors' (Sciortino 1991a: 95). However, many of their law-breaking offences are generally related to their condition of clandestinity rather than to specific acts of criminality. One major factor in the 'racialisation' of immigrants' problems is the way migrants are represented in the media. In a comprehensive analysis of the political discourse on immigrants in the Italian newspapers between November 1989 and May 1990, ter Wal shows, for example, how oppositions are created in the media reporting through use of language such as 'Italian citizens' versus 'extracomunitari' which creates an ideology of 'ingroup' and 'outgroup'. Often words such as 'clandestines', 'illegals' and 'foreigners' are used synonymously, take on derogatory value and are frequently tied to notions of criminality (ter Wal 1991: 36).

Both in the media and in the political sphere, when restrictionist or exclusionary policy is called for, figures are often presented which show an increase in immigration coupled with terms such as 'uncontrollable masses'. Often waves and flows become tides and floods (ter Wal 1991: 40). The reporting in the media of the Albanian crisis is a case in point. When the Albanian refugees fled to Italy on 8 August, 1991, *La Repubblica*, a national daily newspaper reported it in bold front-page headlines as 'an Albanian invasion'. It then went on to report that thousands were turning towards Italy and that an enormous crowd had been turned back on the pier as the police opened fire. This type of representation can exacerbate fears and prejudices in any community.

Unfortunately, there have been extreme acts of violence towards black immigrants. During 1990–1 there has been a spate of murders both in the north and the south. In the south, the murder of a black agricultural worker brought to light not only the issue of informal racism but also the extremely poor working and housing conditions to which many illegal immigrants are subjected (Ben Jelloun 1991). In Florence, Italian retailers on and around the famous Ponte Vecchio harassed many black street vendors claiming that these immigrants were not only taking away custom from the Italian shopkeepers but that they were also ruining the reputation of the area, which had been developed over centuries. This particular struggle led to the murder of a black street hawker in 1990. In the summer of 1991, Senegalese male workers travelling on a motorway in the north of Italy were shot at by a gang of youths, resulting in one death and severe injuries to the others. These incidents tend to drive many black immigrants from public places, thus dispersing co-nationals who would often meet in places such as parks. There have also been random bomb attacks on immigrant housing and some councils have ordered the removal of squatters. For example, one socialist council in Milan bowed to pressures from resident Italians by booting out immigrant squatters from a housing estate and from the tents which had been set up temporarily for an otherwise homeless group of workers.

On the other hand, according to the Italian press, many Italians took Albanians into their homes, clothed them and fed them during the 'Albanian crisis'. The community response is uneven and varies from region to region. Some research results are beginning to emerge on the attitudes of Italians towards immigrants. One study, on the attitude of Italian workers towards immigrants from the non-EC, was conducted in Bologna in Emilia-Romagna, a region considered to be the most progressive and economically stable in Italy. The results suggest that in Bologna there is very little prejudice directed towards those immigrants (Bruni et al. 1991).

Conclusion

To return to the initial question, my answer is that their own emigration experience has not made Italians better able to deal with immigration, either at the state, labour market or community level. Laura Balbo suggests that emigration has not become a part of the perceived Italian national heritage. Italians have avoided public debate on the mass emigration that occurred in the years following the Second World War. Her suggestion is that Italians found it a rather shameful occurrence that compatriots were compelled to leave because their country could not provide them with the possibility of earning a reasonable living. In addition, the racial laws of fascism have been left out of public debate in the post-war years (Balbo, 1991a).

Another major reason why the emigration experience has not made Italians better able to deal with the problems of immigration is that Italian emigrants, when they returned to Italy either for good or for holidays, rarely mentioned the racism they experienced and the difficulties of integration. In fact, many of those who remained behind gained the impression that the migrants were becoming or had become rather wealthy in their new countries. Indeed, migrants who returned often displayed a sense of wealth, whether they had made it or not. Many found it necessary to return with new cars and expensive clothing in order to signify to those who had remained that the migrant's departure and pain had not been in vain. Often the flashy cars had been bought second-hand before the visit and were sold again on their return to their country of immigration.

Recent public opinion polls seem to suggest that Italians do not feel that their country is destined to remain a country of immigration. According to Koch (1988: 198), '[c]urrent immigration is not [seen] as a long-term problem destined to have complex repercussions on the economic, social, demographic, ethnic and cultural fabric of the country; it is more an abstract issue involving humanitarian justice and solidarity'. These feelings and ideas of justice and solidarity 'are not accompanied by concerns for the integration of immigrants. On the whole, Italians are uninterested in the role of immigrants as members of society' (Koch 1988: 198). So where there is no hostility, there is indifference and marginalisation.

Currently, there is a redistribution of people occurring between the poorer and wealthier nations, and there is a call for sharing of resources which the citizens of the wealthier nations have considered rightfully theirs. Livi Bacci's (1990) suggestion that a continuing flow from the south to the north may be, in the long run, the best aid to co-operation and development, seems to be a fruitful approach. Although Italy sent back the second wave of Albanians and has been deporting many nationals from African countries, the flow into Italy continues. Italy is dealing with this by ignoring the long-term effects of this redistribution and by refusing to plan an immigration policy that could benefit both Italy and its immigrant population. Instead, Italy's political actions set her in a bind. On the one hand, the state and the community have determined that exclusion is the best policy and the best way to take control of the situation (Balbo 1991b). However, by taking that position, Italians are in fact losing control of the situation because there is no policy to develop and plan for resources directed towards migrants, as well as planning for a manageable level of intake. This refusal on the part of the state to develop a plan for immigration is due to the fear that this would encourage further entries. Therefore, immigration ends up being treated arbitrarily. This will clearly contribute to problems experienced by migrants. Ultimately, these problems are likely to be blamed on the migrants themselves or on their cultures.

7

The Thorny Road to Europe: Swedish Immigrant Policy in Transition

Aleksandra Ålund and Carl-Ulrik Schierup

In 1975 multiculturalism became an important element in the famous Swedish model of welfare state politics. Sweden's multicultural immigrant policy is known throughout Europe for its consistent rejection of a 'guestworker' strategy for labour import, its ambitious quest to create social equality among ethnic groups, its respect for immigrant culture, and its emphasis on providing immigrants and ethnic minorities with resources with which to exercise political influence. An emphasis on international solidarity forms the basis of an ambitious programme to accept and integrate refugees. In the official oratory of Swedish multiculturalism, welfare ideology objectives centred on 'equality' (*jämlikhet*) occupy a central position. Other policy objectives include 'freedom of choice' (*valfrihet*) and 'partnership' (*samverkan*). Tomas Hammar (1985: 33) summarizes the original intent of these three overarching principles (boldly paraphrasing the French revolution's *liberté, égalité, et fraternité*), in the following way:

> The goal of *equality* implies the continued efforts to give immigrants the same living standard as the rest of the population. The goal of *freedom of choice* implies that public initiatives are to be taken to assure members of ethnic and linguistic minorities domiciled in Sweden a genuine choice between retaining and developing their cultural identity and assuming a Swedish cultural identity. The goal of *partnership* implies that the different immigrant and minority groups on the one hand and the native population on the other both benefit from working together.

Contained within these goals, which were formulated in the mid-1970s, was the implication that not only would foreigners enjoy the same legal privileges as Swedish citizens, but also that the general public would accept multicultural aims. The proclaimed egalitarian and multicultural ideology has considerable legal backing; formal equality before the law holds true in almost all important matters, including equal access to unemployment contributions and a large number of other social welfare benefits.[1] One of the most important legal achievements of Swedish immigrant policy has been the granting to foreign citizens of the right to vote in local elections; this right was first exercised in the local elections of 1976.[2] The voting rights amendment to the Swedish constitution was conceived of as a way of giving immigrants access to the advantages of the welfare state, while simultaneously safeguarding their right to autonomous cultural development. A number of state-sponsored research commissions have been busy formulating policies to control and combat racism and discrimination. Under the heading 'knowledge on immigrants' (*invandrarkunskap*) the state has encouraged the growth of a plethora of educational courses aimed at engendering a spirit of ethnic tolerance and an anti-racist morality into local administrations and the general public. Thus a legal and moral foundation was provided to support 'freedom of choice', to encourage 'partnership', to give 'equality' a social basis, and to prevent uncontrolled ethnic conflicts and the development of a segregated society. A general moral and political consensus was inaugurated, which embraced government and state institutions, political parties (right across the traditional left-right spectrum) and important socio-political organizations and movements like, for example, the trade unions and the national association of local municipal administrations (*Kommunförbundet*).

This broad and stable consensus on the importance of multicultural rights and of an anti-racist morality is probably unique to Sweden. It has relied on a generally 'tolerant public opinion' (Westin 1987) and a sober and respectful treatment of 'immigrant questions' by the media. Today, however, along with the multicultural ideology as a whole, these premises are being jeopardized. Critical disjunctures between ideology and practice have taken the form of prescribed 'equality' versus discrimination and a segmented cultural division of labour, 'freedom of choice' versus exclusiveness and segregation, 'partnership' versus bureaucratic control and techno-scientific monitoring. Obvious disjunctures between liberal and egalitarian ambitions and actual social development tend to be increasingly rationalised through the language and institutional practices of a dominant pragmatism. A liberal multicultural

1. One exception to legal equality, however, is that in the case of a criminal offence, in addition to paying their regular penalty in Sweden, foreign citizens risk the additional penalty of being deported from the country.
2. During the 1980s attempts were made to extend the voting rights of foreign citizens in Sweden to national elections. The main proponents of this prospective reform were the Social Democratic Party and the Swedish Communist Party. However, the necessary support for the required amendment to the Swedish constitution has never existed in parliament. In consequence, providing easy access to double citizenship has been discussed as an alternative to giving foreign citizens actual access to voting rights at the national level.

ideology's construction of cultures and ethnic groups as ready-made objects for public consumption in order to direct a harmonious 'cultural multitude' is imperceptibly drifting towards a more and more explicit labelling of 'foreign cultures as a problem' for the administration and as incompatible with a 'modern society'. Under the impact of drifting definitions at the level of everyday encounters and practices, and confronted with the objective reality and increasing structural discrepancies of an 'organized capitalism' (Lash and Urry 1987) in rapid transformation, both the overall politico-moral consensus and the policy aims have come under serious pressure.

These tensions from within articulate with growing tensions at the international level to, seemingly, bring Swedish government policies and administrative practices into harmony with the ideologico-political scenario of 'fortress Europe'. At the same time, in the context of practical politics, and affected by a dominant 'culturalist' perspective in the public debate, the 'freedom of choice' and 'partnership' propounded by the multicultural ideology has evolved into a situation in which immigrant culture attains the status of a preserved and controlled 'reservation'. We are at a crucial juncture at which we need new, more sensitive cultural politics, new definitions of 'partnership' and a reconsidered and reworked moral consensus, as well as new popular movements to transcend ethnic and national boundaries.

Patterns of Immigration

Before moving on to deal with the political and policy debates it may be useful to indicate the nature of the migrant groups to be found in Sweden. Swedish policy in this field operates with two main categories, namely immigrants and foreign citizens. The category of immigrants usually covers all individuals born abroad and includes even individuals born in Sweden but with at least one foreign-born parent. 'Foreign citizens' covers exclusively individuals, domiciled in Sweden, but with foreign citizenship. In 1991 there were 1,212,000 immigrants in Sweden (of whom 67 per cent had been born abroad and 33 per cent being second generation born in Sweden). There were in the same year 484,000 foreign citizens. Immigrants made up 13 per cent of the total population in Sweden (1991) and foreign citizens 5.7 per cent. The most numerous group of immigrants are designated as Nordic, with a total of 439,683 (Finland 28 per cent, Norway 6 per cent, Denmark 5 per cent = 40 per cent of all immigrants). Next comes 'other European' with 'Yugoslavia' (65,000), Poland (50,000), Germany (49,000), Greece and Hungary (19,000 each), the UK (18,000) and Romania (10,000) as the most important 'countries of origin'. From Asia there are 207,000 'immigrants', with Iran (48,000), Turkey (40,000), Lebanon (20,000), Iraq (14,000) and India (11,000) as the most important sending countries. The number of 'immigrants' from Latin America is 60,000 in total, from Africa 42,000, from North America 20,000 and from the ex-Soviet Union 9,000.

The total number of 'immigrants' from countries outside Europe has increased considerably during the 1970s and 1980s – from 10 per cent in 1975 to 34 per cent in 1991, coming mainly from Asia and South America. This is even more clearly reflected in the changes over time in the number of immigrants each year. Hence the proportion of immigrants of non-European origin among all individuals arriving per year increased from 26 per cent of all in 1976 to 63 per cent in 1991. While the total number of 'immigrants' in the country has increased substantially, the proportion of immigrants of Nordic origin has decreased significantly (from 47 per cent of the total number arriving in 1980 to 18 per cent in 1991). In 1967 immigration into Sweden became subject to strict regulations. Economically motivated immigration which was dominant during the 1960s and early 1970s has since the mid–1970s decreased to very small proportions in favour of family unification and refugee inflow.

The degree of participation in the labour force is somewhat lower among "foreign citizens" (71 percent) and "immigrants" with Swedish citizenship (87 percent) than among the Swedish population as a whole (85 percent). There is a higher degree of participation in the labour force as well as a higher rate of employment among "immigrants" from European countries than among those from extra-European ones. There have always been marked differences in the degree of unemployment among "immigrants" and among the total population. In 1991 the unemployment rate was 66 percent among "foreign citizens" compared to 2,2 among Swedish citizens (including naturalized foreign born Swedish citizens who have a significantly low unemployment rate). Foreign citizens from outside Europe had in 1991 twice as high an unemployment rate as foreign citizens in general. Most "immigrants" work within branches of industry sensitive to economic fluctuations, menial service occupations (cleaning) and health (nurses). As a whole the labour market is markedly segregated along lines of gender and ethnicity, and the opportunity structure for "immigrants" narrow; most significantly so for immigrant women.

Situational Generosity

Since the mid–1980s a 'more realistic', less ambitious tone has sneaked into official Swedish policy declarations and government reports. For a start, the goal of 'freedom of choice' has become a subject for debate. From a recent government bill we learn 'that ethnic conflicts can arise alongside that line which marks the border between the immigrants' freedom of choice and basic Swedish moral and legal conceptions' (*Regeringens Proposition* 1990: 7). Though the overall goals of immigrant policy remain the same and the policy is to be further developed along these ambitious lines, there is still felt to be a need to 'specify and reformulate the goal of freedom of choice' (Karlsson 1990).[3] The notion of 'freedom of choice' has come to be perceived as problematic. Hence, this government motion suggests reinterpreting 'freedom of choice' to include 'respect for the identity and integrity of the individual as well as opportunities to develop one's own cultural heritage within the framework of those basic norms which in Swedish society apply to human coexistence' (ibid.). But rather more problematic than these qualifications to the notion of 'freedom of choice' is the question as to what extent goals as ambitious as 'partnership' and co-operation should be upheld (ibid.: 13). The same government motion tells us that 'the multitude which immigration has brought about can never be void of problems and risks of conflicts ... it is not possible to construct a society without conflicts, ethnic or other' (*Regeringens Proposition* 1990: 5–6). Against this background it is now held that 'peaceful coexistence based on mutual respect between individuals and groups of individuals will do well as a goal' (ibid.: 6). In relation to the very ambitious goal expressed by 'partnership', this seems to signify a retreat. 'Peaceful coexistence' suggests a defensive rather than a forward-looking attitude.

It is highly significant that these subtle reformulations of official policy are taking place at a historical moment when openly expressed racism is growing within the country. With the increased immigration of Third World refugees during the 1980s, the ideological climate has gradually changed in ways that seem to bring Sweden into line with the sombre face of 'fortress Europe', i.e. with the new scenario emerging from the restructuring of the international migratory system which was begun in the 1980s. While western Europe is reorienting itself towards the selective import of labour from a 'second Europe' on the verge of economic and social collapse, attitudes and policies towards Third World refugees are becoming more and more brutal. The European Community's frontiers are being more intensely policed. Internationally co-ordinated control policies are reducing refugee immigration to a trickle; the Mediterranean has been turned into a new Rio Grande (Tunander 1990), with navy patrols confronting millions of prospective labour migrants from the south. As the Berlin Wall is being torn down

3. This reformulation had already started in 1986.

the old ideological wall between the 'European Christian' and the 'Muslim' world is being reconstructed.

The current reconstruction of orientalist stereotypes can be seen to legitimate the further dominance of European economic and political interests in a rapidly changing 'Muslim world', as well as the rejection of a historical and moral responsibility for the consequences of proletarianisation, impoverishment and warfare. It is replicated in changing images of what Blaschke and Greussing (1980) call 'the Third World in Europe', namely labour migrants and refugees. Those who manage to cross the borders of 'fortress Europe' are subjected to an ethnically segmented and discriminatory labour regime and strong forces of political marginalization. Similar forces act to reproduce a repressed labour force among the young descendants of foreign immigrants (Castles et al. 1984). In France, Britain, Germany, Italy and other EC countries, Muslim communities and other minorities of Third World descent tend to be conceived of as a fifth column, an inner enemy. As in the 1950s, this inner enemy is used to foment a cold war and cement a political wall (Tunander 1990). New racist populist parties (such as the Front National in France and the so-called 'Progress' parties in Denmark and Norway) find support among disillusioned working-class and petty-bourgeois people and are given ideological respectability and legitimacy by new right-wing intellectuals writing about 'European civilisation'. 'Christian believers' (in the east as well as the west, from the Urals to Gibraltar) unite, as in earlier times, against the external threat from the Muslim world and from the new 'enemy within'. The 'Turkish peril' is revived and turned into the ideological glue with which to stick a fragmented Europe together (ibid.): a new European fundamentalism.

It is probably only a question of time before Sweden becomes part of this 'new Europe'. The issue of political neutrality became less important with the fall of the Berlin Wall. The argument being put forward by employers and the political right that an accelerating flight of capital and prospective economic decline can be stopped only through full membership of the European Community has gained ground. Also the political left has prepared itself to enter the Community. Sweden, we are told, has an ethical and moral responsibility to help develop a common democratic Europe. As Stefan Edman (1990), a left-wing member of the social democratic movement puts it, 'Swedish social democracy must urgently work out a vision, according to which the whole of Europe becomes an arena for its ideals of solidarity, internationalism and environmental struggle.'

If this traditional Swedish ambition to represent the avant-garde of the international community is to be taken seriously in the 'new Europe', then it is necessary to reconsider Sweden's own changing position in the world community. It is important to ask *where* and *how* Sweden actually leads the league of solidarity and internationalism. Sweden's changing immigration policy is as good a place as any to start the self-criticism. While a refugee policy characterised by 'solidarity and generosity' is still the order of the day according to official proclamations, actual developments since the beginning of the 1990s suggest that Sweden is moving closer to the exclusiveness, selectivity and increasing brutality of 'fortress Europe'. This trend in Swedish refugee policy is criticized most emphatically by Peter Nobel (1990), the former head of the anti-discrimination board (*diskrimineringsombudsman*): '[It] is stupid, inhumane and void of any solidarity. Moreover, quite personally, I am unwilling to live in a society which is a glossy supermarket for some nationalities and a rigid police state for others.' The situation has thus developed into one in which the government, with support from the administrations concerned, is constantly pulling in one direction, while the country's humanitarian forces (churches, Red Cross, Amnesty etc.) and warm-hearted, well-intentioned individuals are pulling in another (ibid.). And a restrictive and selective refugee policy tends to accompany a selective import of labour from eastern Europe. Selection, in turn, tends to be determined by immediate labour market trends – Sweden's so-called 'employment line' (Ålund and Schierup 1991: 21ff). A third element in this new migratory scenario is the continued reliance being placed on an insulated form of 'guestworker system' in which international subcontractors exploit a growing labour force of 'new helots' (R. Cohen 1987), who are unprotected by civil law and the labour regulations of the national state.

In an article in Sweden's largest morning newspaper, Sverker Åström (1990), a now retired senior member of the politico-administrative state elite proposed that:

> As a matter of principle we must argue that Sweden has the right and duty to consider and weigh a number of social, economic, cultural and political factors in relation to one another. It is neither amoral nor against the law to investigate whether an applicant has a criminal past, maybe as a terrorist; nor to ask oneself whether the individual in question appears to be willing or is capable of becoming a loyal member of Swedish society and whether he has what it takes to thrive; nor to try to judge whether he or she comes from a country or culture whose customs and usages are so extremely different that a reasonably harmonious adaptation is difficult or impossible; nor to consider whether extra labour at a certain time is desirable and whether the applicant has enough competence to allow him or her to make a useful contribution to Swedish working life.

This intervention in the debate is an example of how discourses on 'culture' have become both discriminatory and increasingly important in legitimating selective immigration and refugee policies. Even more alarming than this statement by a retired government official is the fact that the (former social democratic) minister responsible for immigrant matters was enthusiastic about Åström's comments. She referred to the article as 'a brilliant problem-description, very interesting to read', even though, as a matter of principle and existing legal regulations, she had to reject the proposal to introduce new criteria for judging applications for asylum based on an applicant's perceived ability to adapt to Swedish customs. The question is, however, whether or not this kind of practice has already become established. If so, Åström's argument is merely a convenient rationalisation and legitimation of the restructuring inherent in a pragmatic policy of selection according to 'cultural' and labour market considerations. A polarised climate has been created when certain categories of people are considered undesirable and when extreme measures are taken to get rid of them; a logical corollary to this, Nobel (in an interview with Albons 1990) argues, is the belief that those who are undesirable are also less worthy of respect. Following this argument, a discriminatory programme at the borders will legitimate racism within the country, including the adoption of discriminatory practices in the municipalities. This would authorise situationally determined preferential treatment in favour of selected educational profiles and individuals, which in turn would depend on shifting labour market needs and would justify the reproduction and development of a labour market segmented by ethnic and cultural stereotypes.

'Orientals ante portas!'

The mere fact that such overtly discriminatory statements appear at all in the language of the state elite (which would have been impossible a few years ago) can be taken to signify that the moral compact on which Swedish immigrant policy is built is gradually disintegrating, giving way to a culturalist construction of new discriminatory boundaries. There are many examples. The hidden logic of a new commonsense cultural racism (demarcating, in terms of a fixed cultural essence, 'other cultures' as different from 'our culture' and disturbing to the normal order) finds its way into the language and practices of public servants and professionals, and into the everyday commonsense discourses of ordinary people (Ålund and Schierup 1991: 47ff, 69ff).

Deliberately or accidentally through Freudian slips, this kind of stigmatising orientalist thinking unwittingly enters speeches, television programmes and newspaper articles dealing with 'immigrant questions'. Through hidden insinuations, decay, pathology and threats to public order become associated with 'the foreign presence'. The following pastiche (Jerkert 1990), depicting decay and social problems in the residential neighbourhood of Biskopsgården in Gothenburg, may serve as an illustration:

> Here the outsides of many houses look terrible, the colour around the windows has gone, rainwater has run down the walls, roofing materials and plaster have come loose, metal plate and concrete have slipped down from the balconies. The holes in the walls look like bullet holes, plywood has been placed in front of empty windows, not a single entrance door has its lock left, and during our visit Arab music echoed through the housing blocks.

While the public starts to regard immigrants and refugees as social problems, individual solutions increasingly come to dominate government schemes. This is reflected in the emphasis on the refugees' and immigrants' individual resources. When Sweden decides to hand-pick immigrants at the borders, pressure to assimilate tends to increase within the country, and the conditions under which immigrants can act as organised collectivities fundamentally change. The dominant ideological trend has been towards culturalising the 'problematic' rather than problematising the structural restraints. Ethnocentrism seems to go hand in hand with cultural determinism and an emerging new cultural racism (Ålund and Schierup 1991: 69ff). The fact that a proposal for culturally defined selection at the borders could even be considered for serious debate articulates in complex ways with a deterioration in the level of public opinion. A gradual change occurred in the character of public discourses during the 1980s, especially after 1988 when there was an intense debate about 'refugees as a problem' (ibid.: 33ff). Public discourses have become increasingly preoccupied with problems, with immigrants' alleged criminal behaviour (see, for example, Baldo 1989; Naumann 1989) and with drawing boundaries between 'cultures', and racist populist organisations have mushroomed.

Hence, at many different levels, a general shift in ideological orientation and institutional practices seems to be taking place at the beginning of the 1990s. Complex processes of reorientation range from the heavy-handed symbolic manifestations of new (ideologically and politically marginal) racist groups at the street level (the burning of crosses, numerous violent assaults on refugee camps) to the discreet, almost imperceptible reformulations in government reports. The trend towards a 'new realism' seems also to be reflected in a current centralisation of finance for research on immigrants and ethnic minorities into a state research fund which is, in general, oriented towards a focus on 'social problems'.

It is important to ask where these trends may lead. Will we come to see the cementing of a future 'cultural multitude' of segregated unequals: a society in political and identity crisis in which growing sections of the general public, confronting anxiety and fragmentation, are confirmed in their distrust of a transcultural 'partnership', gathering instead around the symbols of national or ethnic identity and purity? As Arne Ruth (1986) explains in the *Dagens Nyheter* (Sweden's largest daily), such a development could result from 'an alliance between two varieties of populism, two ways of demonstrating truths ostensibly produced from the sanctuary of the nation', two parallel tracks in a process of culturalisation, leading to 'a footstep in the ultimate direction of cultural apartheid'. He describes Swedish society in the 1980s as representing a juncture at which the 'new realism' of a disillusioned left is turning cynical in its attempts to embrace 'rosy stereotypes of immigrants' and is aligning 'with the great movement away from the optimistic view of human nature marking the 1960s: men and women are totally unlike one another, criminals cannot be rehabilitated, immigrants should be regarded with suspicion'. Another strand of culturalism, a pessimistic 'new racist' romanticism, continues to mystify and draw stereotyped images of the 'alien' against a background of traditional nationalist symbolism: Swedish identity and customs should be conserved and at all costs protected against those foreigners who deviate too much.

In analysing 'multiculturalism adrift', at this point in a state of ideological crisis and reorientation, it is essential to discuss critically the social realities and ideological configurations in which a prescribed, allegedly 'tolerant' multiculturalism is embedded. The crux of the matter is that a discussion about tendencies towards a 'new realism', or different forms of a 'new racism', legitimated in cultural terms, is not residual to the analysis of multiculturalism as an official political ideology and institutional practice.[4] On the contrary, such a discussion could be seen to represent ever present latent possibilities in the ideological construction of multiculturalism, even in the social democratic version stressing egalitarianism and social justice.[5] We are presented with a type of situation in which all social agents – tolerant 'multiculturalists' and 'anti-racists' as well as intolerant 'racists' and 'new realists' – tend to speak in terms of the same discursive formation (cf. Feuchtwang 1990: 4) and through the same basic categories. Following on from the premise that a culture is a community of deep-seated values of a fixed and exclusive almost organic or 'genetic' quality, populations are, in terms of the dominant culturalist orientation of the public debate, sorted by ethnic origins according to a presumed cultural essence. 'Culture'

4. For detailed discussions about 'cultural racism' or 'the new racism' see, for example, Barker (1981), Duffield (1984), Gilroy (1987), Essed (1987), Solomos (1990) and Feuchtwang (1990).
5. See, for example, the argument of Castles et al. (1990: 45).

has become a universal scientific platitude, a central ideological category in the political struggle, an indispensable tool for a techno-scientific administration and a general commonsense popular cliché which, depending on the situation, appears alternately as a 'panacea' and a 'problem'.

A 'Pragmatic Shift'

Changes in public discourses seem, as we have argued, to be connected with the increased import of unstandardised human raw material from what a Swedish government report (Arbetsmarknadsdepartementet 1990: 49) has recently endowed with the technically sounding neologism of, 'the refugee-producing countries'. Changing public discourses articulate with general socio-economic restructuring, cultural change and the establishment of new and more sophisticated forms of public agency under 'post-modern' conditions.

Gaunt and Olsson (1990) speak of a major 'paradigmatic shift' – maybe we should rather call it a 'pragmatic shift' – in Swedish public institutional practices, which started in the mid-1970s and continued throughout the 1980s, in which the mass-production of bulky goods characteristic of the industrial boom of the 1960s gave way to the differentiated production of increasingly handy vacuum-packed 'delicacies' (ibid.: 44). Public institutions are increasingly 'living their own lives' and refining their goods to meet discerning consumer needs. To the extent that immigration has made the composition of the population more heterogeneous, these differences have to be rationalised through public discourse and the population 'integrated' and controlled by the institutional umbrella. Novel experiences associated with immigration have to be institutionalised by new professional bodies. The most striking example of this process is the creation of a ramified refugee bureaucracy, especially during the late 1980s (Ålund and Schierup 1991: 34ff). Here, refugees have tended to be turned into helpless 'clients'. During a complex process of socialisation to Sweden they have become exposed to blatant forms of psychological stress and therapeutic restructuring of their personalities (ibid. referring to Olsson 1989; Westin 1990; see also Kebrome 1990; Mendes 1990). The treatment and transformation of their subjectivity has even been described as being equal to the forging of a 'raw-material, a vacuum-packed raw-material which must be belaboured and "sold" to the Swedish People's Home' (folkhemmet) (Gaunt and Olsson 1990: 44) and to the labour market through the creation of 'an ordered life'. The 'right skin colour' is essential for the success of this production and marketing process (ibid.).

One might qualify Gaunt and Olsson's statement about modern Swedish institutional practices by adding that the central issue could become the inert competence to structure a complex production and distribution process that effectuates the assignment of articles with different colours (phrased in the idiom of the 'relevant cultures') at convenient points in time to the appropriate supermarket shelves. A less metaphorical conceptualization of this problematic may present it as the ramification of institutional practices through a setting in which an ethnicisation of the public discourse comes to contribute to a realisation of immediate needs and to the continued reproduction of an increasingly differentiated and stratified cultural division of labour (Ålund 1987; Ålund and Schierup 1991: 124ff). Thus, in this sense the 'categorisation of human populations by culture or ethnic origin is no different from racial categorisation when the ascription of origin assumes a fixed cultural essence in the individuals categorised. It just sorts people into cultures and cultures into places. "Place" may be a division of labour or of territory or both' (Feuchtwang 1990: 4). These procedures represent a terrain for the formation of institutional ideologies and practices where 'multiculturalism' may imperceptibly, but thereby also more effectively, merge with cultural racism under conditions of 'post-modern' differentiation, political fragmentation and administrative sophistication. In this type of situation in which, in the name of 'multiculturalism', 'culture' has become an increasingly important ideological battleground (Wallerstein 1990), immigrants themselves have also tended to argue in the static terms of 'ethnic absolutism' or 'roots radicalist' nostalgia.

An Ethnic Tower of Babel

Sweden is probably alone in western Europe in the extent to which its public life is controlled, tamed and regulated. Probably no other western European state has been as successful in controlling and transforming radical claims and spontaneous organisation by disciplining and institutionalising them through incorporation and co-optation – a fact which has been closely linked with Sweden's elaborate corporate structure. But the organisation and exchange of experience is a social and political resource. The constitution of social identity is essentially the constitution of certain forms of communication resting on the organisation and expression of collective experience. A central question in understanding the position of immigrants in Sweden therefore hinges around what possibilities exist, in what von Kreitor (1980: 105) calls a Swedish 'sanctioned public', for the organisation and expression of their authentic experience.

The framework for the growth of new alternatives is the development of 'the global village' and of a 'world culture': i.e. the world becomes 'one network of social relationships' with a 'flow of meanings as well as of people and goods', characterised by an 'organization of diversity rather than by a replication of uniformity' (Hannerz 1987: 1; see also Hannerz 1990 and Ehn 1990). New cosmopolitan local communities, in Stockholm's multi-ethnic suburbs as well as in other European cities, harbour the preconditions for transcending narrow social and cultural boundaries (Ålund and Schierup 1991: 89ff). Here, in a dynamic interplay and articulation of 'tradition' and 'modernity', the antagonisms and struggles of the past are linked to the present dilemmas and ordeals of the immigrant experience, producing new amalgamated forms of cultural expression and political alternatives. These authentic forms of plurality still, however, mainly have the character of informal life rhythms hidden behind a legitimated 'cultural multitude' criss-crossed by constructed ethnic boundaries. This dominant culturalist construction of ethnicity is replicated in projects for 'partnership in society activities' which, centred around institutionalised co-operation between Swedish 'folk movements' and immigrant associations, have become a privileged strategy for the organised socialisation of immigrants in Sweden. Here, in the context of disciplinary institutional learning processes, the informal potentials of 'immigrant culture' tend to become adversely categorised as an 'obstacle to cooperation' (ibid.: 69ff).

Popular social movements, or so-called 'folk movements' (folkrörelser), are the traditional vehicle of political socialisation and moral supervision in Sweden. Also, today they form the cornerstone of social democratic strategies of popular mobilisation and national integration. Swedish folk movements can be defined as highly institutionalized popular movements in a symbiotic relationship with an enlightened and reforming state-bearing elite. Folk movements have functioned as effective vehicles for ideological integration and popular mobilisation in the construction of the Swedish social democratic welfare state in general (see, for example, Hirdman 1989) and, more recently and more specifically, as a tool for integrating multiculturalism into the welfare edifice on genuine Swedish terms. The Swedish folk movement par excellence is the trade union movement. It still represents a broad and, compared with other European countries, unusually unitary organisational framework which embraces over 80 per cent of Sweden's working population. But there are many other folk movements: the women's movement, the youth movement, the movement for workers' education, to mention just a few. New folk movements related to popular mobilisation around specific issues spring up continually. A couple of the more recent examples are the ecology movement and the anti-racist movement. But characteristically such movements are very quickly wooed by the state, which tries to co-opt their leadership, translate their claims, transform and adapt their strategies and integrate them into the praxis of state institutions. On the one hand, this may open up communication with centres of political and administrative power. But excess institutionalisation and close integration may, on the other hand, become the movement's bureaucratic kiss of death.

A Swedish 'ethnic pluralism' has been constructed as an integrated, albeit peripheral, part of a centrist, corporate political system (Ålund and Schierup 1991: 113ff). 'Ethnicity' has been established as an authorised and standardised collective ordering principle, largely internalised by immigrants themselves, but in principle purified of 'polluting' political or religious affiliations. 'Grey zones' of 'blurred' or 'inconsistent' ethnic loyalties have largely been treated as 'weeds' by a selective system of state subsidies, which is the most powerful instrument for structuring the Swedish 'cultural multitude'. These culturalist political and administrative practices have helped create a fragmented political stage populated by many parallel 'national organisations' (*riksorganisationer*) of separate (or separated) ethnicities with close ties to the state apparatus, but with very little communication and co-operation between themselves. At the same time a polarisation has taken place between the grassroots and centres of each single ethnic organisation. The scenario of state-sponsored multiculturalism hence appears to have turned into a tower of Babel, with immigrant organisations configuring the particular and the particularising 'cultural' at the expense of the culturally amalgamating and structurally common. This tends to draw immigrants into a politically paralysing separateness and disconnectedness *vis-à-vis* one another as well as in relation to society in general. Caught in between structurally grounded discriminatory practices embedded in the formal political system, on the one hand, and imprisoned in the culturalist tower of Babel of state-sponsored ethnic organisations on the other, immigrants (and especially immigrants of Third World origin) tend to end up in a political backwater. Faced with a credibility gap between incipient ethnic elites and their grassroots, the agency of immigrants and ethnic minorities becomes relegated to various evasive or subversive grassroots strategies of a more or less clandestine, 'pre-political' nature.

The Swedish experience could be depicted as one in which, as the result of specific forms of articulation between radical ethnic claims and the institutional practices of an enlightened leftist technocracy, authentic forms of agency have become blocked. The objective materialisation of the proclaimed multicultural goal of 'freedom of choice' was turned into the state-sponsored containment of immigrant organisational life on the prescribed basis of narrow ethnic particularity, closely monitored within a bureaucratic corporatist framework. Enlightened social engineers constructed a cultural multitude held together through an elaborate system of subsidies and minority services, but marked by the conspicuous absence of trans-ethnic communication and the active formulation of political claims. Hence, in both intent and practice, what probably became the most generous public subsidy system in any western European immigration country did not combine the material assistance it granted and the alleged right it allocated to 'conserve', 'choose' or 'develop' one's own 'ethnic identity' with a licence to extend political pluralism or to constitute effective political pressure groups. 'Partnership' was in practice to be realised through restricted forms of 'consultation' between governmental commissions, administrative agencies and officially acknowledged and state-sponsored ethnic organisations. 'Equality' tended to be interpreted within the framework of a 'therapeutic' welfare ideology. The welfare bureaucracy acquired 'knowledge about immigrants' to enable it to compensate for what were believed to be the immigrants' culturally related problems in adapting to a modern society. A limited number of middlemen with a designated 'ethnic' background were brought into various corporate agencies to help adapt institutional practices to particular culturally classified needs. In conclusion, within the framework of a corporatist political process dominated by institutionalised interest monopolies and an administrative structure controlled by technocratic rationality and therapeutic treatment, 'equality', 'freedom of choice' and 'partnership' have forged the intersecting wires of an 'iron cage', restricting the agency of ethnically or racially defined minorities to one of 'counselling' or acting as 'middlemen' between the administration and immigrant grassroots. Through this a multitude of corporate ethnic bureaucracies (in miniature) did indeed gain some marginal and restricted access to the political process, and certain groups of ethnic professionals have been able to find for themselves restricted niches in administration, education and the social welfare sector. But caught between their own marginal position in the state structure and the needs and claims of their fellow 'ethnics' among the grassroots, a variety of incipient elites have, to paraphrase Dench (1986), remained 'prisoners of ambivalence'.

To escape from the ethnic tower of Babel it is necessary to transcend the static character of the conception of culture, which has so far come to represent the conventional wisdom for the production of 'knowledge on immigrants' in Sweden. It is, likewise, essential to question the definition of 'ethnicity' as a hegemonic ordering principle structuring the multicultural scene and for immigrants and ethnics themselves to reconsider the 'ethnic absolutism' (Gilroy 1987) which has been instrumental in fragmenting their political agency. A composite strategy for democratisation under culturally mixed and spuriously post-modern conditions needs more thoroughly reflected notions of 'politics', 'class', 'state', 'civil society' and 'everyday life' to be conceived of within a wider analytical framework that includes the complex processes of globalisation-localisation circumscribing an ongoing restructuring of the national state (Ålund and Schierup 1991: 137ff). This could help reformulate increasingly difficult struggles against the dismantling of the Swedish welfare state into struggles for a *welfare society* which could better actuate the potentials embodied in a genuinely trans-ethnic 'partnership'.

8

Political Participation and Civil Rights in Scandinavia

Tomas Hammar

Introduction

My central question is: Who are entitled to full political rights in a democratic nation state? Or phrased otherwise, if your answer is: All members of the state should be entitled to full political rights, then I would like to ask: And who are entitled to be members?

The conventional answer to my question is of course: Citizens are members of the state, and only they enjoy full political rights. These rights are given to all citizens whether they are citizens by birth or by naturalisation. Most countries today combine – in one way or another – the two basic principles that citizenship is inherited from the parents (*jus sanguinis*) and/or that it is granted to persons born on the country's territory (*jus soli*). According to these principles most children born in a country acquire its citizenship. But there are also some who do not, but obtain another citizenship from their parents, or because they were born on another country's territory.

I want to argue here that there is another criterion than citizenship based on birthplace and family, which should be – and also increasingly is being – honoured, namely the length of legal stay in a country (*a jus domicilii*). To make this last point absolutely clear, let us think of those foreign citizens who have already lived more than twenty years in a country and let us assume that they are well settled and established there.

For naturalisation, many countries require a residence period of at least five years. The idea is of course that integration takes time and that a certain adaptation should take place, and that at least the language should be learnt. All this takes at least five years. Naturalisation will be a national interest, as soon as there has been large-scale immigration. Every country has a long-term interest in controlling the size of its population of non-citizens. If a large number of foreign citizens are allowed to settle during a period of time, the country of immigration should, not immediately but by and by, start the naturalisation of this new population. In a recent document of a committee of the Council of Europe, this idea was expressed in the following way:

> Seen from the point of view of States it is not in a country's national interest that a large section of its population should remain from generation to generation without the nationality of the country which has become its home. Seen from the viewpoint of long time immigrants, who in practically all respects are acknowledged in the host country, the absence of full participation in the political life there can only be felt as deplorable. (Council of Europe, March 1991)

Serious considerations are given within the Council of Europe to a partial extension of the now existing practical opportunities to obtain and hold dual citizenship. No country seems to have a rule, however, saying that all those who have been legal residents for a long time, e.g. for at least twenty years, shall be offered an automatic naturalisation, which they of course could renounce.

In many states other decisive criteria are in use, however, as to who shall be seen as a member. I am thinking of ethnicity and race. The concept of the German nation has been increasingly employed during the last few years to decide who shall be entitled to a citizenship in the Federal Republic of Germany. German ancestors and German language have given many immigrants from the east enough evidence that they belong to the German nation. In contrast, immigrants from Turkey with more than twenty years of residence, say in Berlin, have seldom been naturalised. And to take another example, a large minority of Koreans are in a similar way excluded from membership in Japan. Many other examples may be given.

Each sovereign state enacts its own nationality Act and applies it according to its own interpretation. Such are the laws which at present are given. But what I want to discuss here is *de lege ferenda*, or what future laws we would wish to have in this field. And my point is of course that individuals and groups under certain conditions may be said to have a moral right to a membership of a state and to political and civil rights.

While personally supporting the right of states to control and regulate their immigration, I suggest that states should not be free to deport immigrants without consideration of their domicile, their residence period, and their relations to the country and its population etc. Nor should a state be free to treat such immigrants as non-members, when this state has once at least tacitly accepted the immigration and then allowed them to stay, work and settle during a long period of time.

This is the reason why I am prepared to consider an automatic naturalisation after twenty years of residence, or the French system of an automatic citizenship at the age of majority to those born in the country as foreign citizens (my third category above). This is also why I am stressing the point that all foreign citizens are not the same. Some are indeed foreigners with no connections to the country, others are legal residents with many ties, and it is in order to bring this latter category into strong relief that I have started to use a special term for them calling them 'denizens', as they are not just aliens, but also not yet citizens.

Aliens, Denizens and Citizens

In many of Europe's immigration countries aliens make up 10 to 25 per cent of the labour force. They were in the beginning expected to return after a few years, but they have in fact settled permanently. They are formally aliens, but they have gained a secure residence status. After many years in the country, they are denizens with many strong ties to the country.

Denizens are not citizens of the country where they have their domicile. They are foreign citizens with a legal and permanent residence status. They enjoy full social and economic rights, and they are often well integrated in the host society. They may even have some political rights, but they are normally not given political representation. During the 1980s the number of denizens has grown in western Europe (to approximately seven or eight million in 1989), and so have their demands for civil rights and for full political participation.

In German and Scandinavian languages the word for foreigner is *Ausländer* or *utlänning*, where 'Aus' or 'ut' mean from the outside, while *Inländer* or *inlänning* could perhaps be used to refer to persons who are permanent residents. Atle Grahl-Madsen (1985) suggests that any future aliens Act should distinguish not merely between citizens and foreigners but also between two types of non-citizen, giving three categories of people in all:

1 foreigners (*Ausländer, utlänningar,* strangers, *étrangers*);
2 denizens (*Inländer* or foreign citizens with full residential rights);
3 citizens (*Staatsangehörige, medborgare*).

This idea provides a useful starting point for a discussion of civil rights and political participation of foreign citizens in west European countries, as it can help us better to understand the need for more secure legal protection for those who are neither complete foreigners nor citizens of the country in which they reside.

Changing Perspectives in the 1970s

The 1948 Universal Declaration of Human Rights signified a break with previous principles which completely excluded foreign citizens from political life in their country of residence, granting political freedom to everyone without discrimination against non-citizens. This innovation caused most western European states to re-examine their policies and change their previous restrictions. The process started early in some countries and late in others, but the direction was everywhere the same.

The right to reside permanently in the host country is a basic prerequisite for political activities. Those who fear that political participation may cause them problems with their residence status and perhaps lead to refusals when they apply for extended permits, will often refrain from politics. On the other hand, if there is not much risk of such consequences, foreigners will make more use of the rights given to them.

In the 1980s many more foreign residents have obtained the privileged position of a permanent resident, and in several countries new kinds of permits have been introduced which allow longer residence periods and easier renewals. As a consequence, the legal status of foreign citizens has improved, and they are now for the first time able to make realistic plans for their future stay in the host country, even if they are not granted its citizenship, or do not wish to acquire it.

Civil Rights

A prerequisite for political participation of aliens is the legal protection of life and personal freedom, as well as a protection against inhuman and degrading treatment or punishment. In European countries – but far from in all countries of the world – foreign citizens have the right to liberty and security of the person. They are equal before the court and enjoy the minimum guarantees given every citizen charged with a criminal offence. Residence and work permits with short duration, and discretionary decisions about prolongation of permits, may be major hindrances to the political mobilisation of foreign residents in the host countries, but civil rights are in general granted on an equal footing to citizens and non-citizens alike, and therefore foreigners in most countries do not encounter legal obstacles to th ir free participation in political debates, associations and political parties.

However, one major exception to their civil rights is found in the aliens control established everywhere. The police are, in one way or another, empowered to arrest foreign citizens and to keep them in custody for a short time in order to check their identity and their permits, deport them or ask for their expulsion. For the same purpose, foreign citizens may also be forbidden to move within the country's territory and from one employer or job to another, although freedom of movement is otherwise considered a fundamental right of everyone in the country. It is worth noting that these exceptions to civil rights caused by the need for an aliens control system do not usually embarrass those foreign citizens who have obtained long-term or permanent residence permits and can easily prove their identity.

In a national emergency situation, for example when a country is at war or under the threat of an impending war, civil rights normally granted to aliens are often suspended. This may be explicitly foreseen in the law, or follow from special decisions and ordinances of the kind that were taken in most countries during the Second World War.

In most European states, foreign citizens enjoy freedom of speech, expression, the press, assembly, demonstration, and association to the same extent as citizens. Freedom of association is more often restricted, but in general the practice is more liberal than the letter of the constitution or the law. Freedom of opinion, association and assembly may in most cases be exercised by aliens, except that a 'sword of Damocles' is hanging over their heads.

Have Foreigners Voiced their Demands?

How are civil rights utilised by foreign citizens? This question is much more difficult to answer because it requires analysis of the political participation of foreigners in the European host countries.

First of all, we must not assume that political activities exist only when civil rights are granted. It is obvious that foreign citizens can be members of political parties even when they are not allowed to vote in local elections. If they are barred from forming their own associations, they may join existing associations in the host country. If they are forbidden to publish their own periodicals, they may publish articles in domestic magazines or give interviews to newspapers.

Foreign citizens and foreign workers have not been silent and inactive in the European host countries. They have from the beginning of the 1970s taken part in a variety of political actions and protests aimed at improving both their status and their working and living conditions. As foreign citizens, they have not been granted voting rights and representation, except in a few cases at the local level, but they have made use of the civil rights that have been given to them. Some have even been prepared to take illegal action, with all its attendant risks, when there were no alternatives.

Political Representation

Foreign citizens have also joined trade unions and other organisations and associations. They have become members of political parties and they have taken part in electoral campaigns.

As long as only citizens are allowed to participate in political life, non-citizens are excluded from representative democracy. The larger this category is in a state, the greater are the consequences of this limitation. The fact is that a substantial proportion of adults, and especially of adult workers, are not represented, and the political balance between the working class and other social classes is therefore also somewhat changed. Denizens' demands are not taken seriously as long as they are not represented in the political councils and assemblies. If democracy means that all those who are affected by political decisions shall also have a chance to take part in these decisions ('no taxation without representation') then we have to admit that political democracy has not functioned well in the 1980s and does not function well at the beginning of the 1990s, for *pro primo* several countries do not grant political rights to denizens, and *pro secundo* others which do, find that, for several reasons, many denizens abstain from using their new rights.

Sweden, the other Scandinavian countries (Denmark and Norway), the Netherlands, two Swiss cantons, and partly also some other states (Iceland, Finland) have granted denizens voting rights in some elections (local and regional) but not in the most important and most publicised national elections. It has been said, for instance in Sweden, that local elections more than national are salient to newly arrived immigrants. Local political rights will give them an opportunity to voice their demands about local issues, like child care, schools, housing etc., and this should lead to improvements in local immigrant policies.

Fifteen years of experience with this system may be said to give some support to this hopeful programme. There is evidence that more denizens have become members of political parties and been elected to political positions etc. And the local political parties have taken more interest in the conditions of denizens living in their municipalities. But great problems remain, especially the low and decreasing political participation among immigrants in general.

As already stated here, formal rights are not enough. Even in states where denizens have obtained electoral rights, their participation has often been low, much lower than the general rate of participation in the host countries, probably also indicating an unsatisfactory political integration.

Take Sweden as an example. Thanks to the electoral reform of 1975, many candidates with an 'immigrant background', i.e. first or second generation, have been elected to political office. In 1988 about 600 foreign-born candidates were elected to the municipal councils all over Sweden, and among them about a hundred were foreign citizens, while the rest (about 500) were either first-generation, naturalised Swedish citizens, or second-generation citizens born in Sweden.

It is probably easier to be nominated and elected as a minority candidate in a proportional list system than in a majority vote system. Nevertheless, only between 4 and 5 per cent of all those elected in Sweden are 'immigrants', compared to about 10 per cent of the electorate. The number of elected immigrants is slowly increasing but does not seem to reach a level corresponding to the size of the electorate. The political parties, first anxious to find candidates from the minority groups, seem more and more reluctant to further increase the number of immigrants in the councils.

Table 8.1 Persons elected to the municipal councils, 1979–1988.

Country of origin	Foreign-born persons				Foreign citizens
	1979	1982	1985	1988	1988
Denmark	47	60	61	70	10
Norway	55	54	61	53	12
Finland	253	272	283	260	56
Yugoslavia	8	10	11	13	5
Greece	7	8	7	7	–
West Germany	35	49	48	69	–
Other countries	85	79	93	117	23
Total	490	532	564	589	106

On the other hand, the influence of elected immigrants seems to be increasing. This may be expected to follow almost automatically for, in practice, the longer time a person has functioned in the councils the more does he know about local politics and the more influential is his position. But there is also a risk that his gradually more successful integration into politics means that he more and more departs from his minority origin, till he finally considers himself to be just another regular politician among all the others.

Participation

In local elections in the Nordic countries and in the Netherlands, the turnout of foreign citizens has been considerably below the average for all those entitled to vote: in Sweden 30–40 per cent below, in Denmark 12–17 per cent, in Norway about 25 per cent, and in the Netherlands also far below the average. Full participation is impeded by a series of *hindrances*, that cannot simply be removed inasmuch as they follow from the composition of the immigrant groups or from their situation as temporary migrants in the host society, as for example:

1 Over-representation of persons with characteristics that usually lead to low participation: low age, unmarried, low income, not members of associations, newly arrived.
2 Faulty knowledge of the electoral system, political parties and issues, aggravated by a lack of language ability and social isolation.
3 Low salience of elections and political issues because of plans to return, or no decision to stay. Immigrant issues are not disputed in party politics and do not play a great role in the electoral campaigns.
4 Attachment to the political system is vague or non-existent. No pressure of group norm to participate.
5 Cross-pressure between political values and modes of behaviour from the country of origin and the country of immigration, between traditional and modern, between rural and urban, and between religious and secular.

These factors which may cause low electoral participation are probably most significant during the first years in a new country, and several of them may after some years of residence tend to lose their power. We would therefore assume that the rate of turn-out would increase year by year, as immigrant voters become more experienced in politics and more integrated. As already noted, we have found the opposite to be true in Sweden. Participation has actually declined election by election.

One explanation for this decline is the fact that in each new election, a large part of the foreign electorate - already somewhat trained and experienced – is lost because of remigration and naturalisation, and replaced by inexperienced, newly enfranchised, first-time voters. In Sweden the total number of foreign voters has been stable, around 240,000, but each election about 70,000 voters have been replaced by new immigrants (having arrived three to six years before), who are probably less active voters than for instance those who voted as denizens in the previous election but who have since then obtained citizenship. This system of repeated exchange of 25 to 30 per cent of the foreign electorate seems to prevent the expected increase in the turn-out, but it cannot explain the continuous decrease, which has taken place in all the Scandinavian countries, and which is especially striking in Sweden.

In many parts of the world it is normal to get an electoral turn-out of around 50 per cent. Even in those political elections, which might be seen as the most important of all, the presidential elections in the USA, the turnout can be less than half of the electorate, which of course has been regretted but mostly not seen as a total failure of the political system. Furthermore, abstentions used to be more frequent in local than in national elections. In countries where the turnout is 80 per cent in parliamentary elections (as often in France and in Denmark and Norway etc.), only 65 to 70 per cent participate in municipal elections.

Table 8.2 Participation (per cent) in five local elections and in one referendum in Sweden, 1976–1988.

Country of citizenship	Local elections					Referendum
	1976	1979	1982	1985	1988	1980
Greece	76	65	61	49	46	75
West Germany	67	64	61	59	52	73
Great Britain	67	57	55	54	50	–
Yugoslavia	66	56	52	45	38	27
Poland	64	59	54	47	40	–
Turkey	63	62	61	54	54	–
Italy	61	60	58	52	50	–
Norway	59	54	52	49	45	67
Denmark	57	46	49	46	41	60
Finland	56	51	49	45	39	49
USA	45	45	47	45	44	–
Chile	–	–	–	77	70	–
Iran	–	–	–	38	39	–
Others	60	55	56	52	44	63
Total mean	60	53	52	48	43	53

Sweden has changed its electoral system in order to abolish this difference between national and local turnouts, conducting three elections simultaneously. National, regional and local elections take place during one and the same day and in the same polling station. As a result the difference in participation has been reduced to a minimum of only a few per cent. But this is also exactly why the difference between non-citizen and citizen voters has become so striking. As foreign voters cannot vote in the national elections, they abstain much more frequently than regular citizen voters, entitled to vote in all three elections.

Is a very low participation rate alarming? As we have already shown, the rate of participation among denizens is negatively influenced by a number of factors. Among these factors, we have also included (those grouped under 3 above) a low salience of elections and of political issues, especially low to denizens uncertain about their future stay in the country, and (under 4) a vague attachment to the host country's political system. What is more, denizens are not granted full political rights, but limited to local voting rights. As we have seen, this must also lead to a lower rate of turn-out, in Scandinavia about 10 to 15 per cent lower.

In spite of all this, the low rate of electoral participation and its continued decline is alarming. Democracy is not just formal rights but first of all real rights, employed by voters with resources to make efficient use of them. It is alarming that one specific group of voters – the denizens – in practice do not use their formal rights and therefore are clearly distinguishable as less active and less interested, voters with less weight in the eyes of the political parties.

This brings us back to the fundamental question which this electoral reform from the beginning was meant to give an answer to: how can denizens get their democratic rights to full political representation in those immigration countries, where they live, work and pay taxes?

The Reform Went Only Half The Way

It was a radical break with constitutional law and practice when a few countries granted non-citizens voting rights in the 1970s. The first elections were seen as rather successful, and the public interest was enhanced by the initial publicity and the following lively discussions. But the reform was a compromise, it went only half the way and stopped in between the two poles of no representation and full representation. Denizens were given some political influence but they were discriminated against, not getting national voting rights.

Can such a system last? What are the consequences in the long run of giving political rights only halfway? One thing must be expected: demands for full political rights will come from those discriminated against. But if they do not obtain full rights, and when time goes by and the chances of a change seem to be increasingly slim, then political passivity, apathy and indifference may grow, and electoral participation may drop.

Several west European immigration countries have – instead of local voting rights – created consultative councils to which denizens have been invited to elect their representatives. Some of these experiments have resulted in improvements in local immigrant policies and have given denizens a voice and to some extent also satisfied their primary demands. But these consultative councils have also met with a big and increasing indifference. They were only meant for consultation and had no power to make their own decisions, nor given any tax money to distribute or administrate. Representatives often felt that their demands were not listened to, and many denizens felt that their votes did not result in anything. This was not real democracy, they said, only a substitute for it.

Something similar may be happening to the Scandinavian–Dutch model of only local voting rights. Even if this means full rights on the local level, it is not full political rights. And even if some national immigrant groups have got a relatively fair representation with full power to make decisions in the local assemblies, denizen representatives are only a small minority in the local councils, a handful of 'immigrant politicians' within a political body of fifty to a hundred representatives. And they are all elected as members and representatives of the regular political parties, divided among themselves and bound by loyalties to the parties.

Can anything be done to ameliorate this situation? At the present time, little or nothing seems to be done in Scandinavia. The political parties are of divergent opinions. In Sweden, the three non-socialist parties in parliament do not favour an extension of voting rights to national elections (which the two socialist parties do), and they hesitate to open up for a more tolerant attitude towards dual nationality (hesitate more than the socialist parties do). Policy changes are therefore not to be expected in Sweden, at least not in the near future, and much less could they be expected in Denmark and Norway.

Why Denizens do not Naturalise?

If denizens quickly and at low cost shifted from one formal citizenship to another, no large populations without political rights would cause problems for democracy. Let us imagine that every immigrant after twenty years of legal residence received not only a permanent residence permit but also automatically and without application a formal citizenship. This fictive (and up to now unrealistic system) would reduce the problem of representation, as immigrants would then after twenty years obtain full political rights, including the right to vote and to stand for election.

There are countries (and Canada is one of these) which strongly encourage immigrants to naturalise, and which do this without demanding that they renounce their previous citizenship. Most countries, however, are much more restrictive and many countries apply severe citizenship requirements and examine each applicant individually.

A country's naturalisation policy affects its naturalisation rate, but even the most liberal country usually finds that a substantial proportion of its immigrants are reluctant to shift citizenship and, although settled permanently, long prefer to remain citizens of another country. This may be a result of the laws of the country of emigration, forbidding foreign citizens, including those who have renounced their citizenship of that country, to inherit or purchase property, or even to visit the country without a visa.

A generally low propensity to shift from one formal citizenship to another is first of all due to another factor, however. It is caused by strong emotional ties to the country of origin, and not least by ties to relatives still living there. Even those who have left the old country for a long time or even for good, continue to identify with its culture and acknowledge a belonging to its nation. In several important respects, they are still 'members' of this state and of this nation, although they have started to acquire another membership also, a membership of the host country.

It is important to note here that citizenship has both a formal meaning (in French, 'nationalité') and a substantive meaning ('citoyen') (Brubaker 1989). In its formal sense, citizenship ('nationalité') is understood as membership of the state, acquired at birth or later, for instance by naturalisation. An individual may possess more than one citizenship at the same time. He may be a dual citizen, and we shall return to this dual status later. But in relation to a certain state, say Sweden, he either is a citizen of that country, or he is not. And as a proof that he is a citizen, he can normally get a passport for travel abroad.

In substance, citizenship means the possession of a number of rights and duties, such as the rights to enter the country, to take permanent residence there and to work there, the right to enjoy social benefits, the political rights, and the duty to do military service. Many of these rights are dependent on a formal citizenship: electoral rights and military service, for instance, while others are available also to some denizens or to all visitors to the country etc. In other words, not only formal citizens, but also many others, denizens and even foreigners on temporary visits, enjoy social and economic rights.

In fact, I have started to use the term 'denizens' just to demonstrate that there is not only one type of membership of a state. Denizens are not citizens of the country where they stay. In this sense they are indeed 'foreigners' (foreign citizens or stateless), but they enjoy a legal and permanent resident status, as well as many rights and duties in relation to the host country. They therefore belong to a new status group.

Because of the reasons given here, we cannot expect denizens to naturalise very fast and *en masse*. We cannot either expect many of them to return to their origins. Most will stay, and many will later obtain citizenship. In the meanwhile, however, the problem of non-representation of large populations will remain unsolved, and it is safe to say that most observers agree that this could in the long run bring several unfortunate consequences.

Dual Citizenship

Most legal experts maintain that dual citizenship, i.e. the possession of a formal citizenship in more than one state, is something harmful which should be avoided, and a number of European states have ratified a European Convention of 1963 on the 'reduction of cases of multiple nationality'. Many states, both parties to this convention and others, are nevertheless in practice increasingly tolerant, allowing naturalisation for various reasons without renunciation of previous citizenship. The number of dual citizens has in this way increased tremendously, and at the end of the 1980s a reconsideration of the convention of 1963 started within the Council of Europe (Darras 1986; Kamman 1984).

Some disadvantages of dual citizenship can be handled through international agreements, for instance agreements about military service and taxation. Dual voting rights, i.e. the right to vote in political elections in two states, has seldom been regulated or restricted in this way, however, perhaps because this consequence of dual citizenship has so far been of little significance.

There are, however, in several states already residential requirements according to which voters must be residents, registered within a constituency. This means that citizens abroad cannot automatically vote. Dual citizens can in such a system vote only in the country where they are domiciled.

Based on a Spanish–Latin American example, a 'sleeping citizenship' has sometimes been discussed, meaning that rights and duties which normally used to go with a formal citizenship, should remain passive or sleeping as long as a citizen is domiciled abroad, but this sleeping citizenship should easily and without delay be reactivated as soon as this citizen returns and again registers as resident in the country.

If dual citizenship were more generally accepted, a number of beneficial effects would follow, especially with regard to the democratic problem discussed here. More denizens would be willing to apply for naturalisation in the host country. The number of denizens without political rights would be strongly reduced, and dual citizens would of course, get full electoral rights in the country of domicile, i.e. voting rights not only in local but also in national elections. It is fairly unrealistic to believe, however, that dual citizenship will be generally accepted within the immediate future, even if some states proceed along these lines, even if some regional solutions are found, and even if the ongoing economic integration may have great political implications in the future, not only in Europe.

–9–

Migrant Women, Racism and the Dutch Labour Market

Helma Lutz

Introduction

Throughout Europe there is an overwhelming tendency in public discourse to put ethnic minorities to the fore. This is also the case in contemporary political discourse in the Netherlands, where one of the main topics concerns the 'minderhedenprobleem', the *problem* of ethnic minorities. It is perhaps noticeable that in general it is taken for granted that ethnic minorities constitute a problem which has to be solved. As this occurs elsewhere in Europe at the same time this may not be called a Dutch specialty. However, what certainly is special for the Dutch discourse is that in the Netherlands the labour market has become the focus of the discourse on minorities.

This paper aims to cast some light on this labour market discourse. I will approach the topic by deconstructing the main ideas of Dutch policy-makers, which are specified in government reports. I will question the implicit notions of the social function of labour and the labour market used in these reports. In particular I will focus on the position of migrant women in the labour market. Finally I will turn to a case study on the position of educated migrant women, because schooling and education are seen as their main access to the labour market; in the light of the results of this study questions are raised concerning contemporary minorities policy.

By May 1989, when the most recent report on ethnic minorities appeared ('Allochtonenbeleid', a report published by WRR, the Scien-

Thanks to John Schuster and Kathy Davis for critical remarks on an earlier version of this paper.

tific Council of Government Policy), it became apparent that there was a significant gap between the tolerant discourse on minorities on the one hand, for which the Netherlands had become famous through their liberal reports and policy-making since the end of the 1970s, and the facts of living conditions of the groups in question on the other hand. Figures showed that unemployment among the different migrant groups was high, even much higher than in other European countries (see table 9.1). This situation has not at all changed since the report was first published. It may be interesting to mention some general facts on minorities policy before looking further into the details of the report.

In 1979 the first overall policy report on ethnic minorities acknowledged that the non-Dutch population was no longer resident in the Netherlands on a temporary basis, but that they had settled down permanently. On this basis the position of both colonial (Surinamese, Antillean and Moluccan) and certain groups of labour migrants (Turkish, Moroccan) was analysed as being marginal, and demands were made for equal opportunities and rights. As a result of the acknowledgement that Dutch society was no longer monocultural but multicultural, and that society and its institutions would have to take this change into account, emphasis was put on the right of minorities to develop a proper 'ethnic/cultural' identity in order to improve their independence and self-esteem. The hallmarks of the report concerned investment in schooling, in support of group emancipation and in social and cultural care and supply. This eventually led to a situation in which large sums of money were invested in social work and schooling.

The hallmark of the second report – published exactly ten years later – is the emphasis it puts on the labour market. Schooling is then connected to the notion that lack of schooling is a reason for high unemployment rates. The change in the central focus of both reports may be interpreted as a result of the shocking truth about the minorities' current unemployment figures. Strikingly enough, any analysis of what actually happened in the ten years between the publication of the two reports is missing. The second report does not start with an evaluation of a decade of minorities policy, but simply announces the need for change. This is even more astonishing as the national and local governments commission most minority research, and minority research output has reached the number of 300 publications per year, almost one publication a day (Sunier 1991: 8, 9).

The preview of the report plainly recommends replacing contemporary policy-making by this new focus on labour market policies 'in order to make the population in question less dependent on public spending and welfare work'. The notion of the necessity of gaining more independence from public spending is central to the argument. The report clearly suggests that ethnic minorities are highly unemployed because they had been regarded by the government as a 'care category'. Because of this policy – it is assumed – they became dependent on public money and the state (WRR 1989: 9). The implicit message of this statement is that ethnic minorities prefer to use or abuse public care. Interestingly enough this argument emerges again in connection with the recent discussions on the government's plans to cut back disability pensions (as laid down in the WAO, the Disablement Insurance Act). Here too a causal connection is made between dependence on social security and care, and the inability to find work, where the individual as a receiver of 'public' money is held responsible for his or her own state of unemployment.

Therefore this notion of 'dependence' has to be seen in the broader context of the discourse on minorities and changes in the discourse on the public duties of the welfare state. We could even – ironically – say that the discourse on ethnic minorities has a 'vanguard' function as it seems to be a laboratory for try-outs, experiments in social policy-making. Those who conduct experiments in this area are assured of very little public protest and resistance because of the lack of political power of the target group.

There is an interesting parallel in the very vivid discussions on the reorganisation of the Dutch welfare state in general, including the emphasis on work – stressing every citizen's duty to participate in the labour market (WRR, 1990: 29–51) – and the discussion on ethnic minority 'problems'. Hence it is the actual focus on the labour market which is the starting point of my argument. While it is not my intention to provide a comprehensive survey of the position of migrants on the Dutch labour market, I will rather analyse the issue of the 'labour market' by asking what it stands for in the discourse on ethnic minorities.[1] Such topics as labour and the labour market are receiving growing attention in connection with the dismantling of the welfare state.

Labour Market and Labour Force

It was already mentioned at the beginning of this article that one has to wonder why so much emphasis is put on the labour market. To begin

1. In this chapter I use interchangeably the terms 'immigrants', 'ethnic minorities' and the term 'allochthonous', which in the Netherlands is used to indicate a group which may even have Dutch citizenship but is of non-Dutch origin; the terminology is in fact dissatisfactory because 'allochthonous' is the collective term for a very heterogeneous group, including immigrants such as Americans, Germans, as well as Turks and Moroccans etc. Yet, using this category, policy-makers generally refer to certain 'allochthonous' groups whose position is characterised by economic, social and political weakness.

with: the figures given by WRR are indeed alarmingly critical. In a country where ethnic minorities make up only 5.5 per cent of the population, they represent 15 per cent of the unemployed. Out of 660,000 unemployed, 100,000 are black or migrant; moreover the situation of youth unemployment is even more critical: 'One out of every two black and migrant youths had no gainful employment' (Choenni and Cain 1991: 6). The question is how the WRR recommendation responds to this situation.

In addition to introducing the labour market as the new focus of minorities policy, the report introduces labour market participation as a necessary precondition for the integration of minorities into Dutch society (WRR 1989: 16). The authors of the report assume that work is a major meeting point and a possible way to get better acquainted with one another's lifestyles. This notion is extremely interesting because it indicates the shift in the argumentation and a departure from former policies. While ten years ago – as I mentioned before – culture (expressed in cultural or ethnic identity) was at the core of the integration strategy, now it is labour through which 'a mutual adaption of values and norms can take place' (WRR 1989: 16). Obviously policy-makers have a conception of labour as being organised in a collaborational form: people working together on the shop-floor or in offices, and the office and the shop-floor as the only (physical) situations in which migrants and the Dutch can get to know each other face to face.

According to this view, the labour market is supposed to function as an educator for integration. A close look at the preconditions for this 'education' raises some questions, however.

1 Though the report does not deny the fact that migrants are concentrated in the unskilled and low-paid sectors of the labour market (WRR 1989: 109), the implications of this fact are not mentioned: the greater part of this kind of labour is dirty, noisy shift work with short breaks and hardly any opportunity to talk to one another. The majority of the workers are of migrant origin, except for the foremen or forewomen. Influence, authority and power in such a setting are structurally determined: one would hardly expect the Dutch foremen or forewomen to 'adapt to the norms and values' of their colleagues, but rather the other way round. Thus it is the migrant worker who has to adapt to the dominant rules of the shop-floor. Meeting these conditions means either to learn to handle them or to adapt to them. Can one really imagine mutual adaptation to ethnic differences?

2 The notion of the shop-floor or the office as a major meeting place assumes a very old-fashioned organisation of labour and production in which all employees work in one building. However, nowadays entire branches of the industries are subcontracted and capital-intensive work has become the domain of a lonely operator. In the service

industries working conditions are rough, hardly allowing the employees to talk to colleagues about anything beyond what is necessary. To which (missing) counterpart is one supposed to adapt?

3 A look at other areas of research underlines the dubious nature of WRR's assumption. It has been shown that the 'hidden rules' of the 'enterprise culture' of different work areas is dominated by (white) male habits, values and norms (Doorne-Huiskes 1979). From case studies we understand that women in general – however skilled, educated and ambitious they may be – have problems coping with an 'enterprise culture' which is usually not prepared to adapt to women's obligations such as child care etc. Even the most recent research on the position of women among university staff (Beckers and Beekes 1991) does not indicate any significant change. Obviously there is very little inclination to adapt to obligations mutually. As a result of this, obligations keep their gendered character.

All this implies that integration by 'mutual adaption through work' can be described more appropriately as an assimilation to dominant structures. Referring to the question raised at the beginning of my article, one could say that integration into the labour market means adaptation to the rules of society through work. To put it in Paul Willis's (1977) words: 'learning to labour' has been and is still seen as the path to social integration.

Summarising this section, one could say that owing to this new emphasis in minorities policy, 'mutual acceptance of each other's culture', which was supposed to be the key to integration a decade ago, has not only been replaced by a somewhat naive idea that everybody who has a job will be integrated, but also that work has an educational task with regard to the social integration of ethnic minorities.

It is certainly worth mentioning that the notion of work as being primarily conducive to social status and social integration is not limited to the Dutch policy-makers' discourse on ethnic minorities (see WRR 1977, 1990). It has become a hot item in the ongoing process of dismantling of public care facilities, which is proclaimed to be necessary for the sake of the welfare state in general. The position of the so-called care categories, the handicapped, ethnic minorities and women, is supposed to be characterised by isolation and dependency, which is to be remedied by means of work and schooling. Work becomes the road to happiness.

What is the Labour Market?

Though the labour market is supposed to be the main instrument of policing ethnic minorities, any definition of it is lacking. If one deconstructs its implicit meaning from the report, one finds a very classical notion.

Classical economists define the labour market as the place of the exchange relationship between employees and employers, regulating the prices that must be paid for labour (see e.g. Kloosterman 1991: 17). According to this definition, labour force is differentiated in terms of (individual) skills, experience, ambition and permanence; labour forces and labour markets are real existing phenomena, measurable in numbers, figures and tables. However, this assumption is highly problematic:

1 The definition is fairly neutral and leaves the conditions of the exchange and allocation of labour out of consideration, disregarding the balance of power and the distribution of power in the functioning of the market.
2 It also assumes a definition of labour which is linked to (un)employment and pay, and fails to take into account labour which is necessary for the (re)production of the official labour force, such as housework.
3 The definition overemphasises the primary sector of the labour market, which is characterised by stable employment of educated employees; it underemphasises the secondary sector, characterised by poor working conditions and unstable employment; and finally it fails to address the tertiary sector of the economy, including non-registered work in the hidden economy. It is an open secret that the importance of the hidden economy is growing and that the majority of people involved in this sector are women and (illegal) migrants.

According to Morokvasic (1991) it is this tertiary sector which, in the face of the establishment of 'fortress Europe', is gaining considerable importance: it provides certain industrial branches (such as the clothing industry, the building industry, and domestic help) with cheap labour, while for (illegal) migrants 'informal' work is the only way to enter the European labour market.

In summary, one has to underline the fact that the classical economic definition of labour and the labour market which is employed in the WRR report fails to consider the underlying distribution of power. In other words, not all participants in the labour market are acting on an equal basis of power.

Another serious omission in the report concerns the absence of any reference to racism on the labour market. In a survey article by Cain and Choenni (1991) it is argued that racial discrimination has become a primary variable on the Dutch labour market. Studies indicate that in a country priding itself on its tolerance as a national virtue, a whole range of subtle and covert racist practices has developed. It is common practice, for example, to demand a proper proficiency in the Dutch language for posts which do not require such a skill. In times of job shortage, employers in the service sector (cleaning work) emphasise language skills and 'western' dressing habits as selection criteria which were not of any significance in the 1970s (Bouw and Nelissen 1986; Den Uyl, Choenni and Bovenkerk 1986). Employers were found to make use of psychological tests to exclude or dismiss migrant employees (Cain and Choenni 1991: 15–16). In the business service sector (banks), employers tend to legitimate the exclusion of better-educated migrant youths holding a Dutch dipoma by their being unacceptable to white clients or Dutch colleagues (Oosterhuis and Glebbeek 1988).

All these studies confirm the assumption that ethnicity as well as gender are central notions of the labour market and have to be taken into account in theory as well as in policy-making.

Migrant Women and the Labour Market

A look at table 9.1 confirms the assumption that female migrants have been affected by the recession even more than their male counterparts: the registered unemployment rates for women of virtually all minority groups outnumber those for men and are significantly higher than those for Dutch women. Because of the absence of this issue from the 1989 WRR report, one has to discuss the question if and how the government is concerned with migrant women by returning to the first policy document on ethnic minorities, which passed through parliament in 1983. I quote from this document:

> The majority of these women lead isolated lives. Their skills and knowledge are too limited for them to be able to function independently in a complex industrialized society. They have little or no knowledge of the Dutch langage, and they lack opportunities to orientate themselves in the society surrounding them .... minority women have hardly taken advantage of the opportunities they are offered through the emancipation policy for support of self-organisation. (Ministerie voor Binnelandse Zaken 1983: 124)

Here as well as in the majority of other reports we find a strong emphasis on the backwardness of migrant women and their incapacity to adjust to 'modern' society and its way of life. However, looking at the position of women on the Dutch labour market in general, the image of the emancipated western woman, counteracting the pitiful passive female migrant, changes.

In the early 1980s women's emancipation policies in the Netherlands had initiated a wide range of programmes to improve the situation of women in general. The percentage of labour participation by Dutch women was extremely low in comparison with other western and west European countries. According to an OECD report of 1986 it was estimated at 28 per cent and was the second lowest in the EEC, next to Ireland, whereas it was 34 per cent in West Germany and 43 per cent in the United States. Between 1987 and 1990 this figure rose to the EEC average of 52 per cent. This served policy-makers as an indication of the tremendous improvement in the position of women.

According to the National Association for the Economic Independence of Women, however, these tables are misleading. There is no other country within the EEC in which the majority of women work in part-time jobs. On the whole, the number of hours women work has not gone up at all. Hence more people work the same hours as before, apparently for lower wages. Despite the official Dutch government policy of encouraging women's labour participation, the result is disappointing because it has obviously not led to a significant redistribution of work and housework (see *Volkskrant*, 11 July 1991).

In the emancipation policy of the 1980s migrant women were one of the target groups of a special programme (VEM, Vrouwen Emancipatie Minderheden), a minority women's emancipation project.

Most of the small-scale educational and vocational training projects developed within the VEM programme were limited to the areas of health, care and social work. Some of the projects such as the 'family helper training', set up for Turkish and Moroccan women, were disastrous failures owing to a total lack of interest in participation in the training programmes. With regard to the output of the projects, one can only note the failure of the programme. By the end of 1988 only a hundred black and migrant women had been helped to attain a secure job, while statistics totalled 36,456 registered unemployed black and migrant women at that time.

In her analysis, Kempadoo (1990) underlines two main reasons for this failure. Firstly, the projects were set up without consulting migrant women at the level of implementation (Kempadoo 1990: 9).

Secondly, the projects meant to give migrant women an orientation towards jobs and professions which require skills for traditional Dutch women's work, such as medical care, social work and handicraft. I share Kempadoo's criticism of this paternalistic approach. Obviously the definition of gender at the level of policy-making is dominated by western paradigms which deny the historical contexts of non-western femininity and the specific experiences and needs of migrant women. Morokvasic (1984), Phizacklea (1990) and Anthias (1991b) point out that migrant women are more likely to work full-time because their salary contribution to the household budget is crucial. With regard to the definition of western women as more emancipated, I argued elsewhere that this definition derives from the obvious necessity to construct a positive self-image of western femininity by using the 'other' (especially the Muslim woman) as a negative contrast (see Lutz 1991b).

Summarising, this policy seems to be an obvious confirmation of Anthias's statement that 'the gender division of the dominant ethnic group as well as the prevailing dominant images of the other affect ethnic minority women's position in society in general and the access to the labour market in particular' (Anthias 1991b: 38)

Education – a Ticket to Integration?

In the following paragraphs I want to draw attention to a group of migrants which is not considered 'problematic' in Dutch labour market policies. According to the WRR report (1989: 116) and other studies (Bovenkerk et al. 1991; Gowricharn 1989) there is not a significant difference between labour market participation of the better-educated Dutch and their migrant counterparts. Bovenkerk et al., however, mention that the majority of migrants are engaged in ethnic work such as social work and native language teaching of migrant children. They conclude their study with the question whether this indicates another ethnic labour market segregation, which in the long run may turn out to be a segmentation and ghettoisation of educated migrants in the Dutch labour market.

My own case study of Turkish women social workers confirms this assumption. Though this study was not meant to be a contribution to labour market research, its findings seem quite useful for further interpretation of labour market data.

The study focused on the experiences of better educated women from Turkey, now living in the Netherlands and west Germany. These women were involved in work with and for compatriots in different institutions of social work: social welfare, community work and teaching. Referring to their professional task of mediating between the migrant (Turkish) community and the institutions of the indigenous society, I called them mediators.[2]

Beyond the description of their tasks, the study focused on the perception these women had of themselves in relation to the views held by the migrant society on the cultural and professional identity of migrant women.

2. The empirical part of this study consisted of twenty-eight biographical interviews, supplemented by information on the work areas.

What makes the study relevant to labour market research? To begin with, it turned out that the respondents' ethnic membership was a crucial condition for their professional tasks. It was found that in many ways through their work they were supposed to functionalise their individual experiences institutionally (as migrants from Turkey) for the integration of their compatriots.

Their ethnic membership turned out both to facilitate and to constrain their participation in the labour market. With the exception of two women, not one of them had ever been given the opportunity to work with Dutch or German people, though most of them had been trained in social work and had obtained a diploma which qualified them to do so.

One half of my respondents had finished their (university) education in Turkey in another profession, and were working in this area because they could not find work in the area they had been trained for. Social work, translation or teaching compatriots were the only employment sectors open to them. However, the other half of the respondents, young 'second-generation' women, daughters of migrant workers, had in fact chosen their educational training. From their biographical narratives it became clear that this choice was based on a very realistic evaluation of their job opportunities. Some of them said they had been influenced by career advisers, teachers or social workers. To many of them, social work seemed to be a profession which they had been doing without remuneration since childhood. By translating, accompanying their parents and neighbours to Dutch (administrative) institutions, filling in forms etc., they had acquired a wide range of knowledge which was relevant to their migrant situation.

Thanks to staff shortages they could usually make their own money in part-time employment during their study time. In this sense their 'choice' to be employed as social workers was a very rational answer to the opportunities offered by the labour market, with its booming sector of social and cultural work for minorities in the wake of minorities policy in the 1980s. Additionally, it may be considered a rational use of their background as human (cultural) capital. So what is wrong with this, one may ask.

Taking a look at other contexts, such as the conditions and the organisation of their work, the picture changes. None of my respondents, not even the ones with long-term experience, held leading positions. Those were held by their Dutch or German colleagues. Because of the way the sector was organised, the majority of my respondents worked in short-term projects and had to apply for another job every two or four years. Social work for migrants has hardly been implemented structurally in the apparatus of the welfare state. It was and still is assumed to be of a temporary nature and has therefore been organised as an additional supply or support to the apparatus. This is why work places are of limited permanence. One may assume that career perspectives are limited in the whole sector.

The majority of my respondents complained about the internal organisation of their work. They described their own position as being considered a 'token' by their employers as well as by their colleagues. They were expected by their colleagues to be experts on all problems concerning their own ethnic group, and they were supposed to have an all-round knowledge of 'culture' and habits, while their white colleagues usually worked for the specific categories they had been trained for, such as lifetime categories (child care, youth work, work with elderly people or work with women). Consequently, the ethnic worker in the group had to solve all problems of the migrant clientele.

Analytically speaking, migrant professionals in social work seem to find themselves in a two-edged position. On the one hand, the inclusion of 'ethnic' social workers is a requirement for the emancipation process of the migrant community. On the other hand, it is only their 'ethnic' capacities which are appreciated at work. Owing to the existence of such tensions as well as the usual overwork etc., two thirds of my respondents had been seriously ill or had suffered from 'burn-out' syndrome for some time. Another stressful factor is the fact that the multiple capacities required for doing this work do not seem to be recognised at all, either by their colleagues or by their employers. Instead of being considered professionals, they are expected to be 'interpreters', as a young 'second generation' psychologist complained: 'I have been working here for one and a half years but the secretary still introduces me as an interpreter.' (Lutz 1991: 244) Her case was not exceptional; all other respondents confirmed this experience of being repeatedly downgraded. From their narratives it became obvious that professional female Turks do not fit the prevailing image of Turkish women in countries such as the Netherlands or Germany, where – according to opinion polls – the Turks continue to rank lowest of all ethnic minorities.

Some of the mediators' problems may derive from the special professional status of social work, which has never been fully respected as a profession. Etzioni (1969) called this sector a semi-profession because it is not really established or even especially desired. Contrary to classical professional training, training for social work is shorter, its status is less legitimated and its basic knowledge less specialised. This eventually makes social workers more dependent on social changes and control. The results of their work determine how it is judged. As Toren puts it, 'The semi-professional is rather judged by the results than by efforts and skills invested in the process' (Toren 1969: 157).

However, not all of the mediators' experiences can be adequately explained by a lack of professional acceptance. Obviously, the ethnicity of the mediators is a crucial precondition for their profession which – in their case – basically links up professional and social relationships with each other. A full professional such as a doctor is prohibited from treating his or her own family. For 'ethnic workers', however, in a symbolic sense treating their own families is required; it can even be seen as a precondition for their work. This causes part of the individual vulnerability of the 'ethnic' social worker.

Summarising, I would argue that if one considers ethnicity as a resource, as a commodity for negotiating access to the labour market, one has to emphasise the feasibility of this commodity. Ethnicity exists because of boundary signification. In the case of the Turkish minority group, it exists because of the assumption that Turks have characteristics in common which stand in some meaningful contrast to the characteristics of the Dutch classifier. According to Wallman, the significance of ethnicity 'is other-imposed as well as self-imposed and serves as a marker on both sides of the boundary' (1979: 5). It is the boundary which counts.

In other words, ethnicity is a resource only if an ethnic group is perceived as such by official policy-makers. The whole area of ethnic social workers would disappear as soon as government policies ceased to define an ethnic group as a problem category.

Putting it in terms of structure and agency, it is the structure of the labour market which imposes the bargaining conditions on the agents involved. However, looking at the agents involved, it would be ignorant to deny the mediators' active involvement in the bargaining process. One necessarily has to call upon ethnicity in order to act as an advocate and a spokesman or spokeswoman for one's group.[3]

I want to argue here that any analytical and sensitive approach with regard to migrant women and the labour market has to take into account the ways in which migrant women as actors call upon their resources (cultural, social and gender) in order to manage and to challenge the structural advantages they have (see Anthias 1991a: 21).

In my view such an approach could avoid overemphasising the structural restraints of the labour market by omitting the active participation of migrants in the process of gaining access to new resources, and it seems much more adequate to understand the great variety of forms and axes of differentiation within the migrant category. While theories referring to migrant labour as a class category (see Miles 1982, 1989) underemphasise the heterogeneity of labour categories and in particular overlook gender differentiations within the migrant category (see Anthias 1990), an alternative approach would have to look at the labour

3. I have focused on these aspects elsewhere see: Lutz, 1991a, chapters 6, 7, and Lutz, 1992.

market as a layered system in which activity, exchange and meaning would have to be differentiated along ethnicity and gender lines.

Conclusion

In this chapter I have outlined discussions on ethnic minorities and the Dutch labour market, paying special attention to the situation of migrant women.

I have argued that the focus of contemporary minorities policy on the labour market has to be interpreted in the context of reorganisation and dismantlement of the Dutch welfare state. As minorities were defined as a problem or care category, they became one of the targets of change. Referring to the ideological implications of policy-making, I have challenged the notion of 'being employed' (no matter how) which is part of the new policy and considered a blessing.

The Dutch labour market is by no means an area of free exchange of forces in which the rules of supply and demand are functioning ethnicity- and gender-blind, and it can not be interpreted in any sensible way if one leaves various kinds of overt or subtle discrimination out of consideration. With regard to migrant labour the different kinds of constraints are a crucial condition for the 'commodity' of labour power.

As the Dutch government invests large sums of money in the improvement of the social position of minorities (contemporary investments have reached the level of 800 million Dutch guilders per year) and the labour market is seen as a crucial mediator on the road to the emancipation of minorities, it is necessary to review the implicit notions of these policies carefully.

Referring to my case study on 'mediators' it must be stressed that it is too facile to legitimate the exclusion of migrants from the labour market by their lack of ability. The implementation of 'contract compliance' programmes or 'positive action' programmes is very poor so far. But even if the realisation of these programmes were encouraged, one still has to wonder if integration into the labour market is achieved by creating 'ethnic job areas'. Ethnically segmented job areas tend to foster exclusion rather than social integration. Ethnic niches might then be an answer to wide-ranging exclusion from primary and secondary sectors. A more appropriate answer, however, would be the acknowledgement that racism is a structural characteristic which society in general and the labour market in particular have to counteract, and that ethnicity and gender have to be analysed in this context.

Such a discussion is not taking place in the Netherlands at the level of policy-making and in public discourse on the discourse on minorities.

The labour market serves as an unquestioned synonym of integration. Deconstructing the labour market then becomes a necessary precondition for using it as a sensible instrument for the social emancipation of minorities.

Table 9.1 Registered unemployment: difference in sex, absolute numbers and percentage of the working population of the group

	absolute (x100)			percentage of the working population per group		
	men	women	total	men	women	total
autocht. Dutch	375.5	219.4	594.8	12	16	13
Surinamese	13.0	6.7	19.7	27	25	27
Antilleans	3.2	1.9	5.1	21	27	23
Turks	18.6	7.6	26.2	40	58	44
Moroccans	13.5	3.3	16.8	41	49	42

Source: Ministry of Social Affairs, 1 January 1988

–10–

The Politics of Marginal Inclusion: Racism in an Organisational Context

Philomena Essed

Introduction

Like several other contributions to this volume, this chapter deals with the discourse of multiculturalism and the denial of racism. Unlike most of the others, however, it deals with these issues in an organisational context rather than on the societal level. At this micro level the contrasts are more articulate between, on the one hand, the dominant group's preservation of a 'tolerant' self-image and, on the other hand, the indifference towards and the exclusion of blacks in everyday organisational life.

This chapter discusses some of the problems related to the idea and practice of positive action in the Netherlands. Positive action is a policy instrument consisting of a range of coherent measures and procedures labour organisations endorse with the aim of equal representation of men and women, blacks and whites in the various sectors, functions and levels in the labour market (Jong and Verkuyten 1990: 12). It is not my intention to evaluate the idea of positive action as such. In fact, the article has a practical orientation. It focuses on the conditions under which positive action is being applied. For that purpose the findings are discussed of a research project conducted in a municipal company. Almost 8 per cent of its workers are from ethnic minorities, most of them being of Surinamese and Antillean descent. The research was instigated by the many complaints about racial discrimination.

The project was carried out by a gender – and culturally diverse – research team over a period of ten months in 1990–1. It consisted of two parts. In the first part of the project we tried to form a general impression

This article is based on a research project conducted by me together with Peter Reinsch, and with the assistance of Tulsa Caupain, Lydia Helwig and Sheela Vyas.

of race and ethnic issues in the company. For that purpose we interviewed thirty-four employees of diverse ethnic, gender and functional background, ranging from the bottom to the top of the company. The resulting picture showed (as we expected) that racism is a structural problem in the company. Most white interviewees either did not perceive discrimination as a problem or they only recognised as problematic the frequent racist jokes and verbal abuse on the shop-floor. Most black interviewees and some of the whites, however, emphasised that managers prevent ethnic minorities from moving on to higher positions. We focused, in the second part of the project, more specifically on these managers. The aim was to investigate whether the company culture was receptive or not to the idea of cultural variety in the composition of the workforce. In particular we were interested in managers' views and experiences on such questions as cultural or ethnic difference, manifestations of racism, and action against racism. We interviewed the whole middle management, twenty-nine people in total. Here, primary attention is paid to this second part of the project. First, however, a general outline is given of race and ethnic relations in the Dutch labour market.

Dutch Policy: From Ethnic Minorities to 'Allochtonen'

In the period after the Second World War the Dutch government used various policy models in order to control the immigration of people from the (ex-)colonies and workers from the south, ranging from *laissez-faire* policies, assimilation and segregation (applied only to the Moluccans) in the 1960s and 1970s to integration and pluralism in the 1970s and 1980s. Today pluralism predominates as a model, but according to economic, political and situational circumstances assimilative, integrative or other elements of the earlier policy models may surface (Mullard et al. 1990). Thus, as from the end of the 1980s, no-nonsense attitudes with strong culturally assimilative undertones characterise the Dutch context of race and ethnic relations.

The move towards more rigid assimilative policies is accompanied by a change in policy language. No longer are the different oppressed groups on the basis of race or ethnic background identified as 'ethnic minority' groups. Any open reference to their cultural background and experiences is removed. Ethnic minorities are now classified as 'allochtoon', originally a Greek word meaning 'those from the outside' or 'outsiders' in plain Dutch. Moreover, 'allochtoon' is an apparently neutral word to set apart those who do not belong from those who are considered to belong, that is Dutch-born for over three generations.

Racism in the Dutch Labour Market

One of the first publications on racism in the Dutch labour market concerned a small-scale replication of a sociological experiment first conducted in the UK by Daniel (1968) and Smith (1977). Briefly explained, the experiment comes down to the following. A black candidate (a member of the research team) applies for a job or an apartment and is rejected. Subsequently, a white applicant (another team member) of the same sex, with matching educational or economic background applies for the same. If the white applicant is accepted that is considered evidence of racial discrimination against the earlier black applicant. An experiment with identical application letters signed with either 'ethnic' names or with obviously native Dutch names showed that in 20 per cent of the cases rejection occurred on grounds of racial discrimination (Bovenkerk and Breuning van Leeuwen 1978).

During the fifteen years following the above experiments, research output on ethnic minorities in the labour market grows and booms. In the meantime, unemployment numbers among people of Surinamese, Turkish, Moroccan, Antillean and Moluccan background keep rising (Veenman 1990). The exclusion of ethnic minority groups from the labour market is due substantially to racism (Choenni and van der Zwan 1987, 1989; Willemsen 1988). Interviewed on various occasions about their preferences, 20 to even 50 per cent of Dutch personnel managers appear to be unwilling to hire non-white employees for functions where they are visible (Reubsaet and Kropman 1985:35; Choenni and van der Zwan 1987). Research into the practice of employment agencies points out that they routinely accept racist requests from employers, such as the wish not to send any Surinamese or other 'foreign' (meaning Turkish or Moroccan) employees (den Uyl et al. 1986). Turks, Moroccan, Moluccan, Surinamese and Antilleans who manage to get jobs are systematically excluded from representative functions. Many experience discrimination from colleagues as well as from supervisors (Essed 1984, 1991; KMAN 1985; Bouw and Nelissen 1986; Sikking and Brassé 1987).

A remarkable feature of Dutch publications on unemployment among ethnic minorities is the researchers' aversion to the terms racism and discrimination (see for further discussion Essed 1987, 1991). Moreover, it is argued that the Netherlands is unique among the other European-type societies in that it has no racism to speak of (Elich and Maso 1984; Penninx 1988; Rath 1991). This denial was modified to a certain extent when, in 1986, the Dutch Ministry of Home Affairs issued a report which strongly supported the case for positive action (Bovenkerk 1986). Making comparisons with policies such as affirmative action in the US and contract compliance in Canada the author of this report argued that ethnic minorities had 'disadvantages' in the labour market. The high numbers of unemployment and the under-representation in middle and higher positions could only partly be explained by historical and cultural characteristics of the ethnic groups. Disadvantage was also due to their 'unfavourable' starting position in the labour market and to 'indirect' discrimination (Bovenkerk 1986: 13). The report became the subject of heated public debate. Thereby some tried to link the case for positive action to the argument that 'women' and 'minorities' are needed in any event because of the shrinking availability of white male workers. Acting upon the recommendations of this report some of the Dutch municipalities are gradually adopting positive action in their policies.

Positive action is not an unproblematic policy instrument. Reasons have largely to do with its main presupposition that ethnic minorities have 'disadvantages' compared to the dominant white group. Thereby, the white (male) group is taken as the norm. Consequently this group is not considered to be part of the problem. Hence, neither will they be seen as part of the solution. In other words, the dominant norms and values in labour organisations, and definitions of quality and relevant qualifications continue to reflect a white (male) profile according to which 'others' are judged. This critique has been levelled by only a few in the Netherlands (Kempadoo 1986; Essed 1991). Kempadoo (1986) outlined in a small research project some of the problematic effects of the implementation of positive action upon women from diverse ethnic minority groups. It appeared that Dutch organisations used as a relevant criterion for hiring these women the degree of their adaptation or their willingness to adapt to Dutch styles of behaviour and thinking. Kempadoo questioned, therefore, the utility of the idea of positive action. Other researchers, in evaluating the workings of affirmative action have pointed at similar problems. Stigmatisation, tokenism and prejudice are likely to become obstacles for hired blacks (Pettigrew and Martin 1989). Without, however, rejecting the idea of affirmative action as such, Pettigrew and Martin argue that these programmes place unnecessary burdens on those whom the programmes are designed to benefit. They discuss various examples of prejudice, such as exaggerated expectations and extreme evaluations of blacks during entry. My own research confirms that mechanisms of exclusion and undervaluation remain active even under conditions of affirmative action (Essed 1991). Apparently programmes to achieve equal representation are not designed to deal with the racism that already exists and which contributed in the first place to the exclusion of blacks. In other words, positive action as such is not an adequate instrument against racism. Moreover positive action becomes an instrument of control when ethnic groups are forced to adapt to the existing dominant culture in the organisations they enter.

With these arguments in mind I now introduce the research project on ethnic relations in a specific company.

Introduction to the Research Project

The company in which we did our research is a relatively large municipal company (4,000 employees) with a predominantly white male labour force. It provides for public services in the city of Amsterdam. The type of services requires that employees have frequent contact with the Amsterdam population. In the second half of the 1980s the company starts to recruit ethnic minorities. It concerns predominantly low-ranking civil servants. Positive action is introduced in the company in 1986.

In practice, positive action regulations are limited to those having to deal with personnel selection procedures. Thereby, the city of Amsterdam recommends the application of a policy of 'preference'. This policy has three variations. The weakest form recommends that labour organisations give preference to ethnic minorities when they are 'equally' qualified as white candidates. The middle form recommends giving preference for ethnic minorities when they are 'sufficiently' qualified. The strongest form recommends that ethnic minorities are hired 'irrespective of' their qualifications. Company regulations recommend the application of the middle variant of 'preference' policy. Thereby, the idea of what quality is, who defines what quality is, and how quality is measured is not being questioned.

These new regulations were formulated in 1985 and explained centrally in various municipal reports. But, the various decentralised municipal organs were free to fill in the details of positive action according to their own needs and wishes. Further, the municipality introduced positive action regulations without providing for a concomitant programme of sanctions and control.

The entrance of largely Surinamese and Antillean workers whom the company hired in the second half of the 1980s does not proceed without problems. The explicit emphasis on positive action and on the (*ad hoc*) opportunities for training for ethnic minority members created the myth throughout the company that ethnic minorities receive preferential treatment and that there is discrimination against white men. The lagging number of ethnic minorities that has been hired (less that 8 per cent in a city with 27 per cent) and the virtual absence of ethnic minority members at the managerial levels of the company prove otherwise. White colleagues and supervisors react. There are racist incidents involving employees who are members of a Dutch racist political party. Acting upon these cases and on complaints that company officials refuse to endorse positive action (correctly) the company directors hire a team to investigate ethnic relations in the company.

When we start with the project we find that company spirits are low. There is a high absentee rate. The company has gone through various reorganisations during the past ten years and yet another, major one is on its way. Cuts are expected and even though the official stand is that no personnel will be fired, there is social unrest. Not only among the workers, but also among the managers, pressures mount and insecurity about the future is a problem. The reorganisation involves the middle and top management positions as well.

The Role of the Management

The success or failure of positive action, or any other policy which addresses race and ethnic relations within an organisation, will depend to a large extent upon the political support of the senior management and upon the availability of resources to implement and monitor the process (Jenkins 1986). Therefore, we focused, in the second part of the project, upon the role of the management. Unfortunately it was no longer feasible to include the top managers, because that level of the company was already being reorganised. Some of these managers were on the point of leaving, others had left and interim managers had taken their place.

Interviews with the managers are interesting not only for research purposes. Their views and experiences form at the same time an indication of the degree to which individual managers can play a role in the process of change from a relatively homogeneous company to a relatively heterogeneous one. We interviewed the complete middle management of the company (apart from two exceptions), twenty-nine in total. Twenty-eight out of the twenty-nine middle managers are white, virtually all are male. In order to gain insight into leadership issues from the point of view of blacks in leading positions we complemented the information gathered from the middle managers with interviews with nine blacks in lower-ranking leading positions such as team leadership.

Using a structured list of open questions we addressed the following issues:

1 What is the attitude and knowledge of middle managers about cultural diversity and (anti-)discrimination?
2 What importance do they give to ethnic relations in general and anti-discrimination in particular?
3 In which way do they implement anti-discrimination and the so-called

policy of preference in personnel selection procedures?

4 What are the views of the managers about leading culturally diverse working teams?

This line of questioning, developing from attitudes and knowledge to implementation, reflects the sequential order of relevance. The first condition, a 'positive' attitude, may encourage the proper fulfilling of the second and third one. This is not to say, however, that a supportive attitude and sufficient knowledge are a guarantee for the successful implementation of anti-discrimination policies.

Attitudes and Knowledge regarding Cultural Diversity and (Anti-) discrimination

How do the managers think about the idea of cultural diversity in the company? The majority of the interviewees react positively to the (direct) question as to whether they feel it is an advantage that the company recruits more ethnic minority members. Many state it is 'good for the company image' and that it is an 'improvement of the company culture' to have ethnic minorities. Contradictions occur after using indirect questioning concerning this issue. If the managers are serious about the positive effects of the entrance of minorities they should subsequently define the (future) identity of the company (partly) in terms of the participation of ethnic minorities in the company. The majority of the interviewees, however, do not include the idea of cultural variety in their view of the company's identity. Most of them mention only factors such as 'honesty' or 'the ability to take a joke' as typical for the company identity.

There are also other indications that the managers are reluctant to deal with cultural diversity and with the issue of racism. All of the managers indicate that they expect black employees to adapt completely to the company culture even when that means that they have to take discrimination. Virtually none of the managers prepares new black employees for the fact that they may encounter discrimination, racist jokes, slurs and the like. None of them makes it clear to the new black employee that discrimination cannot be tolerated and that managers should be informed immediately if there are problems in that respect. The few managers who make mention of racist language on the shop-floor consider this an inherent and unalterable feature of the company culture. The new black employee is urged to learn to live with the situation. One white manager says about his way of greeting a new black employee: 'Remarks like that have nothing to do with your colour (...). One cannot change just like that the attitudes of people who have been working here for twenty-five years. So if you feel that you have to do too much of adapting from your side, you are probably not suitable for working in this company anyway' (Essed and Reinsch 1991b: 15). The findings make clear that none of the managers, and none of the ethnic minority representatives of lower leading positions, expect that the entrance of blacks can or must lead to changes in the company traditions.

Judging from their statements, it shows that black employees will at best be tolerated by the managers. In general, most of the managers have only negative expectations about blacks in the company: 'Those 'allochtonen' will come up with complaints about discrimination (that do not have any basis). This will lead to an anti-'allochtonen' atmosphere on the shop floor' (Essed and Reinsch 1991b: 21). The most frequently occurring objection against ethnic minority employees is that they are poorly qualified. Various managers state that 'allochtonen' do not speak Dutch properly, which they consider to be a problem. Apart from the prejudice implied in the argument that they do not speak Dutch well enough, it is problematic that the Dutch language is taken as the norm in a city with 27 per cent ethnic minorities plus millions of tourists throughout the year who all make use of the company services. Moreover cases have been reported where white employees ask for transfer to other departments when they feel they have to serve too many black customers. Yet, upon being asked about the most important qualities required for company employees the managers put correct and friendly behaviour towards customers on top of their list. Apparently, their picture of the customers, when they so strongly insist that the company civil servants be friendly to them, is a white picture.

In addition to attitudes about black employees and the question of cultural diversity we examined whether the managers have knowledge about racism. This information was important in order to get insight into their motivations for endorsing positive action or refusing to do so. Notwithstanding the fact that the company adopted positive action policies, the majority of the managers deny the structural nature of discrimination. Many blame the minorities themselves for failing to participate in higher numbers in the company, or they blame positive action for hampering equal participation.

To conclude, the managers' attitudes about black employees, and their knowledge of racism and discrimination, are problematic and inadequate given the fact that they are supposed to manage positive action policies. These results suggest that they are not going to give any priority to the improvement of race and ethnic relations in the company. This issue is discussed below.

*Questions of Priority concerning Race Relations and
Anti-discrimination*

The majority of the managers claim that the information they received
about positive action and its implementation was completely inadequate.
In practice positive action comes down primarily to efforts for increasing
the entrance of ethnic minority groups (and white women). More specifically, the role of the personnel managers in this is limited to participating in the job selection procedures. Formally the division manager must
take charge of the implementation of positive action, but none of the
middle managers indicate their accountability to the division manager.
As a result the supervisors and managers are free to define for themselves
how they deal with the policy of positive action. Many complain that this
policy was not their choice. They say they dislike it because it is
imposed. Half of the managers feel positive action is 'nonsense'. Some
of the managers told us plainly they refuse to implement positive action:

'Before we start talking about equal representation, we had better start wor-
rying about where all the Amsterdammers have gone to. Nice talk when you
first do nothing but chase Amsterdammers out of Amsterdam. And once they
have been pushed out you suddenly want the company to reflect the composition of the population of Amsterdam!' (Essed and Reinsch 1991b: 34).

The role of the managers is even worse when it comes to promotions.
The majority of the managers take no initiatives at all to fulfil the company policy that ethnic minorities must be encouraged to move up the
company ladder. The following quotation is probably typical of the attitude of the managers who justify passivity with the quality myth: 'I find
it difficult to swallow that I have to reject a qualified person in order to
take someone who is less qualified' (Essed & Reinsch 1991b: 38–9). To
conclude, the majority of the middle managers feel neither responsible
for nor involved with the implementation of positive action. They take a
passive stand. This is different only for the personnel managers. Most of
them claim that they undertake extra initiatives to encourage equal
opportunities for ethnic minorities.

Implementation of Anti-discrimination Measures

The blaming of victims, for supposed deficiencies that disqualify them
from certain positions, assumes that white managers are no part of the
problem. Moreover, they have virtually no understanding of racism in

general and in the company in particular. To give an example, we questioned the managers about whether and how they register discrimination against black employees. Apart from one, who says that 'you develop a picture of your employees so that you can see things coming', most other managers take a passive stand. Some feel someone would probably come and tell them, or they expect they would notice by visiting the shop-floor regularly. An interesting note on this is that most of the workers we interviewed in the first part of the project complained about the managers 'never being around when you need them'. This suggests that the managers are not on the shop floor often anyway to register discrimination. Some of the managers deny the very possibility of discrimination. These outcomes are consistent with the reactions to other questions concerning the necessity to create an atmosphere that favours anti-racism and discourages discrimination. The managers are indifferent. Only a minority among them feels it is important to encourage anti-discrimination.

Not surprisingly, the majority of the managers are against the monitoring of discrimination. They feel it is unnecessary. When asked, however, how they would react in case of discrimination, reactions are vague and insecure. Most of them say they would talk to the parties involved. Some would report the case to the 'woman of confidence' (an ombudswoman who deals with cases of sexual harassment and racial discrimination). All of their reactions suggest that they would treat the case as an incident, not as the symptom of a pattern. These outcomes suggest that there is a general lack of responsibility among the managers with respect to the problem of discrimination. This is also sharply pronounced by several of the managers when they talk about the problem of racist jokes, which are fluently integrated in the company culture of pestering and joking. They simply do not know what to do about it, many of them say. Therefore, they just ignore it.

From the above it may be concluded that the middle management takes a passive stand with respect to anti-discrimination. Because they do not see discrimination as a company problem, the large majority of the managers do not see it as part of their job to counter racism in the company. The higher levels of management do not call the middle managers to account for the under-representation of blacks on the various levels. This contributes to the fact that none of the managers is motivated to check regularly on such structural features as the percentage of blacks who leave the company and their reasons why, training possibilities, selection procedures for higher functions, absenteeism due to problems of discrimination etc. In other words, there is no anti-discrimination policy to speak of, let alone anti-discrimination being implemented.

Views on Management and Cultural Diversity

Racial and ethnic conflict cannot be solved without making anti-racism and cultural diversity a central issue on the company agenda. Changing labour force compositions call for new forms of leadership (Henry 1991; Sekaran and Leong 1992). With this view in mind, the final part of the project addressed the views of the managers about management in a culturally heterogeneous company. We posed the following question to the managers: 'In light of the current reorganisation of the company leadership we expect that the new managers will be required to have the skills to lead culturally mixed teams. What are the qualifications such a manager needs according to you?' A most interesting result is that none of the managers questions the feasibility of these new requirements. This suggests that they accept, in principle, the idea of the inevitability of new forms of leadership. Accordingly they react differently than in the case of questions about (anti-)discrimination. Whereas the majority of the managers feel next to nothing needs to be done with respect to fighting discrimination, they come up with a whole list of qualifications needed to give leadership in a 'multicultural' company. Obviously, the idea of 'leadership in a multicultural company' appeals to the socially desirable attitude that one has to be 'tolerant' of cultural difference. Therefore it is not surprising that the managers seemed more willing to think constructively with respect to the issue of cultural diversity than they did with respect to the issue of anti-discrimination. Qualifications they mention include such skills as 'flexibility, openness and creativity' (mentioned ten times), 'an anti-discriminatory attitude' (5) or 'a positive attitude towards multiculturalism' (3).

Given the overall pluralistic ideological climate in the Netherlands, it is not surprising that the requirement of 'knowledge about other cultures' scores highest (18). This formal emphasis on the relevance of acknowledging difference is completely contradicted, however, in subsequent reactions to the question about when it is relevant to make a cultural distinction and when not to do so. Apparently this question appeals more to the wish to appear non-discriminatory than to the idea of respecting cultural difference. Almost one third of the group claim colour and cultural blindness: they say that they never differentiate on racial or ethnic grounds. Half of the group say that it is relevant, sometimes, to differentiate. However, the examples they give either express prejudice, e.g. '(we must understand that) these people are extremely grateful when they get a job, because of their low education. They will serve you like a king' (Essed and Reinsch 1991b: 49) or they reproduce clichés of how to control specific cultural expressions. In particular we recognised the tendency of those who adhere to multiculturalism to equate 'culture' with 'religion' (Connolly 1990). Many managers use the argument that one has to take consideration of 'Ramadan'. Ramadan comes up so often that one can rightly speak of a 'Ramadan cliché'. The interviews were taken indeed, during the Ramadan period. However, the argument of Ramadan remains peculiar when only a very small number of the ethnic minority employees working at the company are Muslim.

Not surprisingly, hardly any of the managers emphasise that it is important to differentiate between social, economic and cultural background in order to be able to correct structural discrimination.

In order to avoid any misunderstandings, let me make it clear that I do not consider 'knowledge of different cultures' a primary requirement for effective leadership in culturally heterogeneous contexts. More important are such qualities as the ability to evaluate critically the traditional company culture, the understanding of racism and sexism, the ability to assess the qualities of ethnic minority men and women without bias and the understanding of the experiences and needs of black men and women (see for further discussion Essed and Helwig 1992). In this respect it must be said that in particular the myth that 'promotion is achieved on the basis of merit and fair competition' is persistent. I fully agree with Fernandez (1981: 295) when he says that white men in the company seem not to recognize that many of them would not be in their present positions if they had had to compete on an equal basis with ethnic minority men and women and with white women. The racist and sexist presuppositions which underlie 'blaming the victim' arguments disguise the advantages the discriminated groups have over white men when they get leadership positions. 'Characteristics that many of these minorities and women bring to the corporation, such as an ability to communicate well with subordinates, a more open management style, and a greater orientation toward people, go against many traditional corporate-managerial values. However, they are more conducive to new types of management' (Fernandez 1981: 296). In a racist atmosphere, information about the cultural background of 'other' groups is more likely to aggravate bias than to encourage acceptance. Various scholars have criticised the idea and politics of multiculturalism for not dealing with the issue of racism (Ålund and Schierup 1991). Our research findings confirm the relevance of the anti-multiculturalism critique. For illustration I take the following example. When the managers emphasised the relevance of 'knowledge of different cultures' they created space, in theory, for the acknowledgement of the fact that ethnic minority managers could be expected to be more advanced in this respect than managers from the dominant group. We asked the managers what ethnic minority members, if they were to take the same position in the company as the interviewee, would contribute to the advantage of the company. Half of the interviewees resorts to the 'non-discriminatory' stand: 'It would or should not make a difference', they said, 'whether the person in my position is black or white.' Various others have a hard time thinking of any positive contributions, which we also inferred from the frequent use of the word 'maybe' (Essed and Reinsch 1991b: 50):

maybe they are better in putting things in perspective;
maybe they are a bit less formal;
maybe they have a positive impact for other 'allochtonen' in the company.

Only a few managers thought of the argument that ethnic minorities may have an advantage in dealing with cultural heterogeneity or possibly a better eye for discovering discrimination and dealing with that. Apparently the usual underestimation of the qualification of blacks even blocked managers from acknowledging the most obvious qualification one can ascribe to ethnic minorities within the framework of thinking that knowledge of different cultures is a primary condition for leadership in a company with cultural heterogeneity.

Conclusions

The findings show that the introduction of positive action is not a remedy against racism. The relevance for the company of increasing numbers of white women and of men and women of Surinamese, Antillean, Turkish and Moroccan background is being played down. The politics of positive action are a façade when racism and sexism remain unchallenged. Because positive action is formal policy it is generally believed that ethnic minority employees get preferential treatment. The opposite is the case, however. Managers hardly fulfil even minimal requirements of positive action. Some bluntly refuse to implement positive action. The rhetoric of positive action makes it even more difficult, however, to insist that discrimination continues to exclude ethnic minorities from being hired and from moving up in the company. Despite the increase of black men and women and of white women the management continues to reinforce traditional norms and values. As a result black men and women (and white women) continue to be seen as incompetent. The leadership lacks the skills to evaluate in an unbiased way the qualities of black employees. In addition, black employees who function very well in non-racist circumstances may be affected in a negative way when they have to function in a racist/sexist climate, where they receive little support from superordinates or peers.

Given the above arguments we recommended that the company develops an overall plan for the development of new styles of management, adequate for a company with cultural heterogeneity instead of cultural homogeneity. Given the fact that the managers lack the leadership skills to develop such a plan, professional advising and coaching is necessary. Although the majority of the managers are prejudiced against black men and women and against white women, there is a minority among them who have a flexible, thoughtful and open approach towards these groups. The company may gain by encouraging this group, by developing leadership training that recognises these qualities through promotions, by pay incentives and the like. There is more to it, however, than interference on a management level. Pressure must also come from the black employees and others committed to combating racism, who are caught now in a repressive situation. The denial of racism de-legitimises opposition.

To conclude, one of the hidden currents of positive action is the negation of its cultural implications. Under conditions of culturally homogeneous norms and values it is virtually impossible to preclude that ethnic minorities are stigmatised as less qualified. This suggests that municipal intervention in the management of race and ethnic relations through positive action reinforces the legitimacy of the white (male) company traditions. Also, it may be inferred from the research project that forms of repression used to subordinate ethnic minorities have not been addressed seriously. These and other arguments underscore that opposition against racism must be multidimensional, because interference on one front (increase of numbers) can be neutralised and countered through the continuation of racial and ethnic conflict in other domains. As a result, the inclusion of ethnic minorities in the company risks remaining marginal inclusion.

The Politics and Processes of Racial Discrimination in Britain

John Wrench and John Solomos

A number of chapters in this volume take as their theme a critique of the 'denial of racism' in advanced industrial European countries. This chapter looks not at racism in its broader sense, but at racial *discrimination*, specifically in employment. Britain has a greater tradition of research into racial discrimination than many other European countries, and more comprehensive and detailed anti-discrimination legislation. Nevertheless, there is still a tendency to deny, or at least underplay, the strength of racial discrimination in the UK labour market. This chapter questions the various alternative explanations for persistent racial inequality in the UK by focusing in detail on some examples of research into the way discrimination operates in the labour market. In particular, the chapter focuses on two specific examples of research into the processes of discrimination which exclude young migrant-descended school-leavers from training and employment opportunities. These examples are used to make the broader point that many theories of inequality which understate the role of racism (such as those referred to in the 'underclass' discussion in chapter 1 of this volume) fail to account for the often subtle and indirect way that institutional procedures perpetuate racial discrimination. This in itself is one reason why the existence of racial discrimination is in practice so easy to deny. The chapter shows the direct implications of this for debates in other European countries, and finally looks at the implications of this evidence for anti-discrimination legislation.

As Castles argues in this volume, there is evidence across Europe of an increasing intensity of racism of all kinds, ultimately threatening not only to ethnic minority and migrant communities themselves, but to democratic structures in general. This is most visible at the level of racial violence and the activities of extremist political parties. At the same time there exists a widespread denial of racism in other forms and at other levels, including the allocation of services, housing, and in the labour market. European politicians and policy-makers are more willing to condemn racism if it is seen as the activity of loony extremists, but are less willing undertake action which would imply that racism in both its ideological and practical manifestations forms part of the structure of European societies. The denial of the effects of racism in practice also leads to a denial of the need for anti-discrimination legislation. For example, in an addendum to the Maastricht treaty in 1991 EC leaders made a declaration against racism and xenophobia, but did not consider the implementation of community legislation or measures to achieve closer co-operation in tackling racial discrimination.

In 1990 the International Labour Office (ILO) published a review of evidence of discrimination against migrant workers in six western European countries (Zegers de Beijl 1990). The combined evidence showed that discrimination across western Europe is 'so widespread, systematic and irrefutable that national and international policy-makers are called upon to reflect on ways and means of combating this discrimination' (p.iii). Yet employers, officials and politicians continue to deny that racial discrimination exists. This is particularly true in countries where there is no tradition of research investigation on this subject, and/or no formal anti-discrimination legislation which could generate cases for public view. Sometimes the absence of legal cases relating to discrimination is itself taken as 'proof' of the absence of discrimination (Banton 1991: 160–1).

Racism and Racial Discrimination

First of all, it might be useful to look at some of the differences that have been drawn between the concepts of racism and racial discrimination. Sometimes these two concepts become merged in practice, so that they have little apparent difference. For example, Banton writes that after the International Convention on the Elimination of All Forms of Racial Discrimination was adopted by the General Assembly of the United Nations in 1965, the United Nations has in practice used 'racism' to mean almost the same thing as 'racial discrimination'. However, others wish to identify clear differences between racism and racial discrimination. One difference is that racism is conceived as pathological: 'When referring to racism, speakers and writers often employ medical metaphors, likening it to a virus, a disease, or some sickness that can be spread in the manner of an epidemic' (Banton 1992: 70). Racial discrimination, on the other hand, is more 'normal', 'in the sense that crime, deplorable as it may be, is a normal feature of all kinds of human society' (Banton 1992: 70).

Some see racism as an ideology and racial discrimination as a practice, with corresponding differences in the necessary responses to them. If racism is an *ideology* then anti-racist movements must emphasise methods which counter ideologies, including the use of mass media and schooling. If racial discrimination is an act then anti-racists must emphasise methods ranging from collective action to legislation to fight such acts. Banton argues that in theory 'for every act of racial discrimination someone is responsible and should be brought to account' (Banton 1992: 73). However, in practice things are not quite this simple. Research evidence of the treatment of post-war black migrants and their descendants in the UK shows that we should not only be concerned with acts of discrimination but with processes of discrimination. Processes are established, routine and subtle; only occasionally will an individual 'act' of racial discrimination become visible within these processes, and only intermittently can one individual actor be identified as responsible for the exclusion of another from rightful opportunities. The denial of racial discrimination is common because, quite simply, it can be denied, owing to the normality of its invisibility.

The operation of racial discrimination in employment can be drawn to public attention in a number of ways. Firstly, there can be activities by anti-racists or those discriminated against, such as 'whistle-blowing', strikes, or other collective action called over racist practices (for some examples, see Phizacklea and Miles 1987: 118–20). Secondly, there can be 'discrimination testing' by agencies such as the Commission for Racial Equality (CRE) or the Policy Studies Institute (PSI) in Britain, which have produced a number of notable demonstrations of the pervasiveness of discrimination (Daniel 1968; McIntosh and Smith 1974; Hubbuck and Carter 1980). Thirdly, there can be research, usually carried out by academic researchers, into the operation of discrimination within social institutions.

The Need for Research

As well as providing statistical evidence of patterns of inequality, researchers have been able to provide insights through qualitative research on the detail and processes of hidden discrimination and the economic and political pressures which ultimately lie behind racist judgements and acts. Now some commentators are realising the need for more of this type of investigation. As Banton argues, we need to understand forms of racial inequality at levels on which decisions are taken which, consciously or not, either increase or decrease such inequalities. 'It is necessary to understand the workings of social institutions, such as those which socialise children, which channel job seeking and employee selection so that particular sorts of people end up in particular jobs' (Banton 1992: 84).

The 1990 ILO report on employment discrimination in Europe states. 'In sharp contrast with the wealth of material on migrants' labour market position, little documentation was found on the *accessibility* of the labour market' (Zegers de Beijl 1990: 45). The material compiled by the ILO 'substantiates very clearly the claim that migrants are in a disadvantaged position in the labour market' and similarly demonstrates that 'discrimination, in its various forms, is largely responsible for this situation'. However, having reviewed the existing research which has led it to this conclusion the report goes on:

> Unfortunately, little qualitative research has been carried out to explain the incidence of discrimination by accounting for the various motivations and interests of the respective actors in working life. As long as the reasons why, and the ways in which, people discriminate are not clearly defined, it will prove difficult to design effective means to tackle the underlying feelings of fear, prejudice and intolerance. (Zegers de Beijl 1990: 46)

It is therefore important that researchers should continue to develop this area, showing the ways in which stereotyping and discrimination can operate in the labour market, and identifying those structures of economy and power which work to perpetuate such phenomenon. This is not simply to counter the denial of racism in Europe but also to contribute to current theoretical debates on the perpetuation of structures of inequality, such as the 'underclass' debate referred to in chapter 1.

This chapter looks at examples of research into racial discrimination in the UK labour market. First, however, it is necessary to examine the history of post-war employment of migrants in the UK.

Employment Discrimination in the UK

Migrants to Britain of the 1950s and 1960s came to find work primarily in those sectors experiencing labour shortages. Workers from the Caribbean, India and Pakistan were recruited for employment in foundries in the Midlands, textile mills in the north, transport industries in major cities, and the health service. In common with migrant workers across Europe, these workers experienced a high degree of exploitation, discrimination and marginalisation in their economic and social lives. Despite the need for their labour, their presence aroused widespread hostility at all levels, from trade union branch to government level. Employers only reluctantly recruited immigrants where there were no white workers to fill the jobs; white workers, through their unions, often made arrangements with employers about the sorts of work immigrants could have access to (Duffield 1988). At this time the preference for white workers was perceived to be quite natural and legitimate – immigrant workers were seen as 'an inferior but necessary labour supply' (Brown 1992: 48).

Over time these workers remained in a relatively restricted spectrum of occupational areas, over-represented in low-paid and insecure jobs, working anti-social hours in unhealthy or dangerous environments. Although by the 1970s Afro-Caribbean and Asian people worked in a broader range of occupations than before, these were still jobs that were 'deemed fit' for ethnic minority workers rather than white workers (Brown 1992: 52). In 1984 the Policy Studies Institute published a major survey on the state of black people in Britain, covering housing, education and employment, showing that black people are still generally employed below their qualification and skill level, earn less than white workers in comparable job levels, and are still concentrated in the same industries as they were twenty-five years earlier (Brown 1984).

On top of this, black people have a higher unemployment rate, which increases faster than that of the white population. Particularly badly hit are ethnic minority young people, or the 'second-generation' descendants of migrants. A 1986 review of the statistical evidence reported:

> While employment prospects are discouraging for all young people, the evidence ... shows that black youth unemployment has reached astronomical proportions in some areas. The differential unemployment rates between blacks and whites are in fact generally greater for this age group than for any other. When account is taken of the fact that black people are far more likely to go into further education than whites, we can see that young black people in the 1980s are facing a desperate situation. (Newnham 1986: 17)

However, simple statistics of inequality in employment do not by themselves demonstrate the operation of racial discrimination. The denial of racism draws on a number of alternative explanations for the persistence of inequalities of opportunity for the descendants of black migrant workers in Britain. In societies like the UK, where most post-war migrants have citizenship and civil rights and face no legal barriers to employment opportunity, there are a whole range of forces which could still conceivably lead to the perpetuation of inequality amongst migrant groups and ethnic minorities long after the first generations have become settled and consolidated. These could be factors such as the persistence of language and cultural differences, the existence of 'identity problems' amongst the 'second generation', the educational attainment of the descendants of migrants, the geographical areas they settled in, the particular occupational and industrial sectors the first migrants originally found work in, and their own aspirations, preferences and choices.

There is genuine explanatory value in some of the above factors. The problem is that, as with those in the USA who wish to deny the role of racism in the formation and perpetuation of the American underclass, these factors are all too readily seized upon by academics and policy-makers as the primary causes of inequality, and as an alternative to explanations which emphasise racism and discrimination. Research and other evidence in the UK shows that this particular version of the 'denial of racism' is fallacious, and should be regarded equally sceptically in other European countries where similar arguments are being used.

The 'Second Generation'

Even when the existence of 'discrimination' as a concept and a practice is accepted, there are many who see discrimination against migrants and foreigners to be only a *first-generation* phenomenon. The important characteristic of Europe's ethnic minority/migrant population is that it is a young population, increasingly Europe-born. Often the argument is heard that discrimination is primarily a phenomenon directed against foreigners and non-citizens and is not therefore to be seen as racial dis-crimination. A socially and legally integrated 'second generation' would not experience such problems, it is argued. When, therefore, social inequality is discovered to be perpetuated or even increased for subsequent generations, explanations must be sought.

For example, in 1986 a series of reports were published by CEDEFOP (European Centre for the Development of Vocational Training) on the 'Vocational Training of Young Migrants' in Belgium, Denmark, France, Luxemburg and the UK. Although there exists a great deal of variety in the vocational training arrangements between these countries there were some common themes – higher unemployment and less success in attain-ing quality vocational training by 'second-generation' migrant young people. The reports suggest a number of causes of problems for these young people. The Belgian report talks of the lack of organisation on the part of schools to gear themselves up for receiving migrant children, problems of identity and confusion within the second generation, the 'loss of the work ethos', and language handicaps. The Danish report stresses the need for subjects in vocational training to be taught in the native language, emphasises the need for more teaching of Danish as a foreign language and criticises the teachers' lack of awareness of the cul-tural background of the young people. The French report talks of a 'torn identity' problem and a poor command of the French language, and the Luxemburg report sees language as an even greater problem as migrant workers' children need to be proficient in four languages to be successful. In all of these reports it is noticeable that there is hardly any reference to how racism and discrimination might affect the life chances of these young people, with the exception of the report on the UK.

The UK exception in the 1986 CEDEFOP research partly reflects a historically longer tradition of research into discrimination. This is not to imply that only the UK has an awareness of racism and discrimination and the correct policies to tackle them (for the dangers of this assumption see Lloyd in this volume). In the Netherlands, for example, there has been research into discrimination since the 1970s, and there has been a history of anti-racist organisation and struggle in many other European states, with a growing awareness of phenomena such as hidden and institutional discrimination. Furthermore, as this chapter will show, there is no room for complacency amongst British academics and policy makers on this issue.

This chapter will now consider some examples of research on racial discrimination as it affects the descendants of black migrants in Britain. The first was specifically designed to test labour market discrimination in those jobs for which 'second-generation' young black people would be reasonably expected to apply. In the late 1970s researchers acting in the guise of young applicants from ethnic minority backgrounds 'applied' by letter to non-manual jobs advertised in the local paper of one English city (Hubbuck and Carter 1980). To each vacancy was sent a letter of application from three test candidates, one native white, one West Indian and one Asian. Each 'applicant' was matched in terms of qualifications, previous job experience, age and sex. Standard letters were used to control for content and handwriting, so that the only 'variable' was the ethnic origin of the applicant, which was made clear to the reader in different ways within the letters. This enabled the researchers to test whether there were ethnic differences in the success rates of being offered an interview. A total of 103 jobs were tested across all sectors of industry and commerce.

Where all three candidates were called for an interview, this was seen by the researchers to be 'non-discrimination'. In fact in 48 per cent of the cases the West Indian or Asian 'applicant' was refused interview whilst the white applicant was called for interview, whereas in only 6 per cent of the cases did the reverse happen. The researchers concluded that this represented clear-cut evidence of systematic rejection on racial grounds, and that the fact that there was no difference in the success rates between the West Indian and Asian candidates supported the view that racial discrimination was based on a general colour prejudice. This clearly demonstrated the existence of racial discrimination in employment recruitment. However, it offered few clues as to the specific motives and processes behind this rejection. The second piece of research explored these issues further, by examining in detail the processes of recruitment of school leavers to apprenticeships (Lee and Wrench 1983).

Seeking Apprenticeships

The researchers interviewed employers who were connected with the apprenticeship recruitment of over 300 West Midlands firms, and monitored the fifth form school-leavers of four Birmingham schools. Ethnic minority young people who applied for apprenticeships were found to be just as well qualified as their white peers. However, there were significant differences in success rates in gaining a craft apprenticeship: whites had a success rate of 44 per cent compared to only 15 per cent for Afro-Caribbeans and 13 per cent for Asians. In interviews, employers offered the usual denial of racial discrimination, arguing 'we don't care what colour they are' and explaining the absence of ethnic minority apprentices by saying 'they don't apply' or 'they don't get the qualifications'.

In fact, well-qualified black young people were applying, and the research revealed a number of factors which helped to explain their lower success rate:

1 Some employers had stereotyped perceptions: they labelled West Indians as 'lethargic', or thought Asians were 'weak in mechanical design'. (As one explained, '... look at Indian art, which is flat ...'). One said 'The Asians have funny food. We don't want the whites disturbed by funny practices.'

2 Some employers described 'No go areas' in their firms, where white workers refused to work with a black: these tended to be skilled areas of work, such as craft, toolroom, sheet metal working, maintenance and supervision. 'Some firms can't take one – the skilled workers won't have it... they know they can't force a black in. Never. This is because they can't afford to upset a good toolmaker – this would cost the firm money.'

3 Family preference: many firms rely in significant part on the family members of existing employees. Employers talked of the tremendous benefits to the firm in terms of family loyalty and a parental link with young workers, and trade unions would insist that employees' families get preferential treatment. Thus, in a largely white workforce, this excluded ethnic minorities.

4 Word-of-mouth recruitment: many firms did not advertise their vacancies for apprenticeships. 'I advertised once in the *Birmingham Evening Mail*. We were deluged with applicants so I never did it

again' They relied on word-of-mouth recruitment, with the result that ethnic minorities would be less likely to hear of vacancies than white school-leavers who had contacts within a firm.

5 'Catchment area' recruitment: many employers expressed a preference for 'local lads' when faced with a large number of applicants. When firms are located in white outer suburbs of cities this excluded black applicants from the beginning. However, in multi-ethnic inner city areas firms were much less likely to operate catchment area policies, with recruitment taken from all over the city. So a policy which advantaged white kids in white areas did not advantage black kids in black areas.

The last three factors fall under the heading of *indirect* racial discrimination. Indirect discrimination by its very nature is not always easy to categorise as to whether it is intentional or accidental. Nevertheless the impression was gained that in many cases the racist implications of these practices were known to the employers – it is just that they would not admit to such knowledge in so many words during the interviews. However, although employers may be wary of describing the full detail of their practices to researchers, they do make their racial preferences quite clear to those agencies which are in the business of sending them recruits.

In the early 1990s public notice was drawn to a number of cases of discrimination by external agencies used as a filter between people seeking work and employers looking for staff. Examples of such bodies are private employment agencies, government-funded job centres, and local authority careers services. By quietly making their requirements known to a third party doing the recruiting, racist employers can appear to 'keep their hands clean'. Evidence of this was demonstrated in a Thames Television documentary (Colour Bar, 19 November 90) which revealed how some private employment agencies were uncritically co-operating with instructions from employers not to send them black staff.

In 1991 a major employment agency was reported to have unlawfully discriminated against ethnic minority job seekers by acting on subtle discriminatory instructions received from its clients. The Commission for Racial Equality received a letter from a trainee consultant with the company alleging that a manageress had prevented her from referring well-qualified ethnic minority candidates to two Japanese-owned banks (CRE 1991). Another case was brought to light by the action of job centre staff in July 1991: a manufacturing employer in Rotherham asked a local job centre to help him recruit staff, but stipulated that they should not send him Muslims. (An industrial tribunal in Sheffield ruled that discrimination against Muslims was not covered by the Race Relations Act and that therefore the discrimination was indirect, not direct). It is noticeable that the examples of discrimination described above came to public notice because of the 'whistle-blowing' action of concerned individuals. If we assume that in a far greater number of cases nobody decides to blow the whistle, then many cases must routinely go unnoticed.

A similar agency to a job centre is the local authority careers service, where careers officers give vocational advice to school-leavers and put them in touch with suitable local employers or training schemes. The next piece of research described in this paper fills in more of the picture of labour market discrimination by finding out from careers officers themselves what employers say to them.

The Careers Service

Through the early 1980s formal apprenticeship training in the UK declined, and the gap was filled by the government's Youth Training Scheme (YTS) introduced in 1983, which developed into a two-year programme of vocational training for 16–18 year-olds, and after a further reorganisation at the beginning of the 1990s became simply 'Youth Training' (YT). After the scheme began there was much concern over the fact that ethnic minority young people were less likely to be found on the 'better' employer-led schemes, which are characterised by a greater likelihood of subsequent employment (Fenton, Davies, Means and Burton 1984; Pollert 1985; Wrench 1987).

However, government agencies connected with YTS tended to work with an ideology of 'special needs', defining the problem of black youth unemployment as the outcome of the social and personal disadvantages and handicaps of black youths and the difficulties in responding to the 'special needs' of young blacks in schooling and employment. The problems of the young blacks were assumed to be similar to those of the physically and educationally disadvantaged groups, implying that the reason why young blacks were most likely to be unemployed was due to their own 'problems' rather than to anything that was happening in the labour market or in the structure of British society in general (Solomos 1988: 136).

To examine further the processes behind the continuing inequality in the transition from school to vocational training schemes and employment the researchers (Cross, Wrench and Barnett 1990) studied the Careers Service. This functions as an important and influential bridge between school and work in Britain, being both a provider of vocational guidance in schools and a labour market placement agency, involved in about 90 per cent of the recruitment to YTS.

Data from Careers Service files were collected on 3,000 school-leavers and interviews were carried out with seventy careers officers in multi-ethnic areas. The information gleaned on the processes of subtle labour market discrimination can be divided up into three basic areas: firstly, that on the employers, secondly, that on the Service itself, and thirdly, that on the young people. Careers staff were able to recount many examples of overt racial discrimination by employers, encountered when they were trying to place young people in schemes or jobs. Officers told of stories of employers who provided work experience for training schemes refusing to interview Asian youngsters on hearing their name, and of supervisors on schemes collaborating with such employers who specified, 'We want a white youngster.' Examples from the many quoted in the report were an engineering employer who said that although he employed Asians, 'We don't like West Indians. We find them lazy', and a Midlands YTS employer who instructed over the phone, 'I don't want you to send me any wogs or punks.' The manager of an 'upper class women's clothes shop', on hearing the Asian name of the trainee, said, 'Oh, it's all very well for you but my clients wouldn't like it.'

However, the interviews also revealed that many careers staff were unwilling to challenge such racist instructions by employers. This leads us to explore further the aspect of labour market discrimination which is seldom considered – namely the actions of third parties who in their day-to-day activities play their own part in the processes of discrimination, either by passive or active collusion, with the main discriminator. In the case of careers staff, it was clear that some were afraid to challenge racist instructions from employers and were reluctant to report a case of infringement of the Race Relations Act to the Commission for Racial Equality (CRE). Many careers staff seemed fatalistic, feeling that the Service was powerless when jobs were scarce and 'proof' of discrimination was difficult. The fear of losing a scarce vacancy might well enter their thoughts: 'In training days, that's what I've picked up generally – "try not to lose the vacancy; try to be as tactful as possible".' Some officers complained about the lack of support from senior management in a potential confrontation of racist employers. 'The boss we have has been so hot on relationships with employers and getting vacancies that when you get a vacancy you are very reluctant to do anything that might mean you might lose it, because they are very hard to come by.' If a careers service manager was visibly reluctant to pursue even blatant cases of racial discrimination by employers, this was then reflected in the passivity of careers officers themselves within that service. Careers officers argue that they have very little power – that if they refuse to action a vacancy the employer can simply fill it elsewhere.

Therefore, instead of confronting racist employers, many careers officers would engage in 'protective channelling', directing ethnic minority young people away from firms and schemes where they suspect they will be rejected. For example, a northern officer noted that it would become apparent which schemes were willing to take on ethnic minorities, and the young people would be sent to these in the knowledge that they would be accepted. 'A lot of people would say, "If I sent them to this scheme, they will get on." As a Service we are fairly protective about these kids you know – we don't like to give them to people who perhaps won't take them anyway.' A Midlands careers officer argued something similar: 'It might be that this place has got a history of taking whites only. Rather than disappoint the kid – going for an interview that's a waste of time – you don't send him to that scheme.' He argued that this would not actually be a conscious decision, but might be a result of the 'pressure' on him, in that careers officers were dealing with quite a high case load. 'Putting one kid in YTS might be one of thirty you were doing that day.'

Attitudes and Judgements of Careers Staff

The research also revealed evidence of stereotypes which led to misjudgements by careers staff on the abilities of ethnic minority young people. The researchers matched 900 young people of different ethnic background by educational attainment and submitted questionnaires on these young people to the careers officers. Even when Afro-Caribbean and Asian young people were matched by attainment they were still assessed by careers officers as 'less able' than their white comparison sample. Such judgements carry over when assessed for future occupation – for example, Afro-Caribbean boys who achieved highly were nevertheless likely to be ranked lower by careers officers on a scale of assessment of 'skill' level.

In the questionnaire the seventy careers officers were asked to assess the 'realism' of each youngster's aspirations. In all cases, both in relation to YTS and employment, Asians and Afro-Caribbeans are regarded as possessing more unrealistic aspirations than their equivalently qualified white comparison sample. The taped interviews confirmed that officers saw Asian boys in particular as having ambitions which were quite unattainable – 'their expectations are greater than their academic abilities'. In fact, the statistical data showed that ethnic minority young people in the sample, although ambitious, were not more 'unrealistic' in their aspirations than white young people, pointing to an over-readiness for careers staff to draw upon this particular cultural stereotype.

The Young People

There were a number of ways in which the actions of the young people themselves contributed to their under-representation on the better jobs and schemes. For one thing, ethnic minority young people remained in full-time education for longer than their white peers. Careers officers recognised that they were therefore left with a smaller pool of the better-qualified black youngsters from which to submit to the 'best' YTS. 'The better apprenticeship-type schemes want good O levels but black kids with these stay on in education.'

Another syndrome described by careers officers is that black young people sometimes show active preference for 'less desirable' schemes and jobs, and have actively resisted being placed on the better employer-based schemes. This was often understood to be a response to fears of racist treatment. A Midlands officer felt that black young people saw certain shops as being 'white-oriented' – '"There are no blacks working in them; therefore I'm not going to get a job there because I'm black." It might be quite subconscious, but it's there.' Some prestigious employers were avoided – 'I think there is a grapevine among young people – some youngsters are very aware of the reputation of an organisation' (Midlands careers officer). Similarly a fear of unsympathetic treatment in the labour market was seen by some to explain the preference for going on to college at sixteen, rather than entering YTS, amongst many black young people.

A northern careers officer found that many black young people were unwilling to travel to schemes in the parts of the city where there was known to be overt racism. Trying to suggest that they took up a scheme in one particular area of the city was not usually very productive because 'some black youngsters have been there and been beaten up'. He felt that this made it more difficult for him to argue with employers that they should recruit more ethnic minorities because they say, 'The youngsters are not applying to us.' Subsequent research has confirmed this as a factor which can severely limit the opportunities of black young people. A survey in the Liverpool area found that a majority of the sample of black young people felt unsafe during the day outside their own area of Liverpool 8, because of racial tension or fear of racial harassment or attack (Roberts, Connolly and Parsell 1992). Some felt unwilling to travel alone elsewhere in Liverpool. The result of this was that 'their training, education and employment opportunities were severely restricted' (p.226).

Implications of the Research

The evidence from these particular examples of research shows how the denial of racism fails to acknowledge the complexity of processes of discrimination in practice. Many of the arguments of those who deny the operation of racial discrimination are called into question by such research. Firstly, it is often argued that although blatant racism and direct discrimination were common twenty years ago, UK employers are nowadays more educated on the issue and generally sensitive to equal opportunities considerations. However, the apprenticeship study showed how employers operate to ethnic stereotypes and prejudices, and take account of the racist preferences of their white workforce. Most of this happens quietly, out of the sight and knowledge of the applicants and others external to the organisation. Nevertheless, it is revealed in the directly racialist instructions given by employers to external agencies such as the careers service when seeking recruits. The apprenticeship study also showed how employers routinely use a number of recruitment practices which severely reduce the chances of success of black young people by indirect discrimination.

The second argument frequently heard is that differences of language and culture bar ethnic minorities from many opportunities. As far as language is concerned, in the UK the days are gone when large numbers of ethnic minority school-leavers were rendered less employable through difficulties with the English language. Now, young black British people are likely to have been born in this country, or at least to have received most of their education here. Rather than being linguistically deficient, many Asian young people are, on the contrary, completely bilingual. As for 'culture', the only 'cultural' factor found in this research to be operating is the employers' and gatekeepers' erroneous presumption of cultural characteristics. The operation of stereotypes on the young person's language, abilities and aspirations then forms one part of the process of exclusion.

A third argument is that it must be poor educational performance by ethnic minority young people which accounts for their reduced success in the labour market. The issue of how well a country's educational system serves its ethnic minorities remains an important one. However, in this case the arguments on 'underachievement' are sidestepped by the fact that in both the Hubbuck and Carter research and Careers Service research the ethnic background of subjects was a controlled variable, demonstrating that ethnic minority young people who are just as well qualified as their white peers receive systematically inferior treatment from those who control the gateways to opportunities.

A fourth argument is the geographical factor. It is suggested that as employment opportunities have moved out of traditional urban locations to white suburbs and small towns, ethnic minorities are disadvantaged by their concentration in inner cities. Yet within this research, instances have been given as to how the operation of both direct racism and indirect discrimination makes the geographical factor less 'innocent'. Employers were shown to selectively employ restrictive catchment area policies, so that such policies only ever seem to benefit white young people in white suburbs. Furthermore, the existence of racism and harassment in some white areas of cities also operates to deter ethnic minority young people from seeking work with employers in these areas. Word gets around amongst young people about those areas or employers where black applicants are not welcome. Many stay on in full-time education; others, when they do put themselves forward for training schemes or jobs, choose less threatening environments.

This phenomenon has sometimes led to the fifth argument: that patterns of labour market inequality reflect the ethnic minority young people's own aspirations and preferences. Thus employers will argue that there is little wrong with their practices – it is just that 'ethnic minority applicants are not coming forward'. However, part of this 'choice' by young people is due to their quite accurate perception of the unfairness which often operates in access to schemes and jobs. Thus there operates a vicious circle which will never be broken as long racial discrimination remains untackled.

The Careers Service research also shows how other 'professionals' with influence in the labour market, such as careers advisers and teachers, can play their own part in the processes of labour market inequality. For example, it was clear that where careers staff felt lacking in power and confidence to do anything about racist employers they might fall back on the 'protective channelling' of a young person away from a situation where they may be faced with racism.

Those who argue that racial discrimination is rare fail to acknowledge that the extent of the problem is not identified by how often it breaks the surface. For example, the above-described phenomena – the deflating of 'unrealistic' aspirations, the protective channelling, and the anticipatory avoidance of apparently racist employers by young people – all combine to lessen the likelihood that an act of racial discrimination by an employer will need to occur. But the processes of discrimination are still there, ensuring that black young people are not going to have fair access to opportunities for which they are qualified.

The Careers Service research also demonstrates the importance of considering the broader structural context of discrimination and the imbalance of power in the labour market. The 'natural' power of employers was even further enhanced throughout the 1980s in the UK by the Conservative government, whose ideology advocated the extension of the free market and the reduction of restrictions on employers. In the early 1980s the Careers Service was warned by the British government that its future depended on how efficiently it serviced the needs of employers (Wrench 1990a). The shift in emphasis away from a counselling service for young people towards a labour market placement agency sits uneasily with a need to address more forcefully the issue of racial discrimination in the labour market. The fact that senior staff in particular are made aware of the need to get employers serviced quickly as a major justification for the very existence of the Service means that often junior staff are not encouraged to tackle 'pressure to discriminate' cases, or are not properly supported when they do.

Furthermore, 'powerlessness' might also have less obvious effects than a third party simply turning a blind eye to an employer's discrimination, or engaging in protective channelling. We might also speculate that some of the expressed prejudices and misjudgements by careers staff might be more than just a reflection of the stereotyped and patronising attitudes to black people found in British culture since colonial times. The fact that some careers officers underestimate the potential of black clients or label them as 'over-aspiring' may also be related to an awareness of the relative powerlessness of both the young people and the careers officer in the face of labour market discrimination. Thus part of the 'over-aspiration' labelling process could itself be due to a knowledge of the existence of employer racism – a reaction of officers who are aware of this but who feel powerless to do anything about it. The easier option is to persuade yourself that the young person is not suited for the job, and 'talk them down'. In other words, an individual's attitudes and judgements cannot be seen in isolation from broader structural questions of power.

Conclusion

This chapter has focused on the detail of just a few pieces of research into labour market discrimination in order to make broader points with implications for theories of inequality. The paper shows how the denial of racial discrimination is undermined by evidence from such research, which also undermines the corresponding argument that anti-discrimination legislation is unnecessary. Indeed, recent reports on legislation covering racial discrimination in employment (Zegers de Beijl 1991, Forbes and Mead 1992) argue that such legislation needs to be extended across Europe. For example, a 1991 ILO report looks at the scope and effect of anti-discrimination legislation in the three European countries that are considered to be 'front-runners' in the development of such legislation: the United Kingdom, the Netherlands and Sweden. The UK's Race Relations Act 1976 is seen to offer a more comprehensive codification of migrants' rights than, for example, the rather 'unclear and inaccessible' legislation in the Netherlands. With regard to enforcement, the powers of the Commission for Racial Equality are in practice greater than those of other countries, and the CRE's Codes of Practice are also seen as having a useful role in reducing discrimination. With regard to statutory provisions, the report sees the UK position as 'more or less satisfactory' (Zegers de Beijl 1991).

However, the research described in this paper shows that the existence of racial discrimination legislation by itself is not enough. All the research was carried out when the UK 1976 Race Relations Act was already in force, and this did not prevent the discrimination by employers from happening. Furthermore, the careers officers did not draw on the legislation that was there for them to use against employers who were pressuring them to discriminate. Forbes and Mead's comparative analysis of measures to combat racial discrimination in member countries of the EC recognises that despite Britain's extensive legislation governing racial discrimination in the employment relationship, the small number of cases and lack of successful outcomes shows that potential claimants are discouraged by every step of the process. 'The fear of victimisation and the prospect of emotional stress act as further disincentives to those who might otherwise seek a remedy in law' (Forbes and Mead 1992: 26). They conclude that, despite the substantial legal and practical measures which exist in Britain, 'the evidence shows that the vast majority of instances of discrimination go unpublished under the current arrangements, which militate against the aggrieved individual bringing a case to a successful conclusion. In general, visible minority membership remains a strong indicator of reduced life chances' (Forbes and Mead 1992: 26).

Similarly, the ILO report notes that although migrants in the three countries studied are supposed to be equal before the law, evidence shows that discrimination against migrant workers is widespread and persistent. In order to explain the de jure and de facto discrepancy, the report highlights flaws in the statutory provisions and their enforcement. In all three countries the accessibility of legal procedures for victims of employment-related discrimination was found to be insufficient, and the difficulty in proving discrimination means that victims are reluctant to lodge complaints. Thus the existing enforcement bodies have launched proposals with respect to a partial reversal of the onus of proof in discrimination cases, the establishment of full statutory enforcement bodies with wide investigative powers, and an increase in sanctions on unlawful discrimination. The ILO report concludes: 'Given the shortfall in the respective legislations as pointed out in this report, and their quite evident inability to remove discrimination of migrants in the labour market, the conclusion can only be that such amendments are necessary' (Zegers de Beijil 1991: 32).

Similarly in 1991 the final report of the Community Relations Project of the Council of Europe concludes with a plea for the strengthening of legislation against discrimination. Although the report recognises that in many countries the number of cases brought under anti-discrimination legislation is relatively few, and that only a small proportion of those are upheld, the committee is not of the opinion that this indicates a low incidence of discrimination, but rather that it shows the inadequacy of the legal protection currently available (para. 117). It is recognised that the legal approach needs to go hand in hand with action in the fields of education and information. At the same time, 'education and information will be of little use if it seems to the population that the law is indifferent to racism and discrimination' (para. 123).

The research described above shows that it is not enough to restrict our analysis of the processes of inequality to the phenomena of prejudice and stereotyping. It also reveals the existence of forces which operate to perpetuate and encourage the actions of those individuals who are party to the processes of discrimination. Arguments that the descendants of migrants are over-represented in unemployment because they have been unable to penetrate the more buoyant sectors of the economy (for reasons of geography, culture, educational attainment etc.) must be seriously qualified by this evidence.

The question of the extent to which processes of inequality for descendants of migrant communities in Europe are perpetuated by racial discrimination will be a politically important one. As shown by the American debate on the 'underclass', (see chapter 1) the question has implications for whether social policies should emphasise, for example, anti-discrimination measures, 'universalistic' economic measures, or 'compensatory' training directed at the descendants of migrants themselves. This last option perpetuates the syndrome of 'blaming the victim', something which is easy and convenient to do when the processes of discrimination described in this paper are ignored or denied.

There is a contradictory element to the recognition of racism and discrimination in European societies. At one level, the existence of such phenomena is not denied, as shown by the measures and action against racism which have developed across Europe in recent years, including a number of countries which have institutionalised anti-discrimination measures and legislation. Nevertheless, there is still a common view in these countries that racial discrimination is no longer a major determinant of people's life chances, and that legislation 'covers it'. Racism is seen as something which is manifested in practice only intermittently by rogue bigoted employers or extremist right-wing groups. Politically, this 'pseudo-recognition' of racism is useful. Politicians in Britain can condemn racism and point to the 'better record' of Britain than other European countries, whilst in practice the legislation does relatively little to restrict the freedom of employers to recruit, promote and dismiss whom they like.

The fact that on paper Britain has the strongest anti-discrimination legislation in Europe is politically useful in one specific sense. Britain also has arguably the most unashamedly racist immigration law and immigration control procedures of any EC country. British politicians regularly argue that 'good race relations' are dependent on two things: legislation against racism and discrimination, and a strong immigration policy. The British Home Secretary emphasised in a parliamentary debate in June 1992 the Government's aim to have a fair and integrated multiracial society, and determination to stamp out racial discrimination, adding, 'I believe that good race relations in this country depend on the maintenance of a strict system of immigration control' (*Hansard*, 9 June 1992, cols.160–1) In reality, it is just as likely that immigration legislation has encouraged and worsened racist attitudes and practices. 'The political rhetoric justifying the necessity for immigration control can potentially have the effect of institutionalising racism and, through the use of emotive language and imagery, reinforce the commonsense assumptions which have kept racism flourishing in British society.' (Skellington and Morris 1992: 50). As Bernie Grant, a black British MP, put it, the Government's immigration policy appeases racists whilst storing up trouble for the future: 'The Government are storing up resentment among black people due to the treatment that those people receive' (*Hansard*, 9 June 1992, cols.180–1). At the moment, British government politicians have the best of both worlds: racist immigration laws which are effective, 'balanced' by anti-discrimination laws which are not.

Thus, for those elsewhere in Europe who are interested to see what can be learned from the British experience, we can argue that anti-discrimination legislation is a necessary but not sufficient means of reducing the impact of discrimination. In Britain there is still little incentive for employers to change their practices and implement voluntarily equal opportunity policies. Greater incentives could be provided by strengthened legal measures and by contract compliance. It is important to have an agency with responsibility for the examination of complaints and the power to institute investigation procedures, and which could also play a role in educating and informing the public (Forbes and Mead 1992: 16–17). There should also be arrangements to produce better practice from organisations, with conciliation procedures and codes of practice.

There should be statistical monitoring to reveal the economic and social circumstances of ethnic minorities, and these statistics would be able to point to the processes of inequality which otherwise are revealed only by periodic research investigations. Finally, there is the need for continuing political struggle, and collective grassroots action, whether by informal work groups or trade unions, to make sure that the laws and procedures that do exist are used in practice.

PART III

Issues and Debates

-12-

Denying Racism:
Elite Discourse and Racism

Teun A. van Dijk

Introduction

Within a larger research framework that studies the ways white people speak and write about minorities, this chapter examines one major strategy in such discourse, viz., the denial of racism. The prototype of such denials is the well-known disclaimer: 'I have nothing against blacks, but ...'

Discourse plays a prominent role in the reproduction of racism. It expresses, persuasively conveys and legitimates ethnic or racial stereotypes and prejudices among white group members, and may thus form or confirm the social cognitions of other whites. This is particularly true for various forms of elite discourse, since the elites control or have preferential access to the major means of public communication, e.g. through political, media, educational, scholarly or corporate discourse. Without alternative sources of information or opinion formation, the white public at large may have few resources for resistance against such prevailing messages that preformulate the ethnic consensus. Our (informal) discourse analytical approach is embedded within this complex socio-cognitive and socio-political framework, which will not be spelled out here (for details, see van Dijk 1984, 1987, 1991, 1993).

The Forms and Functions of Racism Denials

The many forms denials of racism may take are part of a well-known overall discourse and interaction strategy, viz. that of positive self-pre-

Parts of this paper were presented at conferences in Amsterdam, Coventry and Duisburg in 1991. A longer version of this chapter, 'Discourse and the Denial of Racism', was published in Discourse and Society 3 (1992), 87–118.

sentation or keeping face (Brown and Levinson 1987; Goffman 1967; Tedeschi 1981). Given general social norms that prohibit explicit discrimination and outgroup derogation, white group members usually do not want to be seen as 'racists'. When they want to say something negative about minorities, they will tend to use denials, disclaimers or other forms that are intended to avoid a negative impression with their listeners or their readers. That is denials have the function of blocking negative inferences of the recipients about the attitudes of the speaker or writer. Such denials may not only be personal, but especially in elite discourse, they may also pertain to 'our' group in general: 'We British (Dutch, French) are not racist ...' That is in talk about minorities, white people often speak as dominant group members.

Denials come in many guises. In general, a denial presupposes a real or potential accusation, reproach or suspicion of others about one's present or past actions or attitudes, and asserts that such attacks against one's moral integrity are not warranted. That is denials may be a move in a strategy of *defence*, as well as part of the strategy of positive self-presentation. Thus speakers may not only deny the incriminated (verbal or other) act itself, but also its underlying intentions, purposes or attitudes, or its non-controlled consequences: 'I did not do/say that', 'I did not do/say that on purpose', 'That is not what I meant', 'You got me wrong', etc. Since lack of specific intentions may diminish responsibility, denials of intentions are a well-known move in defences against accusations of legal or moral transgression, and typical in denials of discrimination. Thus journalists often deny prejudiced intentions of biased news reports about minorities, e.g. by claiming to have only written 'the truth', or by denying responsibility for the effects of their coverage upon the attitudes of the audience.

Another way to avoid negative impressions is to play down, trivialise or generally to mitigate the seriousness, extent or consequences of one's negative actions, for instance by using euphemisms in the description of such actions. Indeed, they may deny that their acts or attitudes are negative in the first place. 'Telling the truth' may thus be the typical euphemism of those accused of saying or writing derogatory things about minorities. Similarly, even the very term 'racism' may thus be declared taboo, for instance in the Netherlands and Germany, where the term is seen to apply only to overt right-wing racism (or to racism abroad), and considered to be 'exaggerated' or totally out of place for the more 'moderate' or 'modern' (Dovidio and Gaertner 1986) forms of everyday racism, especially among the elites. Instead, if at all, the terms 'discrimination', 'resentment' or 'xenophobia' are used to describe various manifestations of such everyday racism (for an analysis of such events of everyday racism, see Essed 1991).

Instead of directly or indirectly denying accusations or suspicions of bias or racist attitudes, white people may of course also have recourse to *justifications*, more or less according to the following pattern of argumentation: 'I did express a negative judgment, but it was justified in this case, and that does not mean I am a racist' (for various strategies of such justifications, see e.g. Antaki 1988; Scott and Lyman 1968; Tedeschi and Reiss 1981). Such justifications also play a prominent role in strategies of excuses (Cody and McLaughlin 1988), for instance in political discourse about immigration: 'That we restrict immigration is not because we are racist, but because we want (a) not to worsen the situation of the other immigrants, (b) avoid further unemployment, (c) avoid (white) popular resentment, etc.' Justifications may also go one step further and blame the victim: 'If they don't get a better education, and engage in crime (drugs), no wonder blacks don't get jobs or are being discriminated against' (Ryan 1976).

Denials may also transfer the charge to others: 'I have nothing against blacks, but my neighbours (customers, etc.) ...' Ultimately, denials may also reverse the charges and accuse the accuser for having (intentionally) misunderstood the actor/speaker, for having accused the actor/speaker without grounds or even for being intolerant: 'Not WE, but THEY are the real racists.' Such reversals are typical for right-wing attacks against anti-racists (Murray 1986; van Dijk 1991).

Denials not only have discursive and interactional functions at the level of interpersonal communication. We have already stressed that they also have social implications: they are intended to 'save face' for the whole ingroup. They express ingroup allegiances and white group solidarity, defend 'us' against 'them', that is, against minorities and (other) anti-racists. They mark social boundaries and re-affirm social and ethnic identities, and self-attribute moral superiority to their own group.

At the same time, denials of racism have a *socio-political function*. Denials challenge the very legitimacy of anti-racist analysis, and thus are part of the politics of ethnic management: as long as a problem is being denied in the first place, the critics are ridiculed, marginalised or delegitimated: denials debilitate resistance. As long as racism is denied, there is no need for official measures against it, for stricter laws, regulations or institutions to combat discrimination, or moral campaigns to change the biased attitudes of whites. By selectively attributing 'racism' only to the extreme right, the mainstream parties and institutions at the same time define themselves as being 'not racists'. 'After all [so the argument goes], discrimination is officially prohibited by law, and punished by the courts, so there is no problem, and there is nothing else we can do. We are a tolerant country. There may be incidental acts of discrimination, but that does not make our society or country "racist".'

It is this overall social and political myth in which denials function. They thus play a role in the manufacture of the ethnic consensus and, indirectly, contribute to the legitimation of white group dominance, that is to the reproduction of racism. Finally denials of racism and affirmation of tolerance also have a cultural function when 'our' or 'western' norms and values are contrasted with those of other, 'intolerant' cultures, such as Islam, with the obvious implication that 'our' culture is superior (Said 1981). Such implications, which were prominent during the Rushdie affair and the Gulf War, function within the broader culturalisation of modern racism, and its transformation into ethnicism.

Analysing Denials

Against this very succinctly sketched theoretical framework, let us now examine various forms of denial in different discourse genres. Although denials, such as the widespread disclaimer mentioned above, 'I have nothing against ... but ...', are also prevalent in everyday conversations about ethnic affairs (for details, see van Dijk 1984, 1987), we shall focus only on elite discourse, viz. on the press and on parliamentary discourse. Note though that many dominant properties of such elite discourses also influence everyday talk and opinions about ethnic affairs: similar topics are being discussed (viz. problems, for us, of immigration, crime, deviance, cultural deviance and ethnic relations), and even similar modes of argumentation, such as the denials that are part of the overall strategies of positive ingroup presentation. In the remainder of this chapter, we shall only focus on these denials (for other properties of elite discourse on ethnic affairs, see van Dijk 1991, 1993).

The Press

Although discrimination is often covered in the press, though usually defined as incidental, racism is denied in many ways. First of all, racism is usually elsewhere: in the past (during slavery or segregation) abroad (Apartheid in South Africa), politically at the far right (racist parties), and socially at the bottom (poor inner cities, skinheads). This is true for both the liberal and the conservative press. This means that it never applies to 'us', that is, the moderate mainstream, let alone to the liberal left or to the elites. Those who accuse 'us' of racism are therefore severely attacked in much of the conservative press or simply ignored or marginalised in the more liberal press, especially when the press itself is the target of critical analysis. Racism, thus, if discussed at all, is explained away by restricting its definition to old-style, aggressive, ideological racism based on notions of racial superiority. Everyday forms of cultural racism, or ethnicism, are at most characterised as intolerance or xenophobia, which may even be blamed on the victim.

Positive Self-presentation

The semantic basis of denial is 'truth' as the writer sees it. The denial of racism in the press, therefore, presupposes that the journalist or columnist believes that his or her own group or country is essentially 'tolerant' towards minorities or immigrants. Positive self-presentation, thus, is an important move in journalistic discourse, and should be seen as the argumentative denial of the accusations of anti-racists:

> (1) (Handsworth). Contrary to much doctrine, and acknowledging a small malevolent fascist fringe, this is a remarkably tolerant society. But tolerance would be stretched were it to be seen that enforcement of law adopted the principle of reverse discrimination. (*Daily Telegraph*, Editorial, 11 September 1985)

This example not only asserts or presupposes white British 'tolerance', but at the same time defines its boundaries. Tolerance might be interpreted as a position of weakness, and therefore it should not be 'stretched' too far, lest 'every terrorist', 'criminal' or other immigrants, take advantage of it. Affirmative action or liberal immigration laws, thus, can only be seen as a form of reverse discrimination, and hence as a form of self-destruction of white Britain. Ironically, therefore, this example is self-defeating because of its internal contradictions: It is not tolerance *per se* that is aimed at, but rather the limitations preventing its 'excesses'.

Denial and Counter-attack

Having constructed a positive self-image of white Britain, the conservative and tabloid press in particular engages in attacks against those who hold a different view, at the same time defending those who agree with its position, as was the case during the notorious Honeyford affair (Honeyford was headmaster of a Bradford school who was suspended, then reinstated and finally let go with a golden handshake, after having written articles on multicultural education which most of the parents of his mostly Asian students found racist). The attacks on the anti-racists often embody denials of racism:

(2) (Reaction of 'race lobby' against Honeyford). Why is it that this lobby have chosen to persecute this man ... It is not because he is a racist; it is precisely because he is not a racist, yet has dared to challenge the attitudes, behaviour and approach of the ethnic minority professionals. (*Daily Telegraph*, 6 September 1985)

(3) (Worker accused of racism). The really alarming thing is that some of these pocket Hitlers of local government are moving into national politics. It's time we set about exposing their antics while we can. Forewarned is forearmed. (*Daily Mail*, Editorial, 26 October 1985)

These examples illustrate several strategic moves in the press campaign against anti-racists. First, as we have seen above, denial is closely linked to the presupposition of 'truth': Honeyford is presented as defending the 'truth', viz. the failure and the anti-British nature of multiculturalism.

Secondly, consequent denials often lead to the strategic move of reversal: Not we are the racists, *they* are the 'true racists'. This reversal also implies, thirdly, a reversal of the charges: Honeyford, and those who sympathise with him, are the victims, not his Asian students and their parents. Consequently, the anti-racists are the enemy: *they* are the ones who persecute innocent, ordinary British citizens, they are the ones who are intolerant. Therefore, victims who resist their attackers may be defined as folk heroes, who 'dare' the 'anti-racist brigade'. Ultimately, as in example (3), the charges may be fully reversed, viz. by identifying the symbolic enemy precisely with the categories of their own attacks: they are intolerant, they are totalitarian 'pocket Hitlers'.

Moral Blackmail

One element that was very prominent in the Honeyford affair, as well as in similar cases, was the pretence of censorship: The anti-racists not only ignore the 'truth' about multicultural society, they also prevent others (us) from telling the truth. Repeatedly, thus, journalists and columnists argue that this 'taboo' and this 'censorship' must be broken in order to be able to tell the 'truth', as was the case after the disturbances in Tottenham:

(4) (Tottenham). The time has come to state the truth without cant and without hypocrisy ... the strength to face the facts without being silenced by the fear of being called racist. (*Daily Mail* 9 October 1985, column by Linda Lee-Potter).

Such examples also show that the authors feel morally blackmailed, while at the same time realising that to 'state the truth', meaning 'to say negative things about minorities', may well be against the prevalent norms of tolerance and understanding. Clamouring for the 'truth' thus expresses a dilemma, even if the dilemma is only apparent: the apparent dilemma is a rhetorical strategy to accuse the opponent of censorship or blackmail, not the result of moral soul-searching and a difficult decision. After all, the same newspapers extensively do write negative things about young blacks, and never hesitate to write what they see as the 'truth'. Nobody 'silences' them, and the taboo is only imaginary. On the contrary, the right-wing press in Britain reaches many millions of readers.

Subtle Denials

Denials are not always explicit. There are many ways to express doubt, distance or non-acceptance of statements or accusations by others. When the official Commission for Racial Equality (CRE) in 1985 published a report on discrimination in the UK, outright denial of the facts would hardly be credible. Other discursive means, such as quotation marks, and the use of words like 'claim' or 'allege', presupposing doubt on the part of the writer, may be employed in accounting for the facts, as is the case in the following editorial of the *Daily Telegraph*:

> (5) In its report which follows a detailed review of the operation of the 1976 Race Relations Act, the Commission claims that ethnic minorities continue to suffer high levels of discrimination and disadvantage. (*Daily Telegraph*, 1 August 1985)

Such linguistic tricks do not go unnoticed, as we may see in the following reaction to this passage in a letter from Peter Newsam, then director of the CRE:

> (6) Of the Commission you say 'it claims that ethnic minorities continue to suffer high levels of discrimination and disadvantage'. This is like saying that someone 'claims' that July was wet. It was. And it is also a fact supported by the weight of independent research evidence that discrimination on racial grounds, in employment, housing and services, remains at a disconcertingly high level. (*Daily Telegraph*, 7 August 1985)

Denials, thus, may be subtly conveyed by expressing doubt or distance. Therefore, the very notion of 'racism' usually appears between quotation marks, especially also in the headlines. Such scare quotes are not merely a journalistic device for reporting opinions or controversial points of view. If that were the case, the opinions with which the newspaper happens to agree would also have to be put between quotation marks, which is not always the case. Rather, apart from signalling journalistic doubt and distance, the quotation marks also connote 'unfounded accusation'. The use of quotation marks around the notion of racism has become so much routine, that even in cases where the police or the courts themselves established that racism was involved in a particular case, the conservative press may maintain the quotation marks out of sheer habit.

Mitigation

Our conceptual analysis of denial has already shown that denial may also be implied by various forms of mitigation, such as toning down, using euphemisms or other circumlocutions that minimise the act itself or the responsibility of the accused. In the same editorial of the *Daily Telegraph* we quoted above, we find the following statement:

> (7) (CRE report). No one would deny the fragile nature of race relations in Britain today or that there is misunderstanding and distrust between parts of the community. (*Daily Telegraph*, Editorial, 1 August 1985)

Thus instead of inequality or racism, race relations are assumed to be 'fragile', whereas 'misunderstanding and distrust' are also characteristic of these relations. Interestingly, this passage also explicitly denies the prevalence of denials, and therefore might be read, as such, as a concession: There are problems. However, the way this concession is rhetorically presented by way of various forms of mitigation, suggests, in the context of the rest of the same editorial, that the concession is apparent. Such apparent concessions are another major form of disclaimer in discourse about ethnic relations, as we also have them in statements like: 'There are also intelligent blacks, but ...' or 'I know that minorities sometimes have problems, but ...' Note also that in the example from the *Daily Telegraph* the mitigation not only appears in the use of euphemisms, but also in the *redistribution of responsibility*, and hence in the denial of blame. It is not we (whites) who are mainly responsible for the tensions between the communities, but everybody is, as is suggested by the use of the impersonal existential phrase: '*There is misunderstanding ...*' Apparently, one effective move of denial is either to dispute the responsible agency, or to conceal the agency.

Parliamentary Discourse

In close symbiosis with the mass media, politics plays a prominent role in the definition of the ethnic situation. In western Europe, decision-making by the administration and the bureaucracy, and parliamentary debates in the 1980s and 1990s increasingly deal with ethnic affairs, immigration and refugees. Persistent social inequalities, unemployment, affirmative action, educational 'disadvantage', popular resentment against immigration, and the arrival of 'waves' of new refugees from the south, are among the major topics on the political agenda, which are 'made public', and possibly emphasised, by the press, and thus by the population at large. Note that since parliamentary speeches are for the record, and usually written in advance, we should not normally expect, except by right-wing speakers, overt derogation of minority groups. However, since restrictions on immigration or refusals to legislate in favour of minorities need to be legitimated we may nevertheless expect negative other-presentation of immigrants, refugees or minorities. These subtle forms of derogation, in turn, require the usual forms of positive self-presentation, and hence of denial. Let us give some examples from parliamentary debates in the UK, France, Germany, the Netherlands and the USA (for detail, see van Dijk 1993). We shall not identify the individual speakers: here we are only interested, more generally, in official forms of talk about ethnic minorities.

Nationalist Self-glorification

Parliament is the prime forum for nationalistic rhetoric. This is particularly true when international norms and values, such as democracy, equal rights and tolerance are involved. Accusations of racism in such a context may easily be heard as a moral indictment of the nation as a whole, and are therefore permitted, though resented, only in partisan debates, in which one party accuses the other of racism. After all, as we have seen, racism is always elsewhere, and always a property of the others.

(8) I believe that we are a wonderfully fair country. We stick to the rules unlike some foreign Governments. (UK)

(9) Our country has long been open to foreigners, a tradition of hospitality going back, beyond the revolution, to the *ancien régime*. (France)

(10) I know no other country on this earth that gives more prominence to the rights of resident foreigners as does this bill in our country. (Germany)

(11) There are so many great things about our country, all the freedoms that we have, speech, religion, the right to vote and choose our leaders and of

course our greatness lies in our mobility, the ability to each and every one of us, regardless of the circumstances of our birth, to rise in American society, to pursue our individual dreams. (USA)

Although nationalist rhetoric may differ in different countries (it is usually more exuberant in France and in the USA, for instance), the basic strategy of positive self-presentation appears in all Houses: we are fair, respect human rights, have a long tradition of tolerance etc. It is not uncommon to hear in each parliament that at least some representatives think of their own country as the most liberal, freedom-loving, democratic etc. in the world.

Fair, but ...

Such self-glorification, especially when introducing a debate on minorities or immigration, has various functions in parliamentary discourse. For those groups or parties that oppose legislation in favour of minorities or immigrants, positive self-presentation often functions as a disclaimer, that is, as an introduction for a BUT, followed by arguments in favour of special restrictions, as is also the case in the following fragment from a radio interview with the Dutch Prime Minister, Ruud Lubbers:

(12) In practice, we should come to opportunities and possibilities for them, but in practice we should also come to a less soft approach. There should be a line like: we also hold them responsible [literally: 'we address them'].

Elsewhere we find a nearly routine combination of fairness on the one hand, and firmness, realism, pragmatism etc. on the other hand:

(13) If we are to work seriously for harmony, non-discrimination and equality of opportunity in our cities, that has to be accompanied by firm and fair immigration control. (UK)

(14) It belongs to this fair balance of interests that the further immigration of foreigners must be limited, because for each society there are limits to the ability and the readiness to integrate. (Germany)

(15) This substitute offers the House of Representatives an opportunity to enact a landmark civil rights bill that is both fair and pragmatic. (USA)

This remarkably similar rhetoric of fairness ('fair, but strict' etc.) in the different countries also seeks to combine two opposed ideological or political aims, viz. the humanitarian values of tolerance or hospitality on the one hand, and the common sense values of 'realism' on the other hand. In other words, the humanitarian aims are recognised, but at the same time they are rejected as being too idealistic, and therefore unpractical in the business of everyday political management and decision-making. The reference to fairness also serves as an element in a 'balance', viz. in order to mitigate the negative implications of proposed legislation, such as limitations on further immigration in the European debates, and limitations on the 1990 Civil Rights Bill (eventually vetoed by President Bush) in the USA. Fairness in such rhetoric usually is supported by the claim that the (restrictive) measures are always 'in their own best interests'.

Denial of Racism

In such a political context of public impression management, the denial of racism plays a prominent role. Whatever the political orientation or party involved, including the extremist right, all parliamentarians emphatically reject any accusation or suggestion of prejudice, discrimination or racism. Indeed, the more racist the opinions professed, the more insistent are the denials of racism, as may be apparent in the following quote from a representative of the Front National in the French *Assemblé Nationale*:

(16) We are neither racist nor xenophobic. Our aim is only that, quite naturally, there be a hierarchy, because we are dealing with France, and France is the country of the French.

Note that an implicit but ('only') follows the denial. The speaker (the leader of the Front National, Le Pen, himself) even claims that it is 'natural' to have a hierarchy between the 'own group', the French, and the immigrants. This assignment of a 'natural' right to a superior position is at the heart of racist ideologies.

Besides the discursive and political strategy of populism, which is very prominent in such debates ('The people would resent it', 'You should listen to what ordinary French, English ... people say'), we also find the element of *euphemism*: we are not racist, only worried. Here is a more sophisticated example of such a strategy:

(17) The French are not racist. But, facing this continuous increase of the foreign population in France, one has witnessed the development, in certain cities and neighbourhoods, of reactions that come close to xenophobia. In the eyes of the French unemployed man, for instance, the foreigner may easily become a rival, towards whom a sentiment of animosity may threaten to appear.

Following the usual 'but', we do not find, as in other disclaimers, a negative statement about immigrants, but rather an explanation of the reaction of the 'common man' (women are apparently not involved). Note that the way this explanation is formulated ('continuous increase', 'rival') suggests understanding, if not an excuse, as in the usual accounts of racism in terms of economic competition. The denial of racism itself is rather complex, however. It is a denial that holds for the French in general. It is followed by a partial concession, duly limited by heavy mitigation and hedging ('coming close to xenophobia', 'a sentiment of animosity may threaten to appear'), as well as limited in place ('in certain cities'). In other words, prejudice, discrimination and racism are local incidents, and should also be seen as being provoked by continuous immigration, arguments we also found in the right-wing British press.

When restrictive measures are being debated, those who support them feel impelled to remind their audience, and the public at large, that such political decisions have nothing to do with prejudice or racism:

(18) I hope that people outside, whether they are black or white and wherever they come from, will recognize that these are not major changes resulting from prejudice. (UK)

Such denials need argumentative support. Saying only that the measures are 'fair' may be seen as too flimsy. Therefore they are often followed by the moves we have found earlier, such as concern for the inner cities. Note that such arguments also imply a move of transfer: we are not racist, but the poor people in the inner cities are, and we should avoid exacerbating the mood of resentment among the population at large. This argument is rather typical of what we have called 'elite racism', which consistently denies racism among the own elite group, but recognizes that others, especially poor white people, may fail to be as tolerant.

Denial and Reproach

In the analysis of the British press, we have found that denials of racism easily transform into attacks against anti-racists. Such a strategy may also be found in parliamentary discourse. Thus, conservative representatives will not accept accusations or even implicit suggestions that their stricter immigration or ethnic minority policies are categorized as racist by other politicians. Since the official norm is 'that we are all tolerant citizens', such allegations are declared unacceptable:

(19) Addressing myself to the people of the left, I repeat again that we are ... I have noted in your words, my God, terms such as racism and xenophobia, that those who do not support your proposals would be judged with the same terms. It should be understood once and for all: we are not racists because we combat your text. (France)

(20) Well, now can we also agree this afternoon that you can have different philosophies about how to achieve through law civil rights and equal opportunities for everybody without somehow being anti-civil-rights or being a racist or something like that. (USA)

One interesting case may be found in a German debate on the new aliens bill. When one of the Green Party representatives qualifies the provisions of the bill as 'racist', a term that is as unusual in official German discourse as it is in the Netherlands, other representatives are shocked:

(21) A chill ran down my back when our colleague ... said that this bill was a form of institutionalized racism. Whereas the older ones among us had to live twelve years under institutionalised racism, ladies and gentlemen, I beg you, and in particular our younger colleagues, to show respect for these terrible experiences, and not to introduce such concepts to our everyday political business.

In other words, evaluations in terms of racism are limited only to the Nazi past, and are banned from official political discourse. At most, the term *Ausländerfeindlichkeit* (literally: animosity against foreigners) may be used. 'Racism' thus is by definition too strong, if only because the present situation cannot be compared to the monstrosities of the Nazis. A similar attitude exists in the Netherlands, where racism is also avoided as a term in public (political, media) discourse because it is understood only in terms of extremist, right-wing ideologies of racial superiority.

Reversal

Although moderate reproaches directed against anti-racist delegates are not uncommon in parliament, reversal is rather exceptional. However, it is quite typical for right-wing party representatives, such as those of the Front National in France. Being routinely accused, also explicitly, of racism, they go beyond mere denial, and reverse the charges. For them, this means that the others, and especially the socialists, allegedly letting in so many immigrants and granting them equal rights, are guilty of what they call 'anti-French racism':

(22) There exists a form of racism, my dear colleagues [interruptions] that is passed over silently, but of which the manifestations nowadays reach an insupportable level and a scope that should concern us: that is the anti-French racism.

Another way of reversing the charges is to accuse the anti-racists of being themselves responsible for creating racism in the country, if only by not listening to the people and by letting in so many non-European immigrants:

(23) Well, France today, according to what those creatures of the whole world tell us who often have come to take refuge in our country ... France is the least racist country that exists in the world. We can't tolerate to hear it said that France is a racist country ... In this respect, this law proposal, because of the debate that takes place at this moment, secretes and fabricates racism!

These examples taken from several western parliaments show that although the debate may be couched in less extremist terms than in much of the right-wing or tabloid press, or in everyday conversations, rather similar strategies and moves are used to talk about ethnic affairs. Most characteristic of this kind of political discourse is not merely the nationalist self-praise, but also the strategic management of impression: whatever we decide, we are fair. Since, especially in Europe, ethnic minorities, let alone new immigrants and refugees, have virtually no political power, this 'balancing act' of presenting policies as 'firm but fair' is obviously addressed primarily to the dominant white public at large. When defined as humane without being too soft, thus, the government and its supporting parties may be acceptable as essentially reasonable: 'We take energetic measures, but we are not racist.'

In other words, besides managing impressions, such political discourse also manages its own legitimation by manufacturing consent on ethnic policies, and at the same time manages the politics of ethnic affairs, immigration and international relations.

Conclusions

Racism, defined as a system of racial and ethnic inequality, can survive only when it is daily reproduced through multiple acts of exclusion, inferiorisation or marginalisation. Such acts need to be sustained by an ideological system and by a set of attitudes that legitimate difference and dominance. Discourse is the principal means for the construction and reproduction of this socio-cognitive framework. At the same time, there are norms and values of tolerance and democratic humanitarianism, which may be felt to be inconsistent with biased attitudes and negative text and talk about minorities. To manage such contradictions, white speakers engage in strategies of positive self-presentation in order to be able credibly to present the 'others' in a negative light. Disclaimers, mitigations, euphemisms, transfers, and many other forms of racism denial are the routine moves in social face-keeping, so that ingroup members are able to come to terms with their own prejudices. At the same time, these denials of racism have important social and political functions, e.g. in the management of ethnic affairs and the de-legitimation of resistance. We have seen that, especially in elite discourse, for instance in the media and in the legislature, the 'official' versions of own-group tolerance, and the rejection of racism as an implied or explicit accusation, are crucial for the self-image of the elite as being tolerant, understanding leaders. However, we have also seen how these strategies of denial at the same time confirm their special role in the formulation and the reproduction of racism.

-13-

Difference, Diversity, Differentiation: Processes of Racialisation and Gender

Avtar Brah

Difference, diversity, pluralism, hybridity – these are some of the most debated and contested terms of our time. Questions of difference are at the heart of many discussions within contemporary feminisms. In the field of education in Britain, questions of identity and community continue to dominate debates surrounding multiculturalism and anti-racism. In this chapter, I consider how these themes might help us to understand the racialisation of gender. However often the concept is exposed as vacuous, 'race' still acts as an apparently ineradicable marker of social difference. What makes it possible for the category to act in this way? What is the nature of social and cultural differences and what gives them their force? How does 'racial' difference then connect to difference and antagonisms organised around other markers, like 'gender' or 'class'? Such questions are important because they can help to explain people's tenacious investment in notions of identity, community and tradition.

One recurrent problem in this area is essentialism: that is, a notion of ultimate essence that transcends historical and cultural boundaries. Here I argue against an essentialist concept of difference while simultaneously problematising the issue of 'essentialism'. At what point, and in what ways, for example, does the specificity of a particular social experience become an expression of essentialism? In reviewing feminist debates, I suggest that black and white feminism should not be seen as essentially fixed oppositional categories but rather as historically contingent fields of contestation within discursive and material practices in a post-colonial society. In similar vein, I shall be arguing that analysis of the interconnections between racism, class, gender and sexuality must take account of the positionality of different racisms with respect to one another. Overall, I underline the importance of a macro-analysis that

Another version of this chapter was published in J. Donald and A. Rattansi (eds) 'Race', Culture and Difference, London, Sage, 1992.

studies the inter-relationships between various forms of social differentiation empirically and historically, but without necessarily deriving them all from a single determining instance. In other words, I shall also be trying to avoid the danger of 'reductionism'.

The article is divided into three parts. In the first, I address the various notions of 'difference' that have emerged in recent discussions of how extensively the term 'black' can be used to define the experience of African-Caribbean and south Asian groups in post-war Britain. The second section is concerned with the ways in which issues of 'difference' have been framed with respect to racism within feminist theory and practice. My primary focus here is on the ongoing debate in Britain. I conclude with a brief examination of some conceptual categories used in the theorisation of 'difference' and suggest that greater clarity in how we conceptualise 'difference' may aid in developing sharper political strategies for social justice.

What's in a Name? What's in a Colour?

Over the past few years the usage of the term 'black' to refer to people of African-Caribbean and south Asian descent in Britain has been the subject of considerable controversy. It is relevant to address some of these arguments as they often centre around notions of difference.

The African-Caribbean and south Asian people who migrated to Britain in the post-war period found themselves occupying a broadly similar structural position within British society, as workers performing predominantly unskilled or semi-skilled jobs on the lowest rungs of the economy. Although the ideologies which racialised them were not identical in content there were similarities in their encounters with racism in such arenas such as the workplace, the education system, the housing market and the health services. Their 'non-whiteness' was a common referent within the racism confronting them. These groups were then commonly described in popular, political and academic discourses as 'coloured people'. This was not a simple descriptive term. It had been the colonial code for a relationship of domination and subordination between the coloniser and colonised. Now the code was reworked and reconstituted in and through a variety of political, cultural and economic processes in post-war Britain.

The term 'black' was adopted by the emerging coalitions amongst African-Caribbean and south Asian organisations and activists in the late 1960s and 1970s. They were influenced by the way that the Black Power movement in the USA, which had turned the concept of Black on its head, divested it of its pejorative connotations in racialised discourses, and transformed it into a confident expression of an assertive group identity. The Black Power movement urged black Americans to construe the black community not as a matter of geography but rather in terms of the global African diaspora. Eschewing 'chromatism' – the basis of differentiation amongst blacks according to lighter or darker tone of skin – 'black' became a political colour to be worn with pride against colour-based racisms. The African-Caribbean and south Asian activists in Britain borrowed the term from the Black Power movement to foster a rejection of chromatism amongst those defined as 'coloured people' in Britain.

The politics of solidarity between African-Caribbean and south Asian activists of the period were also influenced by the history of anti-colonial struggles in Africa, Asia and the Caribbean. The fusion of these two influences in the formation of a project concerned to address the social condition of post-colonial subjects in the heart of the British metropolis meant that the concept of black has been associated with rather distinctive and somewhat different meanings in Britain as compared with the USA.

Recently British usage of the term 'black' has been criticised by commentators like Hazareesingh (1986) and Modood (1988). They argue that the 'black' in Black Power ideology referred specifically to the historical experience of people of sub-Saharan African descent, and was designed to create a positive political and cultural identity amongst black Americans. When used in relation to south Asians the concept is *de facto* emptied of those specific cultural meanings associated with phrases such as 'black music'. The concept can incorporate south Asians in a political sense only, and they therefore conclude that it denies Asian cultural identity. Clearly there is some force in this argument. It is certainly the case, as we have already noted, that the Black Power movement's mobilisation of the term 'black' was an attempt at reclaiming an African heritage that had been denied to black Americans by racism. But, as a historically specific political project located in the socio-political and economic dynamics in the USA, the Black Power ideology did not simply reclaim a pre-given ancestral past. In that very process, it also constructed a particular version of this heritage. Given that cultural processes are dynamic, and the process of claiming is itself mediated, the term 'black' does not have to be construed in essentialist terms. It can have different political and cultural meanings in different contexts. Its specific meaning in post-war Britain cannot be taken to have denied cultural differences between African, Caribbean and south Asian people when cultural difference was not the organising principle within this discourse or political practice. The concrete political struggles in which the new meaning was grounded acknowledged cultural differences but sought to accomplish political unity against racism. In any case, the issue of cultural difference cannot be posed purely in terms of differences between south Asian and African-Caribbean cultures. There are, for example, many differences between African and Caribbean cultures (which also include cultures of people of south Asian descent). Cultures in the diasporas always have their own specificity. In other words, even when the use of the 'black' is restricted to sub-Saharan Africa and its diasporas, it can be said, within the parameters of the terms set by the critics, to deny the cultural specificities of these diverse groups.

A second criticism of the ways in which 'black' has been employed in Britain has been that the concept is meaningless since many south Asians do not define themselves as black, and many African-Caribbeans do not recognise them as such. This assertion hinges partly on the criterion of numbers, but without providing supporting numerical evidence. In my own research I have found that south Asians will frequently describe themselves as 'kale' (black) when discussing issues of racism. But since the whole social being of south Asian and African-Caribbean peoples is not constituted only by the experience of racism, they have many other identifications based on, for example, religion, language and political affiliation. Moreover, as many demonstrations and campaigns show, the concept of black was mobilised as part of a set of constitutive ideas and principles to promote collective action. As a social movement, black activism has aimed to generate solidarity; it has not necessarily assumed that all members of the diverse black communities inevitably identify with the concept in its British usage.

Another area of contention has centred on the distribution of resources by the state to different categories of consumers. It is argued that the term 'black' serves to conceal the cultural needs of groups other than those of African-Caribbean origin. This particular critique is often steeped in 'ethnicism'. Ethnicism, I would suggest, defines the experience of racialised groups primarily in 'culturalist' terms: that is it posits 'ethnic difference' as the primary modality around which social life is constituted and experienced. Cultural needs are defined largely as independent of other social experiences centred around class, gender, racism or sexuality. This means that a group identified as culturally different is assumed to be internally homogeneous, when this is patently not the case. The 'housing needs' of a working-class Asian living in overcrowded conditions on a housing estate, for instance, cannot be the same as those of a middle-class Asian living in a semi-detached house in suburbia. In other words, ethnicist discourses seek to impose stereotypic notions of 'common cultural need' upon heterogeneous groups with diverse social aspirations and interests. They often fail to address the relationship between 'difference' and the social relations of power in which it may be inscribed. It is clearly important that the state should be sensitive to the plurality of needs amongst its citizens. But we need to be attentive to the ways in which 'needs' are socially constructed and represented in various discourses.

There is another aspect to the ethnicist critique of the use of the term 'black' by the local state. Ethnicism does not seem to differentiate between 'black' as a term adopted by subordinate groups to symbolise resistance against oppression and the appropriation of the same term by some local authorities as a basis for formulating policies for the allocation of resources (Sivanandan 1985; Gilroy 1987; Cain and Yuval-Davis 1990). The term has different meanings in the two contexts and signifies potentially different social and political outcomes. But ethnicism seems to conflate these very different sets of meanings. Furthermore, certain politicians may deploy the discourse of 'ethnic difference' as a means to create their own power base rather than to empower those whose 'needs' are supposed to be better met by jettisoning the term 'black'. It is unlikely that replacing 'black' by some other politically neutral descriptions will secure more equitable distribution of resources.

What kind of a terminology has been proposed to replace 'black'? Writing from somewhat different political perspectives Hazareesingh (1986) and Modood (1988) come to rather similar conclusions. Hazareesingh suggests that the use of 'black' should be confined to people of African descent and that people from the south Asian subcontinent should all be subsumed under the concept of 'Indian' on the grounds of a shared 'culture in a historical sense'. But there is an immense diversity of cultures in the subcontinent which have emerged and, been transformed under varying material and political circumstances. Furthermore, these cultures are underpinned by class, caste, religious, regional and linguistic differences and divisions. So in what sense can one speak of a common Indian culture? Hazareesingh's construction of this commonality in terms of a shared experience of imperialism and racism is vulnerable to the same criticism he directs against those who support 'black' as a political colour. He too privileges historical and contemporary processes of domination, and the role of the state in mediating these, as centrally important in structuring people's experiences. His view of a common Indian culture could also be seen by many south Asians as 'an attempt to straitjacket their experience'. Given the position of the modern state of India *vis-à-vis* other countries of the Asian subcontinent, Hazareesingh's concept of 'Indian' might be construed by some as reinforcing a hegemonic project in that region. How will Pakistanis or Bangladeshis recognise themselves in this definition, given the recent history of partition?

Unlike Hazareesingh, Modood employs the term 'Asian' as against 'black', which he claims 'sells short the majority of the people it identifies as black', and against 'south Asian' which he dismisses as an academic term. Leaving aside the fact that Asia covers a much larger part of the globe than the subcontinent of south Asia, it is his definition of 'Asian' which is particularly problematic: 'What I mean by an "Asian" identity', he states, 'is some share in the heritage of the civilisations of old Hindustan prior to British conquest' (p. 397). First, the term Hindustan as used by the Mughals referred largely to the northern states of latter-day India. More importantly, Modood seems to attribute a unified identity to pre-colonial India, which, by implication, was destroyed by the British Raj. Historical evidence shows however, that pre-colonial India was a heterogeneous entity, and that people were much more likely to define themselves in terms of their regional, linguistic or religious identity than as Hindustanis. Indeed, it may be possible to argue that 'Indian identity' as a set of identifications with a nation state was the outcome of resistance and struggle against colonialism rather than something that existed prior to this period.

The main point I wish to stress through this foray into the debate surrounding the use of 'black' in Britain is to highlight how difference is constructed within these competing discourses. That is, the usage of 'black', 'Indian' or 'Asian' is determined not so much by the nature of its referent, but by its semiotic function within different discourses. These various meanings signal differing political strategies and outcomes. They mobilise different sets of cultural or political identities, and set limits to where the boundaries of a 'community' are established. This debate has to an extent been echoed within feminism. And it is against this general background that I turn to issues of 'difference' within feminism.

Is Sisterhood Global?

In 1985 I attended the International Women's Conference in Nairobi. It was a gathering of over 10,000 women from over 150 countries. There we were all gathered together as women to address questions of our universal subordination as a 'second sex', yet the most striking aspect of this conference was the heterogeneity of our social condition. The issues raised by the different groups of women present at the conference, especially those from the Third World, served to underline the fact that issues affecting women cannot be analysed in isolation from the national and international context of inequality (Brah 1988; Mohanty 1988).

Our gender is constituted and represented differently according to our differential location within the global relations of power. Our insertion into these global relations of power is realised through a myriad of economic, political and ideological processes. Within these structures of social relations we do not exist simply as women but as differentiated categories such as working-class women, peasant women, migrant women. Each description references a specificity of social condition. And real lives are forged out of a complex articulation of these dimensions. As is currently being increasingly recognised in feminist theory and practice, woman is not a unitary category. Yet, this does not mean that the noun 'woman' is meaningless. It too has its own specificity constituted within and through historically specific configurations of gender relations. But in different womanhoods the noun is only meaningful – indeed only exists – with reference to a fusion of adjectives which symbolise particular historical trajectories, material circumstances and cultural experiences. Difference in this sense is a difference of social condition. At this level of analysis the focus is on the social construction of different categories of women within the broader structural and ideological processes within societies. No claims are made that an individual category is internally homogeneous. Working-class women, for instance, comprise very diverse groups of people both within and between societies. Class position signals certain commonalities of location within the social structure, but class articulates with other axes of differentiation such as racism, heterosexism or caste in delineating the precise social position of specific categories of women.

The primary objective of feminism has been to change the social relations of power embedded within gender. Since gender inequalities pervade all spheres of life, feminist strategies have involved a challenge to women's subordinated position within both state institutions and civil society. The driving force behind feminist theory and practice in the post-war period has been its commitment to eradicate inequalities arising from a notion of sexual difference inherent in biologically deterministic theories which explain women's position in society as a result of innate differences. Despite evidence that sex differences in cognitive behaviour among infants are slight, and the psychological similarity between men and women is very high, research to establish innate differences continues unabated (Segal 1990; Rose, Kamin and Lewontin 1984). Feminists do not, of course, ignore women's biology, but they challenge ideologies which construct and represent women's subordination as resulting from their biological capacities.

The ways in which questions of biology are addressed and taken account of vary within different feminisms. Radical feminist accounts, for example, tend to identify women's biologically based subordination as the fundamental basis of gender inequality. The relations of power between men and women are seen as the primary dynamic of women's oppression almost to the exclusion of other determinants such as class and racism. Radical feminist perspectives often represent women's procreative abilities as an indicator of certain psychological qualities which are uniquely and universally female. These qualities are assumed to have been undermined through patriarchal domination and thus have to be rediscovered and reclaimed. They may often celebrate sexual difference in the form of presumed unique female attributes and qualities. It has been argued that whilst repudiating biological determinism embedded within patriarchal discourses, some versions of radical feminism in turn construct a trans-historical notion of essential femaleness in need of rescuing and recapturing beyond patriarchal relations (Weedon 1987; Segal 1987; Spellman 1988).

Socialist feminism, on the other hand, has been based on the assumption that human nature is not essential but is socially produced. The meaning of what it is to be a woman – biologically, socially, culturally and psychically – is considered to be historically variable. Socialist feminism has mounted a powerful critique of those materialist perspectives which prioritise class, neglect the social consequences of the sexual division of labour, privilege heterosexuality and pay scant attentions to the social mechanisms which prevent women from attaining economic, political and social equality. This strand of feminism distances itself from the radical feminist emphasis on power relations between the sexes as the almost exclusive determinant of women's subordination.

On the whole, and especially until very recently, western feminist perspectives of whatever kind have paid little attention to the processes of racialisation of gender, class or sexuality. Processes of racialisation are, of course, historically specific, and different groups have been racialised differently under varying circumstances, and on the basis of different signifiers of 'difference'. Each racism has a particular history. It arose from a particular set of economic, political and cultural circumstances, has been reproduced through specific mechanisms, and has found different expression in different societies. Anti-black racism, anti-Irish racism, anti-Jewish racism, anti-Arab racism, different varieties of orientalisms: all have distinctive features.

The specific histories of these various racisms place them in particular relationship to each other. For example, there are several similarities in the social experience of the Irish and black groups in Britain. Both sets of people have a history of being colonised by Britain, their migration patterns to Britain share common features, both groups occupy a predominantly working-class position within the British class structure, and they both have been subjected to racism. But anti-black and anti-Irish racism situate these groups differently within British society. As white Europeans, the great majority of Irish people are placed in a dominant position *vis-à-vis* black people in and through the discourses of anti-black racism, even when the two groups may share a similar class location. In other words, we assume different subject positions within various racisms. Analysis of the inter-connections between racism, class, gender and sexuality must take account of the positionality of different racisms with respect to one another.

A second example may illustrate the above point further. African-Caribbean and south Asian communities have developed differing responses to racism because their experiences of racism, though similar in many ways, have not been identical (Brah and Deem 1986) State policies have impacted differently on these communities. African-Caribbean communities have mobilised far more around their collective experience of the criminal justice system, particularly the police and the courts, whereas Asian groups have been much more actively involved in defending communities against violent racial attacks, racial harassment on housing estates, and in organising campaigns against deportations and other issues arising from the effects of immigration laws. The stereotypic representations of African-Caribbean and south Asian communities have also been substantially different. The gendered discourses of the 'nigger' and the 'Paki' in post-war Britain represent distinctive ideologies, yet they are two strands of a common racism structured around colour/phenotype/culture as signifiers of superiority and inferiority in post colonial Britain. This means that African-Caribbean, south Asian and white groups are relationally positioned within these structures of representation. By their behaviour and actions they may reinforce these structures or alternatively they may assume a political practice which challenges these different strands of anti-black racism.

There is a tendency in Britain to see racism as 'something to do with the presence of black people'. But it is important to stress that both black and white people experience their gender, class and sexuality through 'race'. Racialisation of white subjectivity is often not manifestly apparent to white groups because 'white' is a signifier of dominance, but this renders the racialisation process no less significant. We need to analyse the processes which construct us as 'white female', 'black female', 'white male', 'black male' etc. We need to examine how and why the meanings of these words change from plain descriptions to hierarchically organised categories under given economic, political and social circumstances.

Avtar Brah

Black Feminism, White Feminism

During the 1970s there was a lack of much serious and sustained engagement with issues of gendered exploitation of post-colonial labour in the British metropolis, racism within state policies and cultural practices, the racialisation of black and white subjectivity in the specific context of a period following the loss of empire, and the particularities of black women's oppression within feminist theory and practice. This played an important part in the formation of black feminist organisations as distinct from the 'white' Women's Liberation Movement. These organisations emerged against the background of a deepening economic and political crisis and an increasing entrenchment of racism. The 1970s was a period when the Powellism of the 1960s came to suffuse the social fabric, and was gradually consolidated and transmuted into Thatcherism in the 1980s. The black communities were involved in a wide variety of political activity throughout the decade. There were major industrial strikes of which several were led by women. The Black Trade Union Solidarity Movement was formed to deal with racism in employment and trade unions. There were massive campaigns against immigration control, fascist violence, racist attacks on person and property, modes of policing that resulted in the harassment of black people, and against the criminalisation of black communities. There were many self-help projects concerned with educational, welfare and cultural activities. Black women were involved in all these activities, but the formation of autonomous black women's groups in the late 1970s injected a new dimension into the political scene.

The specific priorities of local black women's organisations, a number of which combined to form a national body – the Organisation of Women of Asian and African Descent (OWAAD), varied to an extent according to the exigencies of the local context. But the overall aim was to challenge the specific forms of oppression faced by the different categories of black women. The commitment to forging unity between African, Caribbean and Asian women demanded sustained attempts to analyse, understand and work with commonalities as well as heterogeneity of experience. It called for an interrogation of the role of colonialism and imperialism and that of contemporary economic, political and ideological processes in sustaining particular social divisions within these groups. It required black women to be sensitive to one another's cultural specificities while constructing common political strategies to confront sexism, racism and class inequality. This was no easy task, and it is a testimony to the political commitment and vision of the women involved that this project thrived for many years, and some of the local groups have survived the divisive impact of ethnicism and remain active today (Bryan, Dadzie and Scafe 1985; Brixton Black Women's Group 1984).

The demise of OWAAD as a national organisation in the early 1980s was precipitated by a number of factors. Many such divisive tendencies have been paralleled in the women's movement as a whole. The organisations affiliated to OWAAD shared its broad aims but there were political differences amongst women on various issues. There was general agreement that racism was crucial in structuring our oppression in Britain, but we differed in our analysis of racism and its links with class and other modes of inequality. For some women racism was an autonomous structure of oppression and had to be tackled as such; for others it was inextricably connected with class and other axes of social division. There were also differences in perspectives between feminists and non-feminists in OWAAD. For the latter, an emphasis on sexism was a diversion from the struggle against racism. The devaluation of black cultures by the onslaughts of racism meant that for some women the priority was to 'reclaim' these cultural sites and to situate themselves 'as women' within them. Whilst this was an important project there was, at times, more than a hint of idealising a lost past. Other women argued that, whilst the empowering aspects of culture did need to be affirmed and validated, it was equally important to examine how culture is also a terrain on which women's oppression is produced and reproduced. The problem of male violence against women and children, the unequal sexual division of labour in the household, questions of dowry and forced marriages, clitoridectomy, heterosexism and the suppression of lesbian sexualities: all these were issues demanding immediate attention. Although most women in OWAAD did not recognise the importance of these issues, there were nonetheless major differences about priorities and political strategies to deal with them.

Alongside these tendencies there was an emerging emphasis within the women's movement as a whole on identity politics. Instead of embarking on the complex but necessary task of sifting out the specificities of particular oppressions, identifying their similarities or connections with other oppressions, and building a politics of solidarity, some women were beginning to differentiate these specificities into hierarchies of oppression. The mere act of naming oneself as a member of an oppressed group was assumed to vest one with moral authority. Multiple oppressions came to be regarded not in terms of their patterns of articulation/interconnections – but rather as separate elements that could be added in a linear fashion, so that the more oppressions a woman could list the greater her claims to occupy a higher moral ground. Assertions about authenticity of personal experience could be presented as if they were an unproblematic guide to an understanding of processes of subordination and domination. Declarations concerning self-righteous political correctness sometimes came to substitute for careful political analysis (Adams 1989; Ardill and O'Sullivan 1986).

Despite the fragmentation of the women's movement, black women in Britain have continued to raise critical questions about feminist theory and practice. As a result of our location within diasporas formed by the history of slavery, colonialism and imperialism black feminists have consistently argued against parochialism and stressed the need for a feminism sensitive to the international social relations of power (Carby 1982; Parmar 1982; Feminist Review 1984; Brah and Minhas 1985; Brah 1987; Phoenix 1987; Grewal, Kay, Landor, Lewis and Parmar 1988; Mama 1989; Lewis 1990). Hazel Carby's article 'White Women Listen', for instance, presents a critique of such key feminist concepts as 'patriarchy', 'the family' and 'reproduction'. She criticises feminist perspectives which use notions of 'feudal residues' and 'traditionalism' to create sliding scales of 'civilised liberties', with the 'Third World' seen at one end of the scale and the supposedly progressive 'First World' at the other. She provides several illustrations of how a certain type of western feminism can serve to reproduce rather than challenge the categories through which 'the west' constructs and represents itself as superior to its 'others'.

These critiques have generated some critical self- reflection on the part of white feminist writers. Barrett and McIntosh (1985), for example, have attempted to reassess their earlier work. They acknowledge the limitations of the concept of patriarchy as unambiguous and invariable male dominance undifferentiated by class or racism, but wish to retain the notion of 'patriarchal' as signifying how 'particular social relations combine a public dimension of power, exploitation or status with a dimension of personal servility' (p.39). Having made this point, they fail to explore in any systematic way how and why the concept of the 'patriarchal' helps us to engage with the interconnections between gender, class and racism. The mere substitution of the concept of patriarchy by patriarchal relations will not by itself deal with the charges of ahistoricism, universalism or essentialism that have been levelled at the former (although, as Walby (1990) argues, it is possible to provide historicised accounts of patriarchy). As a response to recent reconceptualisations of patriarchy, Joan Acker suggests that it might be more appropriate to shift 'the theoretical object from patriarchy to gender, which we can define briefly as structural, relational, and symbolic differentiations between women and men' (Acker 1989: 238). She remains cautious about this shift, however, as 'gender', according to her, lacks the critical political sharpness of 'patriarchy' and could much more easily be co-opted and neutralised within 'mainstream' theory.

Patriarchal relations are a specific form of gender relations in which women inhabit a subordinated position. In theory, at least, it should be possible to envisage a social context in which gender relations are not associated with inequality between the sexes *qua* women and men. I would argue in favour of retaining the concept of 'patriarchal' without necessarily subscribing to the concept of 'patriarchy' – whether historicised or not – because I hold serious reservation about the analytic or political utility of maintaining system boundaries between 'patriarchy' and the particular socio-economic and political formation (e.g. capitalism or state socialism) with which it articulates. The issue is not whether patriarchal relations predate capitalism or state socialism, for they patently do, but how they are manifested within these systems in the context of a history of colonialism and imperialism in different parts of the globe. Structures of class, racism, gender and sexuality cannot be treated as 'independent variables' because the oppression of each is inscribed within the other – is constituted by and is constituted of the other.

Acknowledging the black feminist critique, Barrett and McIntosh stress the need to analyse the ideological construction of white femininity through racism. This in my view is essential since there is still a tendency to address questions of inequality through a focus on the victims of inequality. Discussions around feminism and racism often centre around the oppression of black women rather than exploring how both black and white women's gender is constructed through class and racism. This means that white women's 'privileged position' within racialised discourses (even when they may share a class position with black women) fails to be adequately theorised, and processes of domination remain invisible. The representation of white women as 'the moral guardians of a superior race', for instance, serves to homogenise white women's sexuality at the same time as it fractures it across class in that the white working-class woman, although also presented as 'carrier of the race', is simultaneously constructed as prone to 'degeneracy' because of her class background. Here we see how class contradictions may be worked through and 'resolved' ideologically within the racialised structuration of gender.

Barrett and McIntosh's article generated considerable debate (Ramazanoglu, Kazi, Lees and Safia-Mirza in *Feminist Review*, 22, 1986; Bhavnani and Coulson 1986). Whilst acknowledging the importance of the reassessment of a part of their work by two prominent white feminists, the critics argued that their methods of re-examination failed to provide the possibility of radical transformation of previous analysis, thus leaving the ways in which 'race' features within social reproduction largely untheorised. Although Barrett and McIntosh note that socialists are divided as to whether the social divisions associated with ethnicity and racism should be seen as absolutely autonomous of social class, as reducible to social class, or as having historical origins but articulating now with the divisions of class in capitalist society (p.38), they do not signal their own analytical preference on these issues. This is a surprising silence in an article whose aim is to advance our under-standing of conceptual and theoretical concerns in the field.

I would argue that racism is neither reducible to social class or gender nor wholly autonomous. Racisms have variable historical origins but they articulate with patriarchal class structures in specific ways under given historical conditions. Racisms have independent effectivity but to suggest this is not the same as saying, as Caroline Ramazanoglu (1989) does, that racism is an 'independent form of domination'. The search for grand theories specifying the interconnections between racism, gender and class has been less than productive. They are best construed as his-torically contingent and context-specific relationships. Hence, we can focus on a given context and differentiate between the demarcation of a category as an object of social discourse, as an analytical category, and as a subject of political mobilisation without making assumptions about their permanence or stability across time and space. This means that 'white' feminism or 'black' feminism in Britain are not essentialist cate-gories but rather they are fields of contestation inscribed within discur-sive and material processes and practices in a post-colonial terrain. They represent struggles over political frameworks for analysis; the meanings of theoretical concepts; the relationship between theory, practice and subjective experiences; and over political priorities and modes of mobil-isations, but they should not, in my view, be understood as locating 'white' and 'black' women as 'essentially' fixed oppositional categories.

More recent contributions to the debate make the point that irrespec-tive of the intentions of the authors, anti-racist feminist discourses of the late 1970s and 1980s did not always facilitate political mobilisation. Knowles and Mercer (1990), for example, take the position that Carby's and Bourne's emphasis on the inscription of racism and gender inequal-ity within processes of capitalism, colonialism and patriarchal social systems produced functionalist arguments – that sexism and racism were inherent within these systems and served the needs of these sys-tems to perpetuate themselves. They believe that this approach demand-ed nothing short of an all-embracing struggle against these 'isms' that thereby undermined more localised, small-scale political responses. Their own method of dealing with this is to suggest that racism and sex-ism be 'viewed as a series of effects which do not have a single cause' of abstraction at which categories such as 'capitalism' or 'patriarchal rela-tions' are delineated does not provide straightforward guidelines for concrete strategy and action, and also that racism and sexism are not monocausal phenomena. Nonetheless, I am not sure how treating racism and sexism as a 'series of effects' provides any clearer guidelines for political response. The same 'effect' may be interpreted from a variety of political positions, and lead to quite different strategies for action. Taking up a specific political position means that one is making certain assumptions about the nature of the various processes that underline a social phenomenon of which a particular event may be an effect. A focus only on 'effects' may render invisible the workings of such ideological and material processes, thereby hindering our understanding of the complex basis of inequalities. Although crucial in mobilising specific constituencies the single-issue struggles as ends in themselves may delimit wider-ranging challenges to social inequalities. The language of 'effects' in any case assumes the existence of some causes. The main issue is not whether we should jettison macro-level analysis of gender or racism in relation to capitalism, colonialism or state socialism in favour of empirically grounded analysis of the concrete manifestations of racism in a given local situation, but how each is overdetermined by, and also helps to determine, the others.

I share Knowles and Mercer's reservations about analytical and political perspectives in which social inequality comes to be personified in the bodies of the dominant social groups – white people, men, or heterosexual individuals in relation to racism, sexism or heterosexism – but we cannot ignore the social relations of power that inscribe such differentiations. Members of dominant groups do occupy privileged positions within political and material practices that attend these social divisions, although the precise interplay of this power in specific institutions or in interpersonal relations cannot be stipulated in advance, may be contradictory and can be challenged.

A somewhat different critique of black feminist writing challenges the validity of black feminism as representing anything more than the interests of black women (Tang Nain 1990). By implication black feminism is cast as sectarian in comparison with radical or socialist feminism. This comparison is problematic since it constructs black feminism as outside radical or socialist feminism. In practice, the category 'black feminism' in Britain is meaningful only *vis-à-vis* the category 'white feminism'. If, as I have argued earlier, these two categories are contingent rather than essentialist, then one cannot ask the question as Tang Nain does whether 'black feminism' is open to all women without simultaneously asking the same question of 'white feminism'. Tang Nain's characterisation of radical or socialist feminism as 'open to all women' runs in the face of massive evidence which shows that in Britain and USA at least, these feminisms have failed to take adequate account of racism and the experience of racialised groups of women.

The ideology of 'open to all' can in fact legitimise all kinds of *de facto* exclusion. Socialist feminism, for example, cannot really include women who are subjected to racism unless it is a non-racist socialist feminism, or lesbian women unless it is simultaneously non-heterosexist, or lower-caste women unless it is also non-casteist. But these issues cannot be realised in the abstract, nor can they be settled once for all, but through ongoing political struggles.

For similar reasons Floya Anthias and Nira Yuval-Davis's critique of the category 'black' on the grounds that it failed to address diversity of ethnic exclusions and subordinations seems misplaced (Anthias and Yuval-Davis, 1982). The boundaries of a political constituency formed around specific concerns is dependent upon the nature of the concerns and their salience and significance in the lives of the people so affected. Black feminism constructed a constituency in terms of the gendered experience of anti-black racism. White ethnic groups who were not subjected to this particular form of racism could not, therefore, be part of this constituency. This does not mean that their experiences of, say, anti-semitism are any the less important. Rather, anti-black racism and anti-semitism cannot be subsumed under each other. This becomes patently clear if we compare the experiences of a white Jewish woman and a black Jewish woman. The black woman is simultaneously positioned within two racialised discourses. Anthias and Yuval-Davis make some incisive points about ethnicity as a category of social differentiation but their contention that 'black feminism can be too wide or too narrow a category for specific feminist struggles' (p.63) remains problematic since the emergence of the black women's movement as a historically specific response is a testament that organisation around the category 'black women' is possible. This need not preclude coalitions across other boundaries, and black women have worked with white women on several issues of common concern. Any alternatives to the political category 'black' such as 'women of colour', or some term as yet not in currency may emerge through organic involvement in new struggles set against a changed economic and political climate. But they cannot be willed in the abstract or decided in advance.

My proposition that 'black' and 'white' feminisms be addressed as non-essentialist, historically contingent discursive practices implies that black and white women can work together towards the creation of non-racist feminist theory and practice. The key issue then is not about 'difference' *per se*, but concerns the question of who defines difference, how different categories of women are represented within the discourses of 'difference', and whether 'difference' differentiates laterally or hierarchically. We need greater conceptual clarity in analysing difference.

Difference, What Difference?

It is evident that the concept of difference is associated with different meanings in different discourses. But how are we to understand 'difference'? A detailed discussion of this topic is beyond the scope of this chapter but I would like to suggest four ways in which difference may be conceptualised and addressed.

Difference as Experience

Experience has been a key concept within feminism. Women's movements have aimed to give a collective voice to women's personal experiences of social and psychic forces that constitute the 'female' into the 'woman'. The everyday of the social relations of gender – ranging from housework and child care, low-paid employment and economic dependency to sexual violence and women's exclusion form key centres of political and cultural power – have all been given a new significance through feminism as they have been brought out of the realm of the 'taken for granted' to be interrogated and challenged. The personal with its profoundly concrete yet elusive qualities, and its manifold contradictions, acquired new meanings in the slogan 'the personal is political' as conscious-raising groups provided the forums for exploring individual experiences, personal feelings and women's own understandings of their daily lives.

The limitations of the consciousness-raising method (empowering though it was for some women) as a strategy for systematically challenging the structures of gender inequality have been widely acknowledged. Nonetheless there was at least an implicit recognition in this mode of working that experience did not transparently reflect reality, but instead it was a constellation of mediated relationships, a site of contradictions to be addressed collectively. This insight is quite often missing from current discussions about differences between women where difference and experience are used primarily as a 'commonsensical term' (Barrett 1987). Hence, the need to re-emphasise a notion of experience not as unmediated guide to 'truth' but as a practice of making sense, both symbolically and narratively; as struggle over material conditions and over meaning.

Difference as Social Relation

The emphasis here is on social relations at the level of the social structure. A group usually mobilises the concept of difference in this sense of a social relation when addressing the structural, political and historical basis of the commonality of its experience. Experience is understood here primarily in terms of collective histories.

In practice, the everyday of lived experience and experience as a social relation do not exist in mutually exclusive spaces. For example, if we speak of 'north African women in France', we are, on the one hand, referring to the social relations of gendered post-coloniality in France. On the other hand, we are also making a statement about the everyday experience of this post-coloniality on the part of such women, although we cannot specify, in advance, the particularity of individual women's lives or how they interpret and define this experience. In both instances, the question of how difference is defined remains paramount. Are perceptions of difference in a given context a basis of affirming diversity or a mechanism for exclusionary and discriminatory practices? Do discourses of difference legitimise progressive or oppressive state policies and practices? How are different categories of women represented within such discourses? How do the women themselves construct or represent the specificity of their experience? Under what circumstances does 'difference' become the basis of asserting a collective identity?

Difference as Subjectivity

Issues of difference have been central to theoretical debates around subjectivity. A key question facing us is: how are racialised subjects formed? But the question of racialisation of subjectivity has not yet received much attention within feminist theory, which has been preoccupied primarily with the status of 'sexual difference' in the formation of subjectivity. Feminists have turned to psychoanalysis (notably its post-structuralist and object-relations variants) and to forms of deconstructionist thought to understand the processes of identity formation.

With the growing awareness that women's innermost emotions, feelings, desires and fantasies with their multiple contradictions could not be understood purely in terms of the imperatives of the social institutions and the forces of male domination, feminists have approached psychoanalysis for a more complex account of the trials and tribulations of psychic life. Dissatisfied with the social conditioning approaches to women's psychology, some feminists have looked to Lacan's rereading of Freud for a non-reductive understanding of subjectivity. Post-structuralist accounts have proved attractive to feminism, for they seek to problematise 'sexual difference': sexual difference is something to be explained rather than assumed. Subjectivity is seen as neither unified nor fixed – rather it is something that is constantly in progress. Compelling arguments have been made in favour of the importance of psychoanalysis for feminism against those critics who assume that the notion of a fragmented sexual identity constantly in process is at odds with the feminist project of constructing oppositional consciousness through collective action (cf. Rose 1986; Penley 1989; Minsky 1990).

These arguments are convincing, but certain issues still need to be addressed. The enormous contribution of individuals such as Fanon notwithstanding, much work is yet to be undertaken on the subject of how the racialised 'other' is constituted in the psychic domain. How is post-colonial gendered and racialised subjectivity to be analysed? Does the privileging of 'sexual difference' and early childhood in psychoanalysis limit its explanatory value in helping understand psychic dimensions of social phenomena such as racism? How do the 'symbolic order' and the social order articulate in the formation of the subject? In other words, how is the link between social and psychic reality to be theorised? There is also the issue of how certain psychoanalytical discourses are themselves implicated in the inscription of racism (Dalal 1988).

Difference as Identity

Our struggles over meaning are also our struggles over different modes of being: different identities (Minh-ha 1989). Identity is never a fixed core. On the other hand, changing identities do assume specific, concrete patterns, as in a kaleidoscope, against particular sets of historical and social circumstances. Our cultural identities are simultaneously our cultures in process but they acquire specific meanings in a given context. Social phenomena such as racism seek to fix and naturalise 'difference' and create impervious boundaries between groups. The modalities of difference inscribed within the particularities of our personal and collective historical, cultural and political experience – our ethnicities – can interrogate and challenge the strangulating imagination of racism, but the task is a complex one, for ethnicities are liable to be appropriated by racism as signifiers of permanent boundaries. Hence, the 'Englishness' of a particular class can come to represent itself via racism as 'Britishness' against those ethnicities that it subordinates – such as those of the Irish, Scottish, Welsh, black British, or the ethnicities of the formerly colonised world. But, as I noted earlier, 'white'/European ethnicities are subordinated differently from non-white, non-European ethnicities.

It should be possible through political practice to retrieve ethnicity from racialised nationalist discourses so that it can be manifested as a non-essentialist horizontality rather than hierarchically organised difference. As Stuart Hall says:

The fact that this grounding of ethnicity in difference was deployed, in the discourse of racism, as a means of disavowing the realities of racism and repression does not mean that we can permit the term to be permanently colonised. That appropriation from its position in the discourse of 'multi-culturalism' and transcoded, just as we previously had to recuperate the term 'black', from its place in a system of negative equivalences (Hall 1988: 27)

But the project is always beset with difficulties. Since ethnicities are always gendered they construct sexual difference in specific ways. The appropriation of a particular ethnicity cannot be assumed necessarily to involve challenging gender inequalities unless this is undertaken as a conscious objective. Indeed, the reverse may be the case. Similarly, depending upon the context, ethnicities may legitimise class or caste divisions by proclaiming and stressing only the unity of an otherwise heterogeneous group.

So how can we claim ethnicities that do not reinforce inequalities? The project is complex but broadly will entail a variety of concrete practices at the economic, political and cultural level designed to undermine the relations of power that underlie these inequalities. There will be the need to remain vigilant of the circumstances under which affirmation of a particular collective experience becomes an essentialist assertion of difference. This problem may arise not only in relation to dominant ethnicities but also dominated ethnicities. In their struggle against the hegemonic, universalising imperatives of the former, the latter may also take recourse to constructing essentialist differences. This can be especially problematic for women if the cultural values that the groups in question excavate, recast, and reconstruct are those that underscore women's subordination.

Although I have argued against essentialism, it is not easy to deal with this problem. In their need to create new political identities, dominated groups will often appeal to bonds of common cultural experience in order to mobilise their constituency. In so doing they may assert a seemingly essentialist difference. Spivak (1987) and Fuss (1989) have argued in favour of such a 'strategic essentialism'. They believe that the 'risk' of essentialism may be worth taking if framed from the vantage point of a dominated subject position. This will remain problematic if a challenge to one form of oppression leads to the reinforcement of another. It may be over-ambitious, but it is imperative that we do not compartmentalise oppressions, but instead formulate strategies for challenging all oppressions on the basis of .n understanding of how they interconnect and articulate.

14

The Ideological Representation of Migrant Workers in Europe: A Matter of Racialisation?

Jan Rath

Introduction

Social scientists working in the field of post-migration studies tend to show a greater interest in the situation in surrounding countries than ever before. Although the number of scientists actually involved in international comparative research projects is still relatively low, the tendency to adopt a more 'European' perspective is unmistakable. This tendency is probably due to the remarkable parallelism of the situation in various European countries but also to current political developments, such as the breaking apart of the eastern bloc, the removal of the internal frontiers within the European Community and the subsequent attuning of immigration policies. International researchers generally compare the situation in their own country with the situation elsewhere, thereby producing empirical data with heuristic value or practical relevance. Sometimes, under certain conditions, their projects contribute to the advancement of theoretical debate. However, according to Bovenkerk et al. (1991), who examined a great number of international comparative studies of migration and exclusion on the grounds of 'race' and ethnic background in western Europe, this does not occur very often.

International projects bristle with difficulties and pitfalls, one of them being the problem of conceptualisation. It is not a matter of course at all that 'common concepts' are appropriate for adequately describing and explaining social phenomena in every European country. Bovenkerk et al. ascertain that many international comparative research projects fail to produce valid results because researchers apply theories and concepts with a strong national bias. The specific political and ideological circumstances in a specific country and the prevailing sociological discourse including its epistemological taken-for-granted logic interfere in their work. Bovenkerk et al. argue in favour of a theoretical framework – preferably of a neo-Marxian type – which is sufficiently abstract to enable international researchers to transcend the historical specificity of the countries researched. This does not mean, however, that the historical specificity of the various countries should be ignored. On the contrary, Bovenkerk et al. and also other writers such as Hall (1980) underline the importance of investigating this very specificity. The point is, though, that one needs to have a framework sufficiently abstract to get a sharp picture of it. What Bovenkerk et al. demand is no less than a critical evaluation of existing national research traditions and – if necessary – even fundamental changes. This is a challenging exercise.

This paper is written as a contribution to that exercise. Here, I focus on the ideological representation of migrant workers, and question whether this process can be described and explained in every circumstance by the concepts of *'race'*, *racialisation* or *racism*. These concepts have gained enormous ground in present day sociological discourse on post-migration phenomena. While acknowledging the existence of specific forms of problematisation of migrant workers and practices of social exclusion, I am not sure whether every instance can be caught by these popular concepts. I illustrate my theoretical argument with the case of the official recognition of organisations of Islamic migrant workers in the Netherlands.

Ideological Representation

My concern with this epistemological problematic stems from the following theoretical considerations (for a more extensive discussion, see Bovenkerk et al. 1990; Rath 1991). The point of departure is the assumption that, at a general level, similar processes occur in every social formation, namely processes of production and distribution, and that these processes assume a different, specific form in each nation state. So, on an abstract level, the situation in Belgium, Britain, the Netherlands or Sweden is not unique at all. This theoretical position permits one to distance oneself from the specificity of the national context.

The position of migrant workers (and others) in social relations is the product of a process of distribution of scarce resources. In order to continue the dominant mode of production, to regulate scarcity and to maintain the unity of the nation state, migrant workers take specific class positions and have specific access to scarce goods and services. This process of distribution contains a political component, since it is the result of political decisions on the matter. But it also contains an ideological component. Political decisions on the distribution of resources occur by means of an ideologically constructed hierarchy of social categories, something which assumes a specific form in each nation state. How much or little access to scarce resources someone has depends on his or her position in that hierarchy.

The construction of this hierarchy is part of the process of ideological representation, which is 'the process of depicting the social world and social processes, of creating a sense of how things "really are"' (Miles 1989: 70; see also Hall 1981: 31). This process does not need to be based on undeniable facts nor result in a coherent and rational vision on the entire human race. On the contrary, ideological representations usually assume the form of a set of common sense notions, views and preassumptions about the social world.

A key moment in the process of ideological representation concerns the process of signification, i.e. the process of attributing meanings 'to particular objects, features and processes, in such a way that the latter are given special significance, and carry or are embodied with a set of additional, second order features' (Miles 1989: 70). Out of a whole range of objects, features and processes, only certain ones – such as phenotype, sex, religion, nationality – are chosen to convey additional meaning. They are subsequently seen as a sign of the existence of another real or imagined reality. This ideological process results in the construction of certain social categories. The construction of 'races', for instance, is the result of a process of racialisation, and so is the occurrence of 'race relations' as a certain type of social relations.

The categories constructed are not necessarily ranked in an ideological hierarchy. Only by attaching positive or negative meaning to the signified characteristics are the various collectivities positioned vis-à-vis each other. In practice, the construction of a hierarchy is complicated by the fact that different processes of signification take place at the same time and are even linked with each other, giving rise to new ideological forms and social relations. This does not mean that every representation distinguishable from another is equally important. In a specific conjuncture, some may predominate.

These ideological processes of signification, categorisation and ranking – voiced through discourses – are most important, yet they do not determine political or other processes. Firstly, there are intervening variables, such as the prevailing rules and regulations, the economic conjuncture, political factors of another order etc. Secondly, reverse processes are also possible. A certain political distribution sanctions and legitimises the ideological representation of specific social categories. This can strengthen an unequal distribution of resources, but can also provoke counter-actions or the development of counter-ideologies by the deprivileged categories and/or their allies.

Anyway, for our understanding of the position of these collectivities, the process of signification and the subsequent ideological construction of social categories are essential. Particularly important are the central characteristics that in a specific social formation make up the predominant ideological representation of migrant workers, and the evaluation of those characteristics.

Racialisation and Racism and the Construction of 'Races' in Britain

In Britain, there is a vast literature on these processes, both documenting the problematisation of migrant workers and theorising about the subject (e.g. Anthias 1990; Gilroy 1987; Hall 1980; Miles 1989; Modood 1988; Solomos 1988, 1989). What British authors put forward on this matter – that is to say on the British case[1] – is especially interesting considering the dominance of British sociological discourse in Europe. (As for this, it should be remembered that international researchers often express themselves in English and are inclined to use the available Anglo-Saxon concepts). Notwithstanding the fact that the authors emphasise different sociological aspects and are engaged in debates among themselves on various matters, they share a number of important theoretical notions. They unequivocally argue that a particular group of migrant workers – namely those coming from the Caribbean or the south Asian subcontinent – are constructed as a specific 'race', namely the 'black race' distinguishable from the 'white race' of natives.[2] Furthermore, they argue that additional, negatively evaluated characteristics are attached to the 'black race' and that their presence in British society is seen as causing severe social problems. The consequence of this racist ideology is the ranking of these specific categories of migrant workers and their offspring among the lower positions in the social hierarchy. In the view of these authors, these ideological processes serve to explain why black migrant workers are excluded from privileged positions and resources.

Of course, this simplified description cannot convey the theoretical complexity of the debate, but what matters here is the general under-

1. One should bear in mind that the empirical basis of their theoretical statements is British society only. Their statements should be put in this perspective.
2. At this point, some researchers, Modood (1988) for one, make a sharp distinction between migrant workers coming from the Caribbean and migrant workers from the south Asian continent.

standing that people in Britain are constructed and ideologically represented as 'races' and that racism interferes in these processes.

The opinions diverge, however, when it comes to specifying what
exactly constitutes 'race' and racism. This divergence is partly due to
the fact that, in the opinion of many authors, racism is not fixed but historically specific. Racism can thus vary from time and place to political
and economical circumstances. As a matter of fact, this is why Hall
(1980: 336ff; 1989) and others suggest using the concept of racism in its
plural form: racisms. But the acknowledgement of this historical specificity – how much it may be true – does not get us around the real problem: that of conceptualising 'race' and racism. To be sure: the problem
is not conceptual diversity, but the lack of conceptual sharpness (cf.
Miles 1991). The things that need sharpening revolve, amongst others,
round the following questions: Is racism restricted to the process of ideological exclusion on mere grounds of phenotypical characteristics (i.e.
colour)? Or does racism also refer to instances in which people are
defined on grounds of ethno-cultural, national or religious characteristics? To what extent is the colonial project relevant for the existence of
racism? Can racism exist outside the ideological domain? The answers
to these questions are important since they determine how the ideological constructions of social categories – in this specific instance: the category of 'race' – can be envisaged.

Conceptual sharpness and clarity have constantly been affected by new
evidence of problematising migrant workers and other people particularly
from so-called Third World countries and new evidence of social exclusion. These 'new' phenomena – seemingly for the first time in history not
only in distant colonial areas, but in the very centre of the British empire –
have caused some people to redefine the concepts of racism and 'race'.
Some include practices of social exclusion of black migrant workers in
their definition of racism; others only include specific discourses.

Barker (1981), for instance, discovered that migrant workers in
Britain are not so much problematised on purely biological grounds but
rather on ethno-cultural grounds. He argues that this ideological representation contrasts with nineteenth-century ideas about racism and is to
be considered as the contemporary manifestation of it. Anthias (1990)
also asserts that racism does not need to have purely biological or phys-
iognomic markers or signifiers. Ethnic signifiers, i.e. signifiers that
according to Anthias might be linked to culture, language or territorium,
can also function as such. Modood (1990b), using a different theoretical
framework, identifies a religious dimension in racism, which is manifested in the form of 'Muslimphobia'.

The content of the concept of 'race' has been changed likewise.
Modood (1990a: 31), for instance, argues that 'race should be under-

stood not only in terms of colour and class but in terms of culture as well'. In so doing, religion is envisaged as an aspect of 'race'.

Broad conceptualisations such as the ones given here certainly have their attraction. They allow widely divergent phenomena to be lumped together and related to each other and this offers interesting perspectives for anti-racist political struggle. Their strength is thus their relative simplicity, which may prove to be useful when mobilising anti-racist forces.

But does stretching the concepts enables us better to understand the ideological representation and social exclusion of migrant workers in a particular nation state? Not necessarily. The social world is complex and cannot always be captured by simple, uniform concepts. It is an *a priori* assumption that (seemingly) related phenomena have a similar sociological origin or meaning. Miles (1989: 41–68) in his book *Racism* dedicates a whole chapter to what he calls the problem of 'conceptual inflation'. This 'conceptual inflation' occurs amongst others by confusing racism with nationalism and sexism. Miles gives a number of theoretical reasons for not stretching ('inflating') the concept of racism. He argues convincingly that racism, sexism and nationalism are ideological processes of an essentially different order with the likelihood of having different practical consequences. Researchers who still use a broader and thus less distinguishing definition of racism will not fully appreciate this. Therefore, a more restricted conceptualisation with greater analytical power is by all means preferable for getting a sharp and less reductionist picture of reality. This may imply the development of new concepts with new terms.[3]

Miles (1989: 76–7) suggests reserving the concepts of racialisation and racism – he distinguishes between the two – for only those instances in which 'meaning is attributed to particular biological features of human beings, as a result of which individuals may be assigned to a general category of persons which reproduces itself biologically'. Further in his book, he argues that not only biological characteristics – real or alleged – but also cultural characteristics can be signified in the processes of racialisation and racism. But, as Miles elaborates elsewhere (1991), he refers only to those instances of signification of cultural characteristics in which these are seen as 'naturalised'. The collectivities thus constructed ('races') are 'represented as having a natural, unchanging origin and status, and therefore as being inherently different' (Miles 1989: 79). Interestingly, this notion can also be found in the work of Anthias (1990, 1991a) who, by the way, applies a somewhat broader

---

3. Riggs (1991: 283–4) argues that the development of new concepts and terms is common in the natural sciences. In the social sciences, though, there appears to be a strong aversion against neologisms.

definition. She also refers to 'race' as something which is constructed 'on the basis of an immutable fixed biologically or physiognomically based difference. This may be seen to be expressed in culture or lifestyle but is always grounded in some notion of stock, involving the collective heredity of traits' (1990: 22). For Miles, the 'naturalisation of domination' (1991) is a typical feature of the predominant ideological process in Britain.

Culturalisation, Immigrisation and Minorisation

Now I turn to the question to what extent this holds for other European countries too. Can racialisation and racism in the strict sense of the term be identified as ideological processes of primary importance in other countries than Britain? Various authors assert that this is the case (see Essed 1991; Silverman 1991; van Dijk 1987; Wilpert, in this volume). While appreciating their accounts, it occurs to me they take the broader Anglo-Saxon concepts of 'race', racialisation and racism for granted and assume *a priori* that the ideological representation of migrant workers in Britain, Belgium, Sweden, the Netherlands or any other social formation in Europe does not really differ. But essential differences do exist at this point. The authors may overlook these differences, simply because they analyse the problematisation of migrant workers as mere varieties of racism. A more restricted conceptualisation would reveal subtle but important nuances. In my view, racialisation and racism *in the strict sense* of the terms are not as significant a process as is sometimes suggested in countries such as Belgium, Sweden and the Netherlands, where at least the *predominant* ideological representation does not turn so much round phenotypical or naturalised cultural characteristics.

Martiniello (1990), for instance, who studied the political empowerment of Italian migrant workers in the French-speaking part of Belgium, identifies a process of *immigrisation*, which is the signification of the 'newcomerness' of migrants. Migrants are represented as a threat to the fragile relations between the two linguistic communities. As newcomers, their loyalty to one community or the other is uncertain as yet. By placing these newcomers ideologically and subsequently politically outside the 'imagined community' of Belgians, the potential violation of the social balance and the public order is neutralised. According to Martiniello, this undermines the political empowerment of migrant workers in Belgian society.

Ålund and Schierup (1991) analyse the situation in Sweden in terms of *culturalisation*. Migrant workers are problematised on the basis of their cultural characteristics. Initially, the Swedish state strengthened their cultural identity in an attempt to anticipate social problems. Today in dominant discourse, their cultural identity is considered as the major obstacle for the desired integration of migrant workers.

In the Netherlands, I have identified and labelled the dominant ideological process as one of *ethnic minorisation* (Rath 1991). This ideological construction of 'ethnic minorities' occurs on the basis of socio-cultural and class characteristics. Socio-cultural characteristics are signified and utilised to typify individuals and sort them in groups. The latter is done by comparing these socio-cultural characteristics with the imagined middle-class standard. So, on the one hand there are people who conform to the Dutch middle-class standard and have a desirable lifestyle and, on the other hand, there are people who do not conform to this standard and have undesirable lifestyles. In practice, the lower one's class position, the more negatively one's non-conformity is evaluated. This is a process which, in a previous historical phase, resulted in the construction of a social category of 'anti-socials' (*onmaatschappelijken*), i.e. a category of indigenous people who constituted the lowest class fractions and who exibited, according to the state and private institutions, undesirable behaviour. Today, the objects of this process are specific migrants, such as Turks and Moroccans, but not American, German, British or Japanese migrants who generally occupy higher class positions. The socio-cultural non-conformity of the former migrants is usually related to their foreign origin. Therefore the term '*ethnic* minorities' is used. This ideology contibutes to the positioning of migrant workers outside privileged social positions. As long as 'ethnic minorities' are defined as people that conform inadequately to the Dutch way of life, they are not considered to be fully-fledged members of the 'Dutch imagined community' and are consequently granted less access to scarce resources.

Minorisation, being an ideology of dominance, differs fundamentally from ethnicisation or ethnic categorisation, which treats ethnic belonging *per se* on an equal basis, whereas in the Dutch case 'ethnic belonging' is reinterpreted as a form of non-conformity and thus undesirability.

Minorisation also differs fundamentally from racialisation in the strict sense of the term. After all, minorisation is not a matter of 'naturalisation'. Contrary to 'races', 'ethnic minorities' (in the Dutch sense of the term) are not 'represented as having a natural, unchanging origin and status, and therefore as being inherently different' (cf. Miles 1989: 79). This is a crucial point. In the eyes of the Dutch, the socio-cultural non-conformity of the lower classes can and ought to be changed. This also holds for the non-conformity of the lower-class fractions constituted by migrant workers. Only then, under certain conditions, are they accepted as members with full access to scarce resources. The state and private agents are willing to help migrant workers to reach this state, amongst other means by supporting and creating group specific institutions *outside the mainstream* that are supposed to serve the processes of adaptation and integration. For the rest, minorisation and racialisation are comparable: as ideologies of dominance they are functionally equivalent.[4]

Incidentally, a more restricted conceptualisation would also allow for distinguishing ideological varieties within one nation state. The discourse about Islamic migrant workers illustrates this argument, since they constitute a social category with somewhat different representations. As for this, it is significant that Modood (1990a) refers to religion and colour next to class when analysing the situation of Muslims in Britain, something which indicates that their ideological representation is the product of the ideological articulation of at least racialisation and Islamisation. At this point, the situation in the Netherlands shows interesting differences. Let us now examine this situation.

Islamic Migrant Workers in the Netherlands

Turks and Moroccans constitute numerically the most important groups of Muslims in the Netherlands: more than three quarters of the total of 400,000 Muslims are Turks and Moroccans. Therefore I focus on their situation. They, or rather the older men among them, were recruited as 'guestworkers' in the 1960s and early 1970s. Their presence had a strict economic function and was generally considered as a temporary affair. Contrary to common belief, many of them stayed and had their families come to the Netherlands. From the very beginning the 'guestworkers' had been minorised, i.e. had been considered as people whose ways of living were different from that of the native Dutch (Rath 1991: 149ff). In many publications of that time, guestworkers were portrayed as having a 'different mentality', 'disposition' and 'character', and as having 'deviating and strange customs', something which was usually related to their foreign origin. These foreign people with their 'southern nature' and 'different cultural background' would be 'frustrated' and 'disorientated'. Particularly 'guestworkers' of 'low calibre' who 'lack the adaptability' to the Dutch way of life would suffer from 'innumerable problems of adaptation'. Their very presence would, in all, be the 'source of social tensions'.

This ideological representation shaped the immigration policies of both the state and private organisations. Both designed various programmes to tackle the problems – defined in the first place as socio-cul-

---

4. To paraphrase Memmi (1983), both can be interpreted as instances of 'heterophobia'.

tural problems – arising from the presence of the Mediterranean 'guest-workers'. State-sponsored group-specific social work and community-building programmes were set up to help the 'guestworkers' adapt their ways of life gradually to the imagined Dutch – i.e. middle- class – way of life. As for this, it should be noted that 'ethnic minorities' constitute a part of the working class. The establishment of an extensive network of group-specific welfare institutions was the result (see also Rath and Saggar 1992: 213ff).

In the early 1980s, the state strongly intensified this policy of 'controlled integration'. Compared to the previous period, the so-called Ethnic Minorities Policy became less welfare-oriented and more oriented towards work, education and to some extent also to the field of politics. The dominant ideological representation of the categories concerned did not fundamentally change, though. The 'ethnic minorities', as they were officially labelled from then on, or 'cultural minorities', were still considered as people who conformed inadequately to the Dutch way of life and who therefore were not considered as fully-fledged members of the 'Dutch imagined community'.

Before the early 1980s, the state and other institutions seldom paid attention to religious matters. It is significant that the report on 'ethnic minorities' by the Scientific Council for the Government Policy (WRR 1979), a report which marks the political changes round 1980, does not contain one reference to Islam or Muslims. Interestingly, the Ministry of Culture, Recreation and Social Work (CRM) did grant some financial aid to places of worship of Muslims, provided that these places were run by Muslims from Mediterranean countries only (Rath, Groenendijk and Penninx 1991). Such a regulation was in force between 1976 and 1981. Among the reasons for giving financial assistance to Islamic institutions was the belief that Islam was an essential element of the Turkish and Moroccan ways of life, and that one ought to take account of that. It was hoped that such assistance would stimulate the integration of these migrant workers in Dutch society (Hampsink 1992). Interestingly, the leadership of Turkish and Moroccan Islamic organisations were not very willing to talk with representatives of the state about any matter unless financial aid was given.

When the implementation of the Ethnic Minorities Policy was in full swing, the Ministry of Culture, Recreation and Social Work designed a new regulation, one which was in force from 1981 till 1984. This regulation concerned financial aid to places of worship for Muslims among the 'ethnic minorities', which means that Surinamese and Moluccan Muslims could apply for a grant too. This underlines once more that Muslims were minorised and that Islam was considered as one of many aspects of 'ethnic minority' culture.

It should be noted that the signification of Islam – Islamisation – affected the representation of the migrant workers, too. This process has a long history which goes beyond the recent arrival of Islamic migrant workers (cf. Said 1978; Lutz 1991b). The relations for example between Dutch institutions, including the state, and institutions of Islamic migrant workers were always complicated by this process. In practice, however, the process of minorisation had more impact.

The articulation of these representations did not always go without struggle. This is well illustrated by the case of the official recognition of organisations of Islamic migrant workers by the Rotterdam local authorities (*gemeente*), a process which began around 1980 and did not come to a conclusion before the mid 1980s.[5] Among the practical consequences of this recognition is the fact that these organisations have become eligible for specific subsidies, and at another level, the development of a more coherent policy regulating the settlement of places of worship within the city. The present leadership of local Islamic organisations considers the recognition as an important move in the direction of improvement in the position of Islam in the Netherlands, whereas the local authorities consider it as an important move in the direction of integration of 'ethnic minority' families. The latter is shown by the following statement from the memorandum 'The new Rotterdammers' in which the Rotterdam municipal executive (*College van Burgemeester en Wethouders*) unfolds its policy regarding 'ethnic minorities' in the 1990s (Gemeente Rotterdam 1991: 5–6):

> We have already established that social disadvantage is not restricted to categories of the population of foreign origin. However, the differences in culture, origin and background between migrants and Dutch are big. This should be given due consideration when setting up a 'revised ethnic minorities policy' ... This begs for optimal commitment of the migrants and their organisations. Particularly Turkish and Moroccan groupings should be approached and encouraged to become active in broader social areas. We expect that in the coming years groupings of which the Islamic religion and the Islamic culture are the sources of inspiration will display greater activities in social affairs ... It takes much prudence to give a suitable answer to that in this age of depillarisation ... When ... the social intercourse of, for instance, Muslims goes off largely separated from the rest of society, this can constitute a serious barrier to their emancipation and integration. The surplus value of group-specific facilities and attainments should be that one can work on equal terms on the emancipation of cultural minorities within the existing social order.

5. The findings here are preliminary results of a research project in progress. This research project goes into the role of various institutions, but in this chapter I focus on the prevailing ideological representations of the local authorities in the city of Rotterdam.

The municipal executive has not always had this ideological position. Fourteen years ago, in the 'Memorandum, Migrants in Rotterdam', the municipal executive defended a rather different position (Gemeente Rotterdam 1978: 71–2). Then, Islamic organisations ('mosques') were thought to be able to contribute to the formation of social structures that would diminish 'the chances of social desorientation'. Next to that it was assumed that Islam – partly through the convergence of Islamic and Rotterdamese opinions – would contribute to the 'mutual integration' of Muslims and other Rotterdammers. The municipal executive emphasised that the state in the Netherlands did not accept 'the slightest responsibility, including financial ones, for the church' and that it could never be its intention to give 'the Muslim community' preference over other 'religious communities'. It also pointed to 'the fact' that Turkish *Grey Wolves* and Moroccan *Amicales* – both being extreme nationalistic, if not fascistic organisations – employed the mosques as 'means of control and even oppression'. The municipal executive had enough reasons to keep their distance from Islam and Islamic migrant workers as much as possible. This attitude basically implied maintaining the status quo, i.e. maintaining the situation in which Islamic migrant workers were not really able to make any claim on public resources such as for a suitable place of worship and financial support for their activities.

Notwithstanding their reserve, the municipal executive did mediate occasionally between Islamic organisations and the Ministry of Welfare, Recreation and Social Work (CRM) which in this period provided small block grants for the foundation of places of worship. The relations with secular, progressive organisations of migrant workers contrasted sharply with this reserve. These organisations were heavily subsidised for their accomodation and socio-cultural and educational projects. Besides, with the encouragement of the local authorities, secular organisations were able to monopolise the relations between the authorities and migrant workers.

But changes were at hand. Within the municipal civil service – particularly within the Migrants Bureau, i.e. the bureaucratic department which was concerned with the development and implementation of the local Ethnic Minorities Policy – there was profound discussion about the question of whether the exclusion of Islamic organisations would be tenable any longer. In October 1981 the Migrants Bureau produced a note about this topic. In this note, civil servants focused on the problem that many places of worship did not comply with building and fire safety regulations. They concluded that something should be done about this. In the light of their function as a meeting place, the closing down of mosques was out of the question, though. Instead, the civil servants recommended the provision of specific 'services' to Islamic organisations, for 'the mosques are *by far the most important self-organisations*. It is important to take mosques seriously and to respect this expression of identity for the sake of the approachability of these groupings' (Gemeente Rotterdam 1981). The latter was particularly significant. The recommended change of policy – which in fact would mark a change in the articulation of the ideological representation of Islamic migrant workers – was basically caused by deep concerns over the absence of contact with – if not control over – a substantial part of the migrant worker population in the city. This 'lack of social basis' was seen as an immense problem because, as a senior civil servant expressed it in an interview, without this basis the local Ethnic Minorities Policy and thus the desired social integration would be doomed to failure.

The note caused various actions within the municipality. One of the follow-ups was a series of talks between the Alderman for Special Groups, who had primary responsibility for the Ethnic Minorities Policy, and a number of leaders of Islamic organisations. Furthermore, in the summer of 1983 a new note was brought out under the auspices of this alderman by the Migrants Bureau (Gemeente Rotterdam 1983). This note contained a plea for 'co-operation with the groupings that are nearest to migrants' hearts. For Turks and Moroccans, these are the mosques.' The note also referred to the social 'isolation' of 'most mosques', a situation which was described as the opposite of integration. While referring to the visits of the alderman to Islamic organisations, it was noted that Islamic leaders 'expressed a strong wish for *recognition* and *support* ... A number of mosques have reached a point where they can do without big words from politicians during their visits. In their view, holding back material support equals non-recognition (or unwillingness to recognise)' (emphasis in the original). This statement was followed by a number of suggestions into which this support could crystallise. The note concluded by remarking that: 'support, in the form of service and (limited) subsidy, and recognition of mosques – implicitly but, if possible, also explicitly – provides us with "*social partners*" in the policy on migrants. This policy is not thinkable without the association or, better, collaboration with the people involved' (Gemeente Rotterdam 1983: 4–7; my emphasis).

What the note boiled down to was equal treatment of Islamic organisations and other self-organisations of migrant workers. Compared to the 1981 paper about mosques, which focused on more technical aspects regarding mosques as buildings, this paper laid much more emphasis on socio-cultural aspects and the interest of the local Ethnic Minorities Policy. This indicates important ideological changes, at least, within the Migrants Bureau of the municipality: the signification of religion *per se* has lost some relevance and the subsequent evaluation of Islam as a religion has become less unfavourable, whereas the signification of socio-cultural characteristics and the subsequent desire to eliminate socio-cultural non-conformity through a policy of integrating 'ethnic minorities' has gained importance. This was underscored by the alderman responsible in a letter to his colleagues in the municipal executive stating that: 'in policy-making with regard to migrants, greater and greater interest is attached to the so-called self-organisations *as representatives of ethnic minorities*. They can become as it were *social partners in the process of integration* ... The predominant form of self- organisation is the mosque organisation' (my emphasis).

After lengthy discussion, the municipal executive for the time being backed up this line of policy, albeit not unanimously, and invited the alderman to come up with detailed proposals; at this stage the local council was not yet called in.

The Migrants Bureau did not want to pay only lip-service to the recognition of Islamic organisations, and as a token of their being serious, representatives of these organisations were invited in 1983 to become members of the working party on self-organisations. This working party was to advise the authorities on the policy on subsidising 'ethnic minority' organisations. For the first time, Islamic and secular – if not anti-Islamic – organisations of migrant workers had to co-operate. This co-operation did not result in unanimous advice to the local authorities. An agreement was reached about the conclusion that activities of 'ethnic minority' organisations should be subsidised, provided that they contributed to the process of integration of 'ethnic minorities' in Dutch society. However, the members of the working party strongly disagreed on the question as to whether Islamic organisations should be eligible to receive such subsidy too, including subsidy for their accommodation. The secular organisations argued that the latter would mean that the establishment of places of worship by Islamic organisations was financially supported by the (local) state, something they were strongly against for various reasons. The working party decided to leave the final decision about the matter to the local politicians. The representatives of the secular organisations probably hoped that the local council would foil the plan to subsidise Islamic organisations.

In April 1984 the Alderman for Special Groups presented the elaborated proposals (Gemeente Rotterdam 1984). In a note attached to these proposals, the importance of Islamic organisation was emphasised once again, and so was the 'extreme isolation' of these organisations and its 'negative repercussions on the willingness to integrate'. It was argued that the local authorities had the primary responsibility to prevent or reduce such isolation. This could be accomplished amongst other things by establishing relations with Islamic migrant workers in the form of a '"critical dialogue" in which differences of opinion will not be not covered'. Next to this 'carefully guided "critical dialogue"', it was proposed that the local authorities provided 'service to key figures, and limited subsidies for costs of accommodation and socio-cultural activities'. The latter was to secure the acceptance of the policy by the people concerned, which was another important goal. The formulation of these goals clearly indicates the instrumental character of the policy: the recognition of Islamic organisations is not an objective in itself, but serves the higher objective of making the local Ethnic Minorities Policy a success.

A number of aldermen initially hesitated to support these proposals. After all, the activities concerned would take place as 'church' activities. Some aldermen wondered why Islamic organisations would be eligible to subsidy when Christian communities would not be; would not this constitute a new form a 'discrimination'? However, the municipal executive eventually did support the policy outlined.

With the process of recognition coming to a climax, the endorsement of the revised policy by the entire local council could no longer be put off. Whether or not to proceed with the process and how to materialise the recognition were the issues at stake. So far, it could be argued that the municipal executive only consulted with representatives of the 'ethnic minority' population. But in the meantime various Islamic organisations had submitted applications for subsidies for concrete projects. So the next logical step in the process of recognition had to be a material one. Not every councillor was immediately convinced of the necessity and desirability of recognising and thus subsidising Islamic organisations on an equal footing with secular organisations of 'ethnic minorities'. It happened that councillors of one and the same party presented opposite positions. Some argued that the separation of state from church did not allow subsidising Islamic organisations. Others held the view that Islamic organisations were strongholds of people who were keen on sticking to their own identity and thus unwilling to integrate with the Dutch. After lengthy discussions, the local council endorsed the proposed policy by majority vote, i.e. they voted for supplying limited block grants for socio-cultural activities (including a proportional part of the costs of accommodation) by Islamic institutions, provided that these were not at odds with the municipal policy and contributed to the integration of 'ethnic minorities' with Dutch society.

Summing up, it may be said that this specific instance of political discourse has undergone an interesting change during the early 1980s. About ten years ago, the local authorities already subsidised organisations of 'ethnic minorities'. This subsidising was grounded in the idea that support by the local state in whatever form served the process of integration of these specific categories of migrant workers. After all, social and cultural barriers were to be overcome, so it was thought, something that paradoxically could be best accomplished by temporarily stimulating the formation of self-organisations. In the process, these migrant workers would gradually adopt the desired Dutch way of life. All this indicates the existence of an ideological representation of the Other as a person who above all shows socio-cultural non-conformity, a quality which is considered as unfavourable. It is important to note that this is not a fixed or naturalised quality. On the contrary, this socio-cultural non-conformity ought to be changed and can be changed. This ideology can be identified as an instance of minorisation.

However, the local authorities did not grant money to extreme right and religious organisations. The latter indicates the existence of at least one other ideological representation, namely one of the Other as a person of religion, *in casu* a Muslim. Being a person of religion, or rather being a Muslim, was then evaluated neutrally to unfavourably. The recognition and subsidising of Islamic organisations was subsequently rejected with reference to formal arguments – such as the (supposed) separation of church from state – or to political arguments – such as the political undesirability of supporting nationalistic or extreme right organisations. In either case, around 1980 the signification of religious characteristics predominated over the signification of socio-cultural characteristics.

Through the years, however, this discourse has changed. Firstly, the signification of religious characteristics has lost its relevance to some extent – at least less weight has been attached to these characterictics compared to the signification of socio-cultural characteristics. At the same time, socio-cultural characteristics have become more and more relevant, probably under the influence of the outlining and implementation of the national Ethnic Minorities Policy. Secondly, the religious characteristics – for as far as they have been signified in this specific instance – have been attributed with negatively evaluated characteristics to a lesser extent. Around 1980, every Muslim in the Netherlands was automatically associated with extreme right nationalism or fascism. Now a somewhat more 'nuanced' idea of Muslims exists. The two processes could be observed first with civil servants of the Migrant Bureau, then with the alderman responsible and the rest of the municipal executive, and finally with the majority of the local council.

In extreme cases during the process of recognition of organisations of Islamic migrant workers, every reference to religion was trivialised. A senior civil servant of the Migrant Bureau said that, as far as he was concerned, it did not matter whether the local authorities were dealing with Islamic organisations or with soccer clubs: 'We couldn't care less.' What did matter was the fact that specific organisations of migrant workers had gained social relevance, and it so happened that they 'had presented themselves as Islamic organisations'. The Alderman for Special Groups harboured the same thoughts:

> The critical dialogue has started on the basis of the growing sense of the municipal executive that seriously talking about the policy on migrants, the difficult situation of migrants and their difficult perspectives, particularly in education, schooling and working, it is irresponsible to let large groups alienate themselves from the municipal executive ... Mosque organisations can influence their own followers and in so doing they can put over to them the possibilities and impossibilities for Dutch society of increasing the chances for migrants. A consequence of the critical dialogue should be some subsidising of those activities that are justifiable and possible in the regular policy. A next subject in the critical dialogue will be the position of women, a sensitive subject in those circles. The municipal executive will not stop bringing forward the Dutch views and ideas. The essence of the critical dialogue is to reach every migrant group in Rotterdam – whatever their origins, spiritual and cultural identities – in order to convince them of the necessity of a certain integration in Dutch society, so that they get more equal chances.[6]

Conclusion

This chapter deals with the ideological representation of migrant workers in Europe and focuses on the question of whether this process can be described and explained in every circumstance by the concepts of '*race*', *racialisation* or *racism*. International researchers show a tendency to use rather broad conceptualisations. The advantage is that (seemingly) related phenomena can be lumped together, and that their affinity can be emphasised. The disadvantage, however, is reductionism and lack of sharpness. Therefore, a stricter conceptualisation is preferable. Following Miles (1989), I set forth the view that the concepts of 'race', racialisation and racism are applicable only to one specific discourse, namely a discourse with references to phenotypical human characteristics or to cultural characteristics in so far as they are seen as fixed, naturalised and inherently different. This is apparently the case in Britain – at least the dominant ideological representation revolves round these characteristics. But it should not be taken for granted that migrant workers in other social formations are problematised similarly. It is most important to distinguish different discourses and to express those differences in the con-

6. Volgens 'Verslag van de openbare vergadering van de commissie voor Gecoördineerd Welzijnsbeleid, de Welzijnsplanning en Bijzondere Groepen B.G.–aangelegenheden, gehouden op dinsdag 26 maart 1985 in het stadhuis'.

cepts used. This is the very reason why such concepts as *immigrisation*, *culturalisation* or *minorisation* have been developed in Belgium, Sweden and the Netherlands respectively. These concepts indicate differences between the discourses in Britain and those elsewhere.

It is, moreover, relevant to appreciate the various discourses that make up the ideological representation of one specific social category. The ideological representation of Islamic migrant workers, for one, consists of the articulation of various different representations: at least one based on the signification of religion, others based on the signification of other features such as phenotype (Britain) or (a changable form of) socio-cultural non-conformity (the Netherlands).[7] The social perspectives of the categories thus constructed are related to the ideological representation that predominates in a specific conjuncture.

7. A third one is the signification of gender; see Lutz 1991a.

15

Unravelling Racialised Relations in the United States of America and the United States of Europe

Stephen Small

Introduction

Most chapters in this book have as a central concern the need to uncover and elaborate upon issues of 'racialised', ethnic and national conflict within and across European countries – and of the interplay between these and other conflicts such as class and gender.[1] Most attention is given to describing, interpreting and explaining the dynamics of migration and 'racisms' as they have unfolded within the parameters (geopolitical, economic and cultural) of the European Community (and of Europe as a whole). Some chapters have also considered the political and policy proposals that might lend themselves to the alleviation of such conflicts (for example, Lloyd). These analyses have made reference to the influence of forces originating outside the European Community – to the changing economic relationships between the so-called 'First World' and the 'Third World', to the politics of the 'new world order', to international migration flows, and to the legacies of former empires (for example, Miles).

All of this is as it should be, given that the primary focus of the volume is on actors within the European stage. But clearly the issues are bigger than this and my concern is that we should not lose sight of the

---

1. There are no 'races' so there can be no 'race relations' between them – instead we should study the process by which boundaries and identities of certain groups are 'racialised' (see Miles 1982). Racialisation is defined as 'the extension of racial meaning to a previously racially unclassified relationship, social practice or group ... it is an ideological process, an historically specific one' (Omi and Winant 1986: 64. See also Green and Carter 1988). This approach is described in the text below.

larger theatre within which these dynamics are generated, directed and constrained. In this chapter I argue the necessity of taking a step back, so to speak, and giving more attention to forces outside the European Community, in particular to the influence of the United States. I want to suggest that at a time when all eyes are turning to the European Community we would do well to save some attention for the USA for reasons which have to do with theory, policy and understanding social change. Some of these reasons emphasise the need to consider outside forces *per se*; others are specific to a consideration of the USA. I will concentrate mainly on the latter, for several reasons.

First, because of the influence the USA has had in the past and at present on relationships within Europe. The economic system, labour relationships, class, and 'racialised' and ethnic relations in Europe have all been influenced by developments in the USA historically. The unfolding of events in the USA at present, particularly in response to the 'new world order', is already impacting upon relationships of numerous sorts in the European Community, while the Community itself continues to look to the USA for political leadership of various kinds, as in the Gulf War and Soviet disintegration.

Second, because of the characteristic combination of continuities and discontinuities in patterns of 'racialised' and ethnic relations which prevail in both regions. While each differs in many major ways there remain striking similarities whose importance must be assessed: the settlement and treatment of 'racialised' immigrants, the discrimination, 'racisms' and hostility which they have experienced, their confinement to disadvantaged sectors of the economy and society, the role of the state in managing such relationships and the resistance and resilience demonstrated by them in their efforts to survive and succeed. An examination of these intricate trends, and of their relationships to broader economic forces and political ideologies, promises much by way of contrast and clarity.

Third, because of the dominance of United States scholarship on the field of 'racialised' and ethnic relations. Although each European nation has its own distinctive tradition of research, nevertheless, the impact of the USA has been phenomenal. Some of the best scholars in England agree that this influence has been pervasive and profound, though not altogether productive (Rex 1970; Banton 1983; Miles 1990). And the USA has exerted a similar type of influence across the European Community, one which has yet to be fully identified, examined and evaluated.

Finally, because although there is far from equality for minorities in the USA today, that nation still offers many precedents, policies and principles to provide insights and ideas about patterns in the United

States of Europe (USE) as a whole and in individual nations. For example, in Britain the USA is seen as the leader in policies to combat 'racialised' inequality, and most of its institutional and legislative framework is begged, borrowed or stolen from across the Atlantic; while in Europe, England is often seen as the leader in many respects in the treatment it has afforded its minorities, and its legislation, notably in extending full citizenship to many of them (Moore 1989: 163). [2] Many problems still remain in the USA, as I have argued elsewhere (Small 1991a). But we must examine these policies to decide what kind of successes have been achieved, what limitations, and how we in Europe might go beyond them.

In this chapter I use a telescope to look at the big picture rather than a microscope to scrutinize the minute details. [3] We can fine-tune these issues later ourselves. My goals are as follows. Firstly, to describe the interplay of continuities and discontinuities in the minority experience in the USA and USE; secondly, to argue that throughout the 1990s and beyond, various forces currently at work will exacerbate 'racialised' inequality; [4] thirdly, to suggest that a useful way forward in unravelling these patterns is offered to those who work within the 'racialisation problematic'; and finally, to call for more systematic and sustained comparisons of the USA and USE for purposes of theory, policy and understanding political action and social change.

2. At a presentation in the Charles Wootton Centre in Liverpool on 7 June 1991, Bernie Grant, MP for Tottenham emphasised this point. He argued that there are few agencies like the CRE across Europe, that 'race' was on the back burner, that there were no black members of Parliament other than a deputy in France. In his travels across Europe, he added, black people looked to Britain for a lead in advice and information. We can note, though, that on some issues, for example mother-tongue teaching, Britain clearly lags behind.

3. I am not a specialist on Europe and do not claim expertise in all countries – my main area of research has been on the USA and England. But I believe that the increased attention inwards in Europe might be misplaced and I want to maintain attention on the USA before this slip down the slippery slope becomes a landslide.

4. These forces and ideologies impact adversely on 'racialised' inequality in ways that are not immediately obvious and for which no clear 'racist' intention to discriminate will be apparent. Actions spurred on by racist ideologies will adversely impact on minority populations, but minorities are also at a disadvantage as members of class or gender categories. Given the centrality of 'racialised' issues in the growth of European and American capitalism, it could be argued that all forces are institutionally 'racialised' (ideologies of racism, stereotypes, discriminatory laws and policies) and those less apparently so (advocacy of enterprise culture, meritocracy, appeal to colour-blind approaches). My intention is to emphasise the increasing complexity of factors that serve to perpetuate the disadvantage experienced by minority populations. This is developed in the text below.

Disentangling Continuities and Discontinuities

The first question that might be asked is why compare a country with a set of nations? Surely, the structural, cultural and ideological differences of the two areas make any comparison inadvisable and fruitless? There are many reasons not to carry out comparisons of the USA and USE, and many theorists will object to such an endeavour. Upon first inspection, such differences are distinct and must be confronted.

The USA is a single nation state, sharing a common official language and welded together through conquest and colonisation, while Europe is a community of nation states, tenaciously holding on to different languages, cultures and traditions, and while both were welded together on the basis of foreign expansion and exploitation, the circumstances have been different. The USA has tried to forge one nation from people of diverse national, cultural and 'racialised' origins as it aspires to become a 'multi-racial', multicultural community, while in the USE they are attempting to devise a common political and economic structure that can accommodate many nations and national identities to reflect the diverse (and often divergent) multicultural realities there. Although *de facto* cultural diversity in Europe is historically longer, the USA has for longer dominated policy discussions and concepts. The political systems display marked differences, and neither plantation slavery nor Jim Crow segregation has any counterpart in Europe. While each zone is markedly capitalistic in its economic organisation, the relative successes of each region have waxed and waned.

The size, pattern of settlement and length of residence of minorities in each region display many differences. The USA has a minority population of over 20 per cent, one which is overwhelmingly urban, and many of its cities have a majority of minorities in them. The minorities there include large numbers of African-Americans and significant numbers of people from central and south America (Farley and Allen 1988; Lieberson and Waters 1988). The proportion of south-east Asians is rising, especially in recent decades. It is also notable that the majority of African-Americans are indigenous (97 per cent) as are many Hispanics. Many in the Chicano population in fact were there before the United States annexed Mexican territory – they did not move to take up USA citizenship, it moved to encompass them (Barrera 1979). In the USA 'more than a third of national population growth in the eighties came about due to migration' while only about 3 per cent of European Community residents are recent migrants, and there are few cities, and no larger areas, in which minorities form significant or majority parts of the population (*The Guardian*, 10 June 1991). Current estimates of the black or minority population in the USE put it in the region of fifteen million. Minorities are more diverse in national and cultural origins and tend to be drawn from North Africa, Asia, the Middle East and the Caribbean.

While such differences remain vivid in the minds of many analysts, any preoccupation with them is bound to blind us to the immediate and striking similarities between the two regions.[5] Both regions are advanced industrial societies based on free market economies, wage labour, rationalisation of bureaucracies and liberal political democracies. Each has a multi-trillion dollar gross national product. Despite this, both have achieved their domination through the systematic exploitation of the labour of people of colour, both in their countries of origin and within these regions. These migrants have been forced into low-paying, unskilled work rejected or vacated by the indigenous majority working class, and people of colour remain minorities in majority white societies.

In each region there are inexorable demographic changes underway with immigrant groups becoming increasingly indigenous, and minorities in each region becoming large proportions, sometimes majorities, of communities and regions. The minority population is also characterised by its youth. For example, in Europe by the year 2000, one third of all under thirty-five year olds will have an immigrant background (Suarez-Orozco 1990). In the USA minority groups collectively will form a majority of the population of the state of California by the year 2010, and the white population for the nation as a whole will become a minority by the year 2065. There remains a continuing flow of dependants despite an effective end to primary immigration as each region engages immigration policies based on family unification.

'Racialised' and ethnic discrimination is widespread in each region – from the point of entry to the regions, to the point of entry into the economy, politics and society – and white exclusionary practices have prevailed. Both have played the numbers game in denying or curtailing entry, whether blacks moving from the south to the north in the USA, or Mexicans in the south-west (Barrera 1979; Lieberson 1980); whether north Africans in France (Lloyd and Waters 1991); Turkish Workers in Germany (Räthzel 1991: 35); Tunisians in Belgium (Merckx and Fekete 1991: 73); or Caribbean and Asian settlers in Britain (Miles and Phizacklea 1984). Belgium stopped immigration for work in 1974, France greatly cut African immigration in the early 1970s, while Germany cut back foreign immigration in 1974. Britain introduced restraints on

5. I have responded elsewhere to those authors who object to comparisons of the USA and England (Small 1991a: 6–10). Other authors have argued for comparisons of European countries on much the same grounds as I offer here (Miles and Räthzel n.d.).

'coloured' immigrants as early as 1962. France, Germany and Britain all introduced the notion of 'voluntary repatriation' in the late 1970s.

Central to this has been the development of multiple 'racisms': ideologies and attitudes that identify, distinguish and lead to discrimination against minority groups in immigration legislation and citizenship rights, in the dispensation of power, property and privilege, and in the advocacy of repatriation (Omi and Winant 1986; Runnymede Trust 1987; Miles 1989). These 'racisms' have been intellectual and they have been working-class; [6] they have been biological and they have been cultural; they have entailed actions by national governments and local governments, by the right wing and the left wing, by trade unions and employers' associations. Whatever different forms they have taken they have all shared one common factor – the systematic denigration and exclusion of people of colour (and culture, e.g. the religion of Islam). [7] And many of these 'racisms' have appealed for legitimacy to a mythologised past in the construction of national identities, and of European identity (Gilroy 1990; Pieterse 1991). [8]

The state continues to play a central, if contradictory, role as it attempts to manage its most primary concern – the crisis of capitalist profitability – and to resolve the contradictions that are invariably thrown up – as in the 'needs' of employers for more labour and the hostility of the working class towards that labour being recruited from minority groups. Immigration (that is 'racialised' immigration) continues to be a matter of political urgency and controversy, with the state trying to monopolise on these matters politically, and its representation of immigration has been ideological, distorted and selective. It has employed the language of 'swamping', 'floods' and 'tidal waves', blurred the distinctions between voluntary and involuntary immigrants, and portrayed immigration as a spectacle of alien cultural invasion.

6. On intellectual 'racisms', for example, the Heidelberger Manifesto, published by a group of professors in the Federal Republic of Germany, emphasised, exaggerated and advocated the cultural separateness of different 'racialised' groups, and was also imbued with biological notions (Räthzel 1991: 41). The invidious role of the writers and supporters of the *Salisbury Review* in Britain has been described elsewhere (Gordon 1990). On working-class 'racisms' see Phizacklea and Miles (1980). The contrivances of the new ideologues of 'racism' in the USA where 'racist' discourse has been 'rearticulated' are described in Omi and Winant (1986).

7. Among the left-wing in particular there has been a failure, duplicity and/or dogmatism in countering or challenging the 'racisms' of their own constituencies (other than on paper), be it trade unions or labour organisations (for Britain see Joshi and Carter 1984; for France, Lloyd and Waters 1991: 55; for the USA Omi and Winant 1986). Many activists have refused to see it as an issue; many failed to involve black people, and many simply refused to invest the energy and resources needed to tackle the issues, often because of fear of upsetting the working-class racists.

8. Bovenkerk et al. note: 'the "race" myth ...[has] found formal political expression in all countries of western Europe in different ways and at different times' (1990: 475).

In particular the state has mobilised support for its activities around the issues of illegal immigrants, drugs and terrorists: from Mexicans, Colombians and Palestinians in the USA to north Africans, Turks and Iraqis in the USE. Whether one consults the Immigration and Reform Control Act of 1986 in the USA, or the Trevi and Schengen arrangements in the USE, one gets the same message (Bean, Vernez and Keely 1989). Some have argued that in Europe these migrants fulfil a more general function in obfuscating the causes and nature of economic crises, and the same can be said of the USA (Moore 1989: 167).

Right-wing movements have aided and abetted the state in this enterprise, albeit often by default rather than design, as they have vocalised and mobilised around the more extremist issues, from the Centrumpartij in the Netherlands and the Front National in France to the Vlamms Blok in Belgium, and the Republikaner in Germany (Bovenkerk et al 1990) and the Ku Klux Klan in the USA. In each region, extreme right-wingers have become more centre-stage in mobilising around 'racialised' hostility, thus David Duke, formerly Grand Wizard of the Ku Klux Klan, recently failed candidate for Governor of Louisiana.

There are many anxieties in the majority communities of each bloc: apprehension over the 'Hispanisation' of the USA , or the anarchy of 'rap' on its youth, has its counterpart in the worries of Europeans over Arab influence. There are fears that national cultural identities (more precisely, 'racialised' national identities predicated on myth) are under threat. And each region has its metaphors to capture its anxieties over 'racialised' immigration: 'fortress Europe' and the 'Watch on the Rio Grande'.

In these patterns it is women who have been most often misrepresented and disadvantaged, as well as having least recourse to resources to challenge discrimination. Penalised in the immigration legislation, persecuted for alleged involvement in marriages arranged for purposes of acquiring entry papers, segregated in the labour force, burdened with the additional responsibilities of house and home, migrant woman have found themselves more economically disadvantaged than men, and have always been victims of discrimination from within their own communities of colour and gender (Davis 1981; Mama 1992; Lutz, this volume). One recent example of their plight concerns the arguments over the headscarves (hijab) worn by Muslim girls in France which was presented as an example of religious tradition incompatible with secular state schools (Lloyd and Waters 1991: 49). Though they have long been the mainstay of resistance to 'racialised' hostility, their voices have yet to be represented in the literature in a way that reflects their numbers and strivings. Responses to such discrimination have been more forthcoming in the longer-established communities of blacks and Hispanics in the United States, but also display a recent increase in Europe (Anzaldua 1990).

Resistance by minorities – physical, ideological, cultural – at the community, national and, increasingly, international level, has been widespread and relentless. Grassroots organisations have mobilised around single issues such as immigration, mother-tongue teaching or education, and multi-issue organisations have been established across nations. Their resilience is reflected in the growth of more organised and assertive migrant movements and in the increasing involvement of youth.

Each region professes legal equality and has developed a range of legislative and bureaucratic mechanisms to guarantee *de jure* equality. The USA introduced fundamental legal changes to end Jim Crow segregation and the suppression of black political rights in the 1960s (Wilson 1978); Britain followed suit in the same decade (Miles and Phizacklea 1984); and similar measures have been introduced elsewhere, for example, in France (Lloyd and Waters 1991: 56). Yet each has systematically failed to achieve, or come close to achieving, such equality in practice. All of this means that both regions have made minorities second-class citizens in terms of opportunities and outcomes, and, as one author suggests, 'The class positions of different groups of migrants in Europe ... are ... more similar to one another than they are to those of indigenous working classes' (Moore 1989: 167).

Finally, both regions play a role in regulating and controlling relationships with so-called 'Third World' nations, the USA primarily in south and central America, and Asia, the USE in Africa. They often come together in ways that throw into stark relief their common economic and political interests – as in the Gulf War. And each bloc still retains an economic and employment role for migrants as demography turns against them.

These continuities and others are bound to persist and will contribute to the perpetuation of 'racialised' inequality. Elsewhere I have used the concept of the 'Colour Line' to refer to the systematic inequalities experienced by black people in England and the USA (Small 1991a). It is clear too that a such a line exists across the USA and USE. But it is not uniform and unchanging; for example, black people in Britain have been referred to as a 'privileged class' compared to minorities across Europe, given the security of residence and the political rights that they enjoy (Moore 1989: 167); while blacks in the USA are less impacted upon by citizenship rights than in Europe, though Mexicans and others remain so. These experiences provide a solid basis for comparison.

The Exacerbation of 'Racialised' Inequality in the 1990s

These patterns are not set in stone. Developments in the 1980s and 1990s suggest that patterns of 'racialised' inequality will become exacerbated and the factors that maintain them will become more complex and difficult to pinpoint. This means policies to combat them will be more difficult to formulate. Clearly our analyses of these phenomena and the theoretical and conceptual frameworks we employ to carry out empirical research will have to become more sophisticated (see Castles, this volume).

The stage for all this has been laid in the changing international economic and political order. In the economic realm this includes the changing strategies of capital and the state to make profits in a context of increasing unemployment; the transformation of labour markets and companies (new tech, high tech, new TECS and higher education) making them more competitive and with a greater demand for credentialed workers. The use of new technology, especially in service industries such as finance and banking, has led to the restructuring of work processes and the reorganisation of industries, as well as redundancies and unemployment. This has occurred alongside a growth in the informal economy. It has also led to the export of jobs to so-called 'Third World' countries and new resentments as European workers come into more direct competition with workers elsewhere. Political developments have called for new arrangements as both USA and USE respond to the disintegration of the USSR, the imbroglios of eastern Europe and the unification of Germany; as numerous 'Third World' countries rebound from the withdrawal of aid (redirected to the east); and as an invigorated emphasis is placed on ideologies supporting the free market economy, economic efficiency and enterprise culture.

In light of these panoramic changes I would like to stress three trends: the movement from a single predominant 'racism' to concurrent and multiple 'racisms'; the increasing significance of broader forces; and an increasingly opaque role of the state.

The role of multiple 'racisms' – direct and indirect, institutional and individual, intentional and unintentional, in complex combinations of scientific and pseudo-scientific, biological and cultural – in maintaining the current pattern of 'racialised' disadvantage will persist and expand (Omi and Winant 1986; Sivanandan 1988). On the one hand some older, cruder, seemingly obsolete forms of 'racism' will continue – that expounded by right-wing movements such as the KKK in the USA, and the National Front and Front National in the USE.[9] On the other hand, there will be a dramatic increase in more furtive and surreptitious methods of denigration and exclusion as 'racists' employ codewords, *doubles entendres* and the like to camouflage the vehemence and virulence of their attitudes and actions.[10] I envisage a continued move from direct, overt and conspicuous 'racialised' discrimination in which it was easy to identify motives predicated on 'racialised' beliefs (for example, immigration legislation) to indirect, covert and inconspicuous 'racialised' discrimination in which motives and intentions are less obvious.

But if 'racialised' discrimination continues as a result of the malicious and vindictive wishes of individuals, it will also continue for other reasons, many of which will be devoid of any purposive 'racist' intent. I want to argue for the increasing significance of forces whose 'racialised' ramifications are not apparent, though they will be immediate and in ways that ensure, rather than erode, 'racialised' inequality. To the extent that minorities are disadvantaged and subordinated because they are members of the working class or gender groups, broader forces and the ideologies that support them will adversely impact upon them (Goldsmith, 1989). These forces will directly exacerbate existing patterns of 'racialised' inequality for two reasons: first, because minorities are at a greater disadvantage compared to the majority, *whatever their class position*; secondly, because the current context of recession marginalises sustained efforts to combat 'racialised' inequities.

Many of these forces are discussed elsewhere in this volume (for example, see Castles) and include the changing strategies of state and capital to make profit, new technologies in industry and the changing contours of labour market demography. To the extent that these forces add pressure to the free market rationale for economic organisation, and lead to an increased emphasis on 'equal' treatment of all workers, 'racialised' minorities will remain (and become more entrenched) in inequality. An example of this from Britain can be found in the expanding higher educational system. Ostensibly it seems to the benefit of

9. Crude yet effective official 'racism' continues in the 'racialised' immigration legislation of most countries. There are other types, for example, in Belgium where foreign workers 'are barred by statute from any kind of public service or government employment' (Merckx and Fekete 1991: 72). They also have no political rights and are subject to deportation (ibid.: 75)

10. Gilroy provides an example from the 1987 British general election in which appeals to patriotism and deference to the law were emphasised. While containing 'no overt reference to race' such language 'acquired racial references' (1990: 269).

minorities, but greater scrutiny demonstrates that it will considerably disadvantage them, making them less likely to pursue higher education. Another example involves the establishment of TECS which offer little help to the long-term unemployed, or those with greater educational disadvantage.

The role of the state in the management – meandering, manoeuvring and manipulation – of 'racialised relations' will be less obvious and thus less susceptible to criticism. I believe the state will continue to play a role in maintaining 'racialised' disadvantage that is less obvious and less conspicuous. The state has demonstrated its ability simply to ignore or deflect criticisms of its more detrimental policies – such as immigration, deportation and aspects of policing – and will continue to do so. And it will continue to find more indirect but equally effective means of discriminating even as it reconciles employers' 'needs' with working-class 'racism' and its own need to stay in power. In the United States, the manipulation of Willie Horton as 'bogey man' of the Democratic Party in George Bush's successful 1988 presidential bid, President Bush's *doubles entendres* about 'racial quotas' in the 1990 Civil Rights Bill, and his show-casing of right-wing African-American intellectuals and politicians are all evidence of this course of action (Piliawsky, 1989). In Europe the abortive efforts to get a black candidate to stand for Cheltenham, the representation of anti-racist activity as dictatorial and dogmatic, the organisation of Trevi and Schengen around issues of 'illegal immigration in lieu of drugs dealers and terrorism' are the counterparts (Gordon 1990).

These ominous trends loom large as obstacles to tackling 'racialised' inequality in both regions, and their various elements must be identified, the relative impact of them evaluated, and the types of responses likely to contain and reverse them highlighted. 'Racialised' discrimination will continue, and 'racialised' inequities be further exacerbated; but it will become increasingly difficult to identify 'racist' intentions, and we will need to change our agenda, particularly if we are concerned with effecting social change. 'Racisms' will be less evident, but no less effective. We will need to spend less time focusing on whether 'racism' is increasing or decreasing, less time on the motivations of 'racists' and less time pursuing a single theory of 'racism', or 'racisms'. In lieu of this we should spend more time assessing the broader economic and political changes, and institutional provisions – especially state activities – for the consequences they will have on 'racialised' inequality. Given past discrimination, and the current pattern of entrenched inequality, even institutional changes that seem to promise equality can have adverse effects, for example, as in the effects of loans on black students. 'Racialised' intentions will continue to figure prominently in much of this, so we must still keep an eye on 'racialised' ideologies of an institutional kind. If we are to achieve these goals then we need to develop clear frameworks for analysis and comparison.

The 'Racialisation Problematic' as Strategy

I do not need to extol the virtues or warn of the pitfalls of international comparisons as there is an extensive literature on this matter (Skocpol and Somers 1980; Bovenkerk et al. 1990). But while certain comparisons abound, others are scarce. Most comparisons of the USA and Europe concern social mobility, class formation, education and industrial relations (Edwards 1983). Consideration of 'racism' and gender is marginalised or absent from this research (Kerckhoff, Campbell and Winfield-Laird 1985); though work on immigration is increasing (Power 1979; Institute for Research in History 1983; Brubaker 1989; Waldinger 1990). Moreover, there is recent evidence of increasing attention to comparisons of 'racisms' across Europe (Cross and Entzinger 1988; Bovenkerk et al. 1990; Suarez-Orozco 1990, 1991). Such comparisons must be extended to include patterns of 'racialised relations' in the USA and USE, and there is a clear need for an outline of the framework within which such comparisons might be undertaken.

First of all we must note, as others have done, that there can be no simple transplantation of concepts, structures or ideologies, and there is no simple American solution to problems that prevail in Europe (Trow 1979, 1988). But after taking such factors into account there remains a tremendous opportunity to benefit from the USA experience. Despite continuing obstacles to minority success in the USA, minorities there still have established agendas, developed strategies and tactics, and achieved goals from which minorities in Europe can benefit. Europe can learn from the diverse ways in which 'problems' have been defined and from the formulation of policies to respond to them; from the initiatives launched, the obstacles encountered and the tactics developed to circumvent them; from the strategies developed for gaining access to power and decision-making positions, the alliances formed and reshaped; and from the practical day-to-day lessons of those who have spent years striving to gain entrance to, as well as working in establishment institutions. The USA has a wealth of experience to offer at this level, and it can be captured by anyone willing to study their situation. [11]

11. As a USA author argues, 'Ideas and programs that in the USA flourished and then wilted in the 1960s and 1970s seem to be appearing in another cycle in European investigations' (Suarez-Orozco 1990: 269).

In all this we can benefit from the spirit of striving and the determination to succeed which characterises so much of the minority experience there.

Comparison will particularly help our understanding of the role of the state in the management of 'racialised relations', the role of multiple 'racisms' and of broader forces and ideologies in maintaining 'racialised' disadvantage. And you can bet it will not simply be those promoting social justice that will take cognisance of these benefits; no doubt the 'special relationship' between the USA and UK will foster special arrangements for the exchange of security, military, surveillance and documentation to manage migration. In light of the fact that a former CIA chief has stated that the European Community represents a threat to USA national security, it is clear that Trevi and Schengen will go transatlantic! (*Guardian* 6 September 1991).

I believe one way to benefit from comparisons is by working within the 'racialisation problematic'. The 'racialisation problematic' represents a paradigm within which competing theories can be advanced for an understanding and explanation of the creation and variations in 'racialised' group boundaries and identities in various socio-historical contexts. The notion of 'racialisation' addresses the question 'if "race" is not biology then what is it?' and it can thus be used to unravel the relative influence of multiple factors (economics, politics, demography, culture, ideology and myth) in patterns of 'racialised relations' across Europe. The range of analysts in Britain and North America working within this problematic suggests the diverse theoretical orientations for which it allows (Banton 1977; Reeves 1983; Omi and Winant 1986; Jackson 1987; Green and Carter 1988; Satzewich 1989; Miles 1989; Smith 1989; Williams 1990). While there are differences between them, it is what they agree upon that links them in a common enterprise. My own approach has involved drawing a distinction between the 'racialisation problematic' as a paradigm, and the process of racialisation (Small 1989; 1991b). The 'racialisation problematic' enables us to escape from the spurious assumptions of 'race relations', to begin to distinguish ethnic differences from 'racialised' ideologies and to untangle both from broader economic and political processes. All of this provides a basis for systematic comparison of the two regions.

One problem with many social scientific analyses of 'race' is that while they often acknowledge that 'race' is a social construct that is flexible and fluid, they go on to talk about 'race' as if it were a naturally occurring phenomenon, treating it as real and adding credibility to its status as an explanatory factor in social relationships. [12] This practice is

12. For a specification and elaboration of these issues, and examples of texts, see Miles 1990.

widespread in the various legislative measures within Britain, is pervasive in the parlance of practitioners and among the general public (Miles and Phizacklea 1984). Similarly the field of 'race relations' is discussed as if it were a distinctive field of study, with a unique set of social relations governed by a specific set of rules. In fact in any context described as 'race relations' attitudes and notions about 'race' are only one aspect of the social relationships involved – and may not even be the most central aspect. As one author notes:

> The use of the terms ethnic or racial relations tempts us into the error of thinking that ethnic or racial consciousness is the *defining* characteristic of the relationship that we are studying, [but in fact] 'ethnicity' and 'racial' consciousness' are *aspects* of social relations and social structures which are defined more profoundly and more tellingly in other terms – and you can't have a sociology of aspects (Fenton 1987: 278, 282).

These relations are inextricably entangled with issues of economics, employment, politics and demography, as well as nationality, language and religion.

One of the most invidious outcomes of all this is that minorities, and black people in particular, continue to be the main focus of the magnifying glass in attempts to understand 'race relations': it is as if the problems inhere in their 'race', an approach which usually ends up pathological. But in fact, the problem is not 'race' but 'racisms', not relations between 'races' but relations which have been 'racialised', not the physical attributes of minorities or their presumed inferiority, but the motivations of whites, and the obstacles they impose. The theoretical, policy and practical ramifications are thus changed considerably.

A second problem is that some analysts often conflate 'race' and 'ethnicity' (Williams 1990). This confuses more that it clarifies because it collapses patterns of ethnic and 'racialised' boundaries and identities into the same matrix. It thus fails to distinguish the processes involved and prevents us from disentangling the real differences they manifest. And, in Britain, there are major differences in the experiences of migrants and settlers from Africa, the Caribbean and the Asian sub-continent as compared with those from Ireland, Italy or Cyprus (Daniel 1968); as there are in Europe between Turkish, north African and Arab migrants as compared with Spanish and Italians (Lloyd and Waters 1991); and in the United States between African-Americans, Hispanics and Asians as compared with European immigrants (Waters 1990).

One criticism of the 'racialisation' problematic is that it is simply semantic. I argue otherwise: this approach changes not just the language but also the framework, focus and facts of the analysis, leads to a very different definition of 'the problem' and to very different types of policy proposals. So there is a fundamental difference between those who explicitly subscribe to the 'racialisation problematic' and those who do not. For the former group the rigorous assessment of the nature and meaning of 'race', and of the differential power relations amongst those who seek to ensure their definitions prevail, is immediate and mandatory, while for the latter it is optional. One cannot discuss 'racialised relations' without being forced to raise what is meant by the term; but for those who talk of 'race relations' – in courses, units, articles and books – this may well be avoided, neglected or postponed. Once it is raised in this way, the likelihood that it will be sustained throughout research, writing and teaching is far greater.

Conclusion

It is clear from the chapters in this volume that the issues raised are broader than the contours of Europe, more wide-ranging than the patterns of migration, and involve ideologies that are more encompassing than 'racisms' (see Castles, this volume). In the light of this, the need for clear principles and priorities in order to construct effective policies and political action is all the greater.

Once again it is clear that the imperatives of industrial society have not demolished 'racialised' or ethnic divisions or identities as predicted by nineteenth-century social theorists. [13] In many respects, twentieth-century industrial society has given rise to new ethnic and 'racialised' structures, divisions and identities, for example, in the creation of northern ghettos and an 'underclass' (or ghetto poor) in the USA (Wilson 1978, 1987); the settlement of minority workers in England and across Europe (Brock 1986; Cohen 1987) and the growth of an indigenous and young minority population which threatens to become a majority in key areas.

One of my goals has been to make a contribution to the systematic evaluation of similarities and dissimilarities in the experience of minorities across the two regions and to draw out some of the implications for theory, policy and social change. At a time when eyes in Europe have turned inward and the lingua franca of 'race relations' has become institutionalised and entrenched, I have taken the opportunity to remind theorists and practitioners of the need to step back and review the larger picture. A critical assessment of the theoretical and conceptual frame-

13. That such a demolition was unlikely was cogently argued some time ago by Herbert Blumer, who outlined how segregated economic practices and labour relations based on 'racialised' differences were resistant to such 'imperatives' (1965).

works which shape the analyses that we produce and the policies that are proposed, and an analysis of the continued impact of United States institutions, ideologies, politics and policies on Europe must be carried out.

There are some who say that in matters of 'racialised relations' Britain, and perhaps Europe, are ten years behind the USA (Humphry and John 1971). While I do not believe it is that simple – especially in light of recent international developments – it is clear that many patterns do follow on and we can learn from them. The US offers many policies for us to examine, including privatisation of industry, health, the legal profession, as well as with regard to 'racialised relations', for example, equal opportunities policies and positive action. Minorities in the US have come some way towards ending legal barriers to equality, but it is equally clear that they have a long way to go. There still remain fundamental obstacles to minority success, and we should learn from their experience before we rush in – it might simply be out of the frying pan into the fire.

What can we do about all this? I suggest a need to maintain systematic comparisons with the USA, even as we turn much of our attention to Europe and the European Community; I suggest a need to re-evaluate the appropriateness of theories, concepts and policies to promote 'racialised relations' in Europe that are borrowed from the USA; and I suggest a need to look more at the broader social, economic and political changes that reveal no apparent 'racialised' content, and to ask questions more about the consequences for the existing pattern of 'racialised relations' and less about 'racist' intentions.

The precise ways in which the lessons of comparisons might be extracted, the information disseminated and the benefits formulated and implemented are matters for discussion and negotiation. But in light of the overwhelming turn of heads to Europe I doubt that such discussion will ensue without the matter being raised and reiterated time and time again. I have little doubt that the immediacies of local and national contexts are bound to take precedence, and it is essential that we examine the unfolding of such factors in local contexts and particular institutions. But unless we go beyond such immediacies our theoretical understanding will remain limited, our efforts at policy formulation dull and our strategies for political action abortive. We need to undertake more grounded comparisons based on a full appreciation of contexts. Such comparisons should be conceptually clear, empirically grounded and theoretically driven if they are to be useful. We need to unravel continuities and discontinuities, disentangle complexities, review principles, establish priorities and identify policies. These steps are the indispensable components of any thorough research programme, any informed policy formulation and implementation, and any progressive political agenda. Those of us who are prepared to take our actions beyond examination and evaluation to action and implementation need to mobilise around these matters to combat 'racialised' hostility. We must push beyond describing what needs to be done to rigorously addressing how such action is to be ensured.

–16–

Research and Policy Issues in a European Perspective

Cathie Lloyd

Adopting a European perspective is proving to be a complex matter in the area of racism and migration. At one level the notion is proving to be illusory in itself. Almost by definition a European perspective will be pluralist or eclectic. Different countries have developed differently. Failure to realise this has led to the development of a rather crude sub-theory of stages as though every society had to go through a set procedure of development or evolution. The conclusion in Britain is that we are 'ahead'. I would argue that this needs to be fully tested and specified.

As is pointed out elsewhere in this volume (Wrench and Solomos) the question of racism and its denial is an important theme in some European countries. It has national dynamics which come out of specific histories. The existence of a discipline in Britain of 'ethnic (or race) relations studies' differentiates us from some other European countries, where there is a broader interface between the more classic mainstream of the humanities and social sciences and this area. In different countries there has developed a different division of labour, with foci on varying aspects of the area. This may also depend on the 'health' of a particular subject area or discipline. There is little and patchy knowledge of the state of the debates in different countries, which also limits the scope for collaboration. In terms of methodology a European perspective might conjure up the idea of comparative work, but comparative ventures have been fairly limited to date.

We are forced to reconsider what is adequate comparison. A group of researchers, Bovenkerk, Miles and Verbunt (1990) in Britain, France and the Netherlands who are studying state responses to migration and racism in western Europe on a comparative basis, have pointed to a series of difficulties. There are practical impediments (such as language, culture, scientific traditions, forms of political and financial organisation of research), the high costs of collaboration, incompatible raw data for comparisons. They further point to poor understanding of cross-cultural methodology in three main categories of study: mirror studies, inventories and analyses.

Mirror studies (such as Bagley, 1973), they argue, are framed to use analysis of one society in order to shed light on another. There are problems with reaching the right level of abstraction, taking sufficient account of international variation to generate discriminatory power. Inventories (examples of better collections of this type given are Brubaker, 1989 and Layton-Henry, 1989)[1] fail because descriptive catalogues are fragmentary and have failed to reach the necessary generality through interpretation in the light of theory. Analyses have proved unable to grasp the contradictory nature of different social realities. Comparisons need to discuss all the major problems that confront the difficult issues behind terminology. They conclude that ethnocentrism is a significant 'source of error in cross-cultural and cross-national interpretation'. There needs to be some balance between the consideration of cases in their own right but at a level of abstraction which can encompass all cases. It is important to recognise the complexity and points of similarity. They should be embedded in an abstract level and not expect facts to speak for themselves.

This chapter aims to take this debate further by briefly surveying work which has taken place to date, to identify some of the problems encountered in collaboration between European researchers and to suggest a perspective which can take European developments into account. By a European perspective we run the risk of entering into a difficult problematic and a confusion with Eurocentrism. In many ways the issues posed by research which adopts a wider European perspective also require a far broader international and anti-racist context. I will look briefly at work which has taken place, at some of the problems and issues generated by this work (particularly the difficulties of collaborative work), and finally suggest how research may be affected by the adoption of a European perspective.

Work to Date

Early Work

The flurry of interest and activity which has accompanied the move to respond to the Single European Market, the harmonisation of legislation

1. This volume for example. Layton-Henry (1990) explores a key theme, that of political rights, instead of conducting a country-by-country inventory.

and the greater integration of Europe has tended to obscure earlier and ongoing work. We are not exempt from collective amnesias and reinventions of established processes when faced with what seems to be a new problematic. In fact, international collaborative research has been very important in the past: for example the work which flowed from the 1950 UNESCO resolution and the earlier meeting of scientists and social scientists which gave rise to the UNESCO papers of 1951 and 1980 (UNESCO 1980). As Rex (1986: 18) points out, the impact of this UNESCO-sponsored activity has had different consequences even within the UK. Elsewhere, particularly in France, the UNESCO day against racism and xenophobia provided a focus for the anti-racist movement during the 1960s and 1970s. It has also had a continuing impact on the usage of the terms 'race', 'racial' and 'racism'.

Apart from international academic conferences there have been regular meetings of academics to discuss developments (for example, in the post-war period a Franco-British colloquium on race relations took place in 1968)[2]. There were discussions then on broader European cooperation with the foundation of the Research Group for European Immigration Problems and the Centre d'Etudes Inter-ethniques (CERIN) at the University of Nice.

In more recent years several important projects have taken place. The European Science Foundation project, 'Identity among the Second Generation in Immigrant Communities', involved teams from France, Germany, the Netherlands, Sweden, Finland, Britain, Portugal and Italy. Three books were published as a result: Rex, Joly and Wilpert (1987) developed a theory of association formation in ethnic groups, Liebkind (1989) applied the techniques of identity structure analysis, and Wilpert (1988) examined ethnic minority youth employment. Another study conducted by the Centre des Etudes et Recherches Internationales (CERI) in Paris with the Centre for Research in Ethnic Relations (CRER) at the University of Warwick among others looked at ethnic minority mobilisation at national and international level. The report to the CNRS included a study of Identity and Mobilisation amongst ethnic minorities in Britain, on three Asian associations in Britain, immigrant associations in Lille and Marseilles, the situation of Turkish immigrants in Berlin and Cologne, on the Tabligh mission in France and the transnational organisation of ethnic minorities in the European Community (Leveu and Kastoryano 1992). European collaboration on the area of ethnic minority mobilisation is thus highly developed.

2. *Ethnies*, Mouton, 1972 in which see: P. Bessaignet, 'L'Organisation des études inter-ethniques en France'; K. Little, 'Approaches to the Sociological Studies of Race Relations in Britain'; R. Bastide, 'Les Études et les recherches inter-ethniques en France de 1945 a 1968'.

A project funded by the International Labour Office (ILO) on the integration of ethnic minorities was led by the Centre d'Analyse et d'Intervention Sociologiques (CADIS) in France. This analysed the interaction between local authorities and ethnic minorities in France, Germany and Britain. Findings were debated at an international conference in Paris in October 1990 and published (Lapeyronnie, Frybes, Couper and Joly 1990). It is not possible to give an exhaustive survey of work here, but there are some useful inventories of research in many European countries (Michel 1962; Campioli 1975; Wilpert 1984; Dubet 1989; Pereda 1992; SOS Racismo 1992).

One important factor, however is that collaboration to date has tended to be sporadic and specific, with researchers coming together for conferences or specific projects rather than the long haul which the new integrated Europe implies. This means several changes, that co-operation in the long-term will necessitate a more systematic knowledge of the field in each different country, and a different approach to the selection of partners which will require a better basis of knowledge of one another's work.

Current Work

Searching last year's output from academic journals to begin to answer the question 'What kind of research is being currently done?', and to reveal trends and gaps, resulted in rather predictable findings. In terms of policy-related literature oriented specifically to the EC, there is virtually no reference to the migration of persons. A recent book on the effects of European integration on the Third World looks exclusively at trade links (Sideri and Sengupta 1992). This reflects the emphasis to date from the EC, which has not been willing or politically able to take up the issue of migration and the effects of integration on migrants, third country nationals and ethnic minorities.

There are signs that this is changing. Since the second European parliamentary inquiry into racism and xenophobia (Evrigenis 1986; Ford 1990) the Council of Europe Community Relations project has been completed. This contained a series of recommendations for member states. There are EC-run social science projects on Co-operation in Science and Technology (COST), Human Capital and Mobility (HCM) and the Third Poverty Programme.

In more academic social science publications the coverage is more varied. Journals concerned specifically with the European Community contained only one reference to 'race' or 'ethnic minority' issues and this was significantly flawed (Ireland 1991). There have been some 'special issues' of journals.[3] Even some prominent social science journals (for instance *British Journal of Sociology*) have had little coverage of 'race and Europe' apart from Allen and Macey (1991). This article recognises that there will have to be accommodations in the new European discourse and welcomes the opportunity to challenge unreflective use of language. However, where comparative work is reported it is most frequently oriented towards north America. The topic is not included at all in journals concerned with international studies.

The journals which seemed to have the most coverage were either the more radical (*Race and Class*, 1989, 1990, 1991), which has developed an analysis of the impact of the new Europe on racism, or publications which are more closely related to policy-making and contemporary developments[4].

Journals published in other European countries would seem to have a more comprehensive coverage of European comparative work, such as *Les Temps Modernes*[5], which is particularly informative in an analytical way about the specific debates in different countries. Some journals have included articles (literature reviews, syntheses etc.) about this subject, for example *Current Sociology*[6] covered the state of sociological research on migration in Yugoslavia, Greece, Spain, Italy, Portugal, Britain, France and Federal Republic of Germany. *Migration*, 9 reports on a conference on the future agenda for research to which I will refer later.

---

3. A special issue of the *European Journal of Political Research* vol. 19 no. 1, January 1991, devoted to an analysis of the Euro-Elections contained only a fleeting reference to the extreme right and the Front National in France and nothing on the general issues of the growth of the right and of racism or the rights of ethnic minorities to vote. However, *Contemporary European Affairs*, vol 3, no.3, 1990, produced a special issue on European Immigration policy defined broadly enough to include articles about education and citizenship. An editorial in *Community Development Journal*, vol. 26 no 2, which was focusing on the impact of 1992 on 'communities' commented on the low level of debate particularly on race issues at Community level and invited contributions in future issues (Taylor 1991). A special issue of *Ethnic and Racial Studies* has been published on France: vol. 14, no. 3, July 1991.

4. *New Community* has regularly included contributions from other European countries and a European dimension in the Reports and Debates, for instance J. Wrench, 'Employment and the Labour Market', vol. 16, no. 2, January 1990. *Race and Immigration*, now *The Runnymede Bulletin* has contained regular items relating to Europe, but note in particular the special Europe issue (February 1992). See in particular P. Nanton, 'National Frameworks and the Implementation of Local Policies: is a European Model of Integration Identifiable?' and M. Baldwin-Edwards, 'Immigration after 1992', both in *Policy and Politics*, vol. 19, no. 3, July 1991.

5. *Les Temps Modernes*, July-August 1991, no. 540–1 is a special issue on the British experience; *Projet*, no. 224 contains articles on Immigration in Holland and Poland; the autumn issue on integration policy contains material on US policies.

6. *Current Sociology*, special number, vol. 32 Nos. 2 and 3, Summer 1984, 'Migration in Europe: Trends in Research and Sociological Approaches: Perspectives from the Countries of Origin and Destination 1960–1983'.

The focus for much work has been the coming of the Single European Market and plans for further political integration which have given a new importance to international contacts, generating discussion on the possible implications of harmonisation of policies, legislation and rights. Many of these discussions have concentrated on the prospect of a 'fortress Europe', a clamp down on asylum seekers and the growth of internal controls (JCWI/CRER 1989; Gordon 1989). There has been an explosion of writing in this area. There is some danger in the less informed variants of this perspective (not cited here but which appear in the popular ethnic minority press and the remaining 'left' journals) in that people (particularly well-intentioned gatekeepers) may be deterred from participating in European initiatives because what they hear is remorselessly negative. Thus we run the risk of ethnic minorities being negatively channelled away from Europe[7]. For instance, educational exchanges may be organised to exclude people who it is thought may encounter racial violence. The problem is that without a better knowledge of the situation, measures to tackle such obstacles will not be sought, and another tier of discrimination and exclusion in this country as well as in others will be constructed.

A further obstacle to closer understanding has been produced in discourses about policies in different countries. There are at least two main aspects of this: firstly the generalised assertion that there is a policy vacuum in other European countries, and that the only way to fill this is by a direct transfer of the experience in the UK. This is expressed in a number of different ways, but what is significant is the effect of this approach. It encourages rather simplistic generalisations of a polemical kind to be made about other European countries. Measures and struggles against racism are largely ignored. Other exaggerated concerns then follow, which reduce the impact of suggestions that anything can be done about the situation elsewhere in Europe. Second, by 'talking up' the provisions against racial discrimination and disadvantage in Britain, there is a risk of undermining arguments for the strengthening and critical assessment of policies here. We may be giving other Europeans the impression that simply to introduce legislation against discrimination along the lines of the 1976 Act will be enough, without emphasising important factors such as citizenship rights and political struggle. Thus in a recent House of Commons debate the Home Secretary was able to say, 'We have a better record than almost any other equivalent country in the western world with a large ethnic minority population. Our political system is responding better to the pressures of this kind than say, the

7. Discussion at Hackney College staff development day about sending ethnic minority students to Leipzig, Germany, 20 February 1992.

political system in either France or Germany appears to be.'[8] Although Clarke then warned against it, there is massive complacency about 'race relations' in the UK, and the failure to look more objectively at the complex situation in other countries is contributing to this.

The other argument (more often found in other European countries than the UK and often developed in anticipatory resistance to the first argument) is that different 'logics' have developed which correspond to the response of the society to immigration but grounded in older political struggles (for instance, the tradition of human rights and universalism of the Enlightenment and the French revolution). This can also be encountered in the incomprehension and distaste with which some antiracists and immigrant associations react to the way in which the term 'race' is used in the UK. To speak in a European forum of 'race equality', as is now fashionable here (rather than the more acceptable 'antiracism' coupled with demands for general equality), is to risk entering into a dialogue of mutual incomprehension.

However, some important areas of comparative research have also emerged. For example, the research in Britain and France on the local policies of integration (Lapeyronnie 1991a, 1991b) suggests growing similarities between the two countries. His analysis (Lapeyronnie 1991b) questions the adequacy of the classic opposition between British communitarianism and French assimilationism. He argues that the basis of these oppositions, different colonial practices, is partial, and situates the greater difference in the way in which French and British society has reacted to immigration. While France used immigration for purely economic ends, immigration to Britain was more closely linked to decolonisation and became a political issue early on. Since the mid-1970s the politicisation of issues in France around the effects of imigration has led to a growing convergence of debates. Lapeyronnie suggests that a problematic could be constructed around three elements:

1 different ways in which immigrant populations have been constructed (i.e. the history of migration processes within the context of the nation state);
2 the effects of the disintegration of major institutions (the family, political parties, education system and 'welfare') and fundamental changes in the economy;
3 the end of the model of the national society.

8. House of Commons Official Report, Parliamentary Debates, *Hansard*, col.173, Tuesday 9 June 1992.

Problems

In the course of this 'new' European research, and in discussions at conferences a number of distinct problems have started to emerge. In many ways they reflect difficult issues in any context. To summarise, they include problems of terminology, different models or stages, different methodologies and the relationship between researchers, theoretical orientations and policy-makers. Finally, there is no obvious answer to the question 'What do we mean by a European perspective?'.

There are also very practical problems of 'doing' European research. It is very expensive, and there is a premium on researchers who know several European languages. There are huge problems for researchers who lack access to the networks. Networking is a complex and very personal business. How to 'break in' to networks can pose a considerable problem, especially for young ethnic minority researchers who may lack the 'right' contacts. There are inevitable tensions between the impulse to respond to invitations for tender from policy bodies with very short deadlines, and the need to do more speculative and long-term research. Research partners may be selected with very scanty knowledge about their work (partly because of the language problem) and under pressure to find partners to meet EC contractual deadlines. New, more formalised networking projects, such as the EC's Human Capital and Mobility may begin to address these issues, and there are also more informal subject-based networks being established[9].

In actually working with other researchers on 'the new agenda' of comparative research there are interesting issues. Researchers from different countries approach the question from the perspective of different disciplines. How to find a common agenda between demographers, criminologists and social policy analysts? There will be different political analyses of the situation (which may be hard to decode from the subject-based or national cultural-based discourse in which it is framed). There may be different ways in perceiving or stating the problem (i.e. racism, institutional closures or problems of integration). People will be coming from different experiences and may not always be able to take this into account; this may create difficulties in determining an agenda and may involve researchers floundering in ill-defined debates.

To turn to some of the key problems which have arisen primarily from the experience of research:

---

9. Two of note: the 'History of National Identities, Migration and Racism in Europe', based at the Ecole Normale Supérieure in Paris, and the International Association for the Study of Racism at the University of Amsterdam.

Terminology

The problem of terminology is a tricky barrier. In some cases there are just problems in translation in communicating the finer points of language. But these difficulties also reflect more fundamental differences in the way in which people think of relationships, or in the basic approach to nation and race. What do the French really mean when they speak of 'immigrants' and the Germans 'Ausländer'? This can only really make sense when seen within the broader context of the social relationship (of migrant worker/settler and receiving society). We cannot take terms on face value: a European perspective will require efforts of contextualisation because the 'taken-for-granted' knowledge that enables us to situate terms, actors or perspectives may be unfamiliar to us. There have been (a few) attempts to offer explanations (for instance Couper 1990; Dummett 1992) which encompass the social, cultural and historical context, but a much more comprehensive treatment is required. The pitfalls and snares which have always existed in this difficult area of the social sciences (where in Britain terminological wrangles are complex enough) are more dangerous when one is trying to pick up signifiers through an interpreter.

Definitions of a European Perspective

It is far from clear what a European perspective actually means. It may be many things. Once the notion of Europe is subject to critical scrutiny, its meaning begins to dissolve. Balibar (1991) questions whether we can define 'Europe' 'by reference either to a political entity, to a historical-cultural entity, or to an "ethnic" entity'. Developments in central and eastern Europe have made this even more complex. It is also important to know if one is referring to the countries of the European Community or to other Europe-wide groupings such as the Council of Europe, or even including eastern Europe. Ann Dummett (1991) argues that there is considerable confusion here. I would suggest that comparative work may be undertaken at the level of the nation state, or to compare different initiatives or experiences at the local or community group level. Such work would be important to avoid a European perspective from being equated with a narrow Eurocentrism. This would merely reproduce the discriminatory institutional structures at European level (notions of 'fortress Europe') and nation state level in academic work. The work will involve quite complex approaches to comparative study.

Cathie Lloyd

Theory

In addition to the challenge of comparative work there is the question of different national and international theoretical approaches. In Britain the emergence of a discipline which addresses 'race and ethnic relations' has provided a forum for theoretical developments, particularly in sociology. In France the study has tended to be more part of the mainstream disciplines in recent years as it has shifted from a marginal preoccupation with psychological explanations for the nature of racism. The experience of working with other European researchers in a different context may lead the British to question some of the key approaches and stimulate important new developments, for instance in the theorisation of 'race'. While some writers argue that in other European countries empirical work is relatively underdeveloped (De Rudder 1992), there has been an interesting number of investigations of life in suburban housing estates (Dubet 1987; Wieviorka 1992) which derive from Touraine's theory of social movements. French historiography, particularly the influence of the Annales school is evident in the work of Noiriel (1988, 1991).

Different Models

It has been suggested that different countries have developed radically different approaches to 'integration'. The French Haut Conseil à l'Intégration (1991) suggests incompatibility between the Anglo-Saxon models based on 'community politics' and the French 'citizenship model'. However Silverman (1992) has used discourse analysis to reveal the 'logics' of French immigration policy. He argues:

> In order to break down barriers of comprehension, there is a need to problematise 'models' which have become stereotyped as binary oppositions ... universalism, assimilation and individualism are not opposites of particularism, difference and the collectivity, the former constituting the French model, the latter constituting the Anglo-Saxon model. Instead, these concepts form part of a more complex whole; that of a tension *within* the fabric of western nations. This is not to suggest that there are no substantial national differences in the formulation of questions of migration, racism and rights. But a reappraisal of the conceptual framework of oppositional models might show that, at a deep level of crisis of the western nation-state, the problems are substantially the same. (p.4)

This sort of work is an important advance over the taking up of positions on the basis of a misunderstanding of a word (Lloyd 1992a). It is evident also, however that there are different agendas which are served by the use of specific models. There is much to indicate (following Lapeyronnie 1991b) that when policies and developments are examined in detail and at different levels (i.e. national, local) then the apparent differences conceal broad similarities. It may be that the notion of these fundamental differences is used by opponents of particular policy approaches as a sort of smokescreen. Research can help to reveal whether these stratagems exist. I have argued that it is more revealing to think in terms of a continuum rather than separate policy universes (Lloyd 1992a). While there may be different national cultures there may also be different responses to similar problems.

Relationship between Researchers and Policy-Makers

This relationship will also vary depending on the mechanisms for research funding and the importance of 'race' in policy-making at different levels in different countries. This will partly determine the kind of research done, questions addressed and even the theoretical and methodological orientation of the studies, which of course may pose serious problems for independent work (Wrench and Reid 1990). In the UK there has been considerable debate about the relationship between the groups studied and researchers. Groups demand information, representation and accountability from researchers.

Future Research Agendas

There have been several attempts to synthesise the agendas which may guide research by academic researchers, policy-makers at national level and activists or community organisations. I suggest there is considerable overlap in their priorities, although there may be differences in emphasis. There have been discussions of future agendas, such as that reported in the journal *Migration*, debates on the future programmes of research centres and in consultative groups at European level. While research will continue to focus on issues of integration, citizenship and racial discrimination in western Europe, there is increasing pressure for new work on migration from central and eastern Europe. The growth of ethnic nationalism and racist violence will be a major theme. There is also, in other European debates, a growing interest in examining the structural causes behind underdevelopment and economic crisis as part of the debate about the north-south divide.

The themes of integration and policies against racial discrimination are seen as of great importance in many countries. In the UK the Commission for Racial Equality (CRE) has linked quantitative research on the extent of discrimination to the development of effective law enforcement strategies. This will be crucial if competence to act against racial discrimination can be established at European Community level and also for national laws to be made more effective. There is clearly much scope for comparative work on terminology and to compare experiences with policies at national and local level. The debate is still at the stage of setting an agreed base line for understanding.

The issue of citizenship is related here and will be an important corollary to advances made against discrimination. In France there is already an important movement to redefine citizenship, and this is likely to gain momentum elsewhere with European integration. The impact of economic restructuring and crisis as it affects ethnic minorities and links to the growth of populist racism is a subject that will be kept on the agenda by events. The upheavals in central and eastern Europe means that the question of ethnic nationalism is desperately important. They have also given rise to new migratory flows.

There are continuous changes in types of immigrations; e.g. refugees, 'illegal immigrants' and social fragmentation in older settled groups will be important objects of study, especially for policy makers and anti-racist organisations. The impact of demographic changes on the demand for immigrant labour (INSEE 1991)[10] may change the terms of debate. So may changes in the direction of immigration, with traditional countries of emigration (eg Greece, Italy, Spain, Portugal) becoming receiving countries. Ethnic relations and immigration policies at the periphery (especially meridional Europe) will be very important. Baldwin-Edwards(1991) suggests three outstanding issues: (i) Southern vs eastern immigration; (ii) Demographic policy; (iii) Guest-worker policy.

New Issues

The new European dimension will give rise to new issues on the research agenda. In the area of social and political change, there is an

10. INSEE, 'L'Horizon 2000', *Economie et Statistique*, July 1991, suggests that France will require an additional 180,000 immigrant workers every year by 2020–9 to maintain the economically active population (see also A. Duval Smith, 'What About Some Workers?', *Guardian* 16 August 1991).

agenda which is itself being created by the developments in Europe. Thus it will be important to examine the impact of European integration on 'race relations' and anti-racist policies. Dimensions which have been neglected in international comparative research such as the position of women will require attention. This may pose questions about the assumed homogeneity of 'ethnic minority' communities. Racism based on ethnicity rather than perceptions about skin colour will be considered. For instance the different orientations in other European countries may enable research to be conducted on communities which have been ignored, for example the Irish and other European immigrant groups in Britain.

The broader political agenda will make it important to examine the link between racism and nationalism. Racial violence is a growing preoccupation, whether it be 'ethnic cleansing' in the context of a new ethnic nationalism, or daily violent harassment on modern housing estates. The influence of research particularly in France (to which I have referred) to examine new questions of a dual society, with effects of inclusion and exclusion may lead to important questioning of our more racialised ways of conceiving of anti-racist strategies (Wieviorka 1992).

As different research traditions begin to draw upon one another, there will be a cross-fertilisation from different schools which have placed varying emphases on the 'post-industrial society', or issues of identity. It may be that old paradigms, and 'normal science' in this area, may be challenged by these new areas. Work in the UK may be renewed by these new influences, while forcing others to reconsider their own premises in the light of experience here.

Bibliography

Abu-Lughod, J. (1989) *Before European Hegemony: The World System A.D. 1250–1350*, New York, Oxford University Press

Acker, J. (1989) 'The Problem with Patriarchy', *Sociology*, 23, 2: 325–40

Adams, M. L. (1989) 'Identity Politics', *Feminist Review* 31: 22–34

Albons, B. (1990) 'Et frö till rasism: Peter Nobel är starkt kritisk mot regeringens flyktingpolitik', *Dagens Nyheter*, 19 February, p. A7

Allen, S. and Macey, M. (1991) 'Race and Ethnicity in the European Context', *British Journal of Sociology*, 41, 3: 375–93

Ålund, A. (1987) 'The Swedish "Vertical Mosaic": European Migrants and the Echo from America', report no. 12, English Series, Uppsala: The Study of Power and Democracy in Sweden

Ålund, A. and Schierup, C. U. (1991) *Paradoxes of Multiculturalism: Essays on Swedish Society*, Research in Ethnic Relations Series, Aldershot, Avebury

Anderson, B. (1991) *Imagined Communities: Reflections on the Origin and Spread of Nationalism*, London, Verso

Antaki, C. (ed.) (1988) *Analysing Everyday Explanation: A Casebook of Methods*, London, Sage

Anthias, F. (1990) 'Race and Class Revisited: Conceptualising Race and Racism', *Sociological Review*, 38, 1: 19–42

(1991a) *Gendered Ethnicities and Labour Market Processes in Britain*, paper presented at the conference 'Transitions' at the Science Centre for Social Research/Labour Market and Employment Unit, 13/14 May, Berlin

(1991b) 'Parameters of Difference and Identity and the Problem of Connections – Gender, Ethnicity and Class', *International Review of Sociology*, Monographic Section, 'Gender, Race and Class', edited by S. Allen, F. Anthias and N. Yuval-Davis, 2, 29–52

Anthias, F. and Yuval-Davis, N. (1982) 'Contextualising Feminism', *Feminist Review*, 15: 62–75

Antwort des Senats (1992) Kleine Anfrage Nr. 1511 des Abgeordtneten Eckhardt Barthel (SPD) von 25.11.1991 über Angriffe auf Auslander, in *Top Berlin International*, January, 56–7

Anzaldua, G. (ed.) (1990) *Making Face, Making Soul: Haciendo Caras*, San Francisco, Aunt Lute Foundation

Arbetsmarknadsdepartementet (1990) *En sammanhållen flykting-och immigrationspolitik*, Stockholm, Arbetsmarknadsdepartementet

Ardill, S. and O'Sullivan, S. (1986) 'Upsetting an Applecart: Difference, Desire and Lesbian Sadomasochism', *Feminist Review*, 23: 31–57

Ascherson, N. (1990) 'A Breath of Foul Air', *The Independent on Sunday*, 11 November

Åström, S. (1990) 'Sätt tak på invandringen', *Dagens Nyheter*, 25 August

Autrata, O., Kaschuba, G., Leiprecht, R. and Wolf, C. (1989) *Theorien über*

Bibliography

Rassismus, Berlin, Argument-Verlag

Bagley, C. (1973) *The Dutch Plural Society: A Comparative Study in Race Relations*, Oxford, Oxford University Press

Balbo, L. (1991a) 'Evolutions en cours en Italie', in *Pluralisme culturel, 'race' et nations en Europe*, Seminar Series, European Culture Research Centre, European University Institute, Florence, October

――――(1991b) 'Il modello italiano per gli immigrati', *Politica ed Economia*, 9, September, 3–4

Balbo, L. and Bevilacqua, A. (1991) Questioni di razzismo: *dieci progetti praticabili*, Rome, Italia-razzismo, 1–24

Baldo, C. (1989) 'Begår invandrare fler brott än svenskar?' *Svenska Dagbladet*, 24 April, p. 18

Baldwin-Edwards, M. (1991) 'Immigration after 1992', *Policy and Politics*, 19, 3: 199–211

Balibar, E. (1988a) 'Racisme et crise' in E. Balibar and I. Wallerstein, *Race, nation, classe*, Paris, La Découverte

――――(1988b) 'Le Racisme de classe', in E. Balibar and I. Wallerstein, *Race, nation, classe* Paris, La Découverte

――――(1988c) 'Racisme et Nationalisme', in E. Balibar and I. Wallerstein, *Race, nation, classe*, Paris, La Découverte

――――(1988d) 'La Forme nation: histoire et idéologie', in E. Balibar and I. Wallerstein, *Race, nation, classe*, Paris, La Découverte

――――(1991) 'Es gibt keinen Staat in Europa: Racism and Politics in Europe Today', *New Left Review*, 186: 5–19

Balibar, E. and Wallerstein, I. (1988) *Race, nation, classe*, Paris, La Découverte

Banton, M. (1977) *The Idea of Race*, London, Tavistock

――――(1983) *Racial and Ethnic Competition*, Cambridge, Cambridge University Press

――――(1991) 'The Effectiveness of Legal Remedies for Victims of Racial Discrimination in Europe', *New Community*, 18, 1: 157–66

――――(1992) 'The Nature and Causes of Racism and Racial Discrimination', *International Sociology*, 7, 1: 69–84

Barkan, E. (1992) *The Retreat of Scientific Racism: Changing Concepts of Race in Britain and the United States between the World Wars*, Cambridge, Cambridge University Press

Barker, M. (1981) *The New Racism: Conservatives and the Ideology of the Tribe*, London, Junction Books

Barrera, M. (1979) *Race and Class in the Southwest*, Notre Dame, University of Notre Dame Press

Barrett, M. (1987) 'The Concept of Difference', *Feminist Review*, 26: 29–43

Barrett, M. and McIntosh, M. (1985) 'Ethnocentrism and Socialist-Feminist Theory', *Feminist Review*, 20: 23–49

Barzun, J. (1938) *Race: A Study in Modern Superstition*, London, Methuen

――――(1966) *The French Race: Theories of its Origins and its Social and Political Implications*, New York, Kennikat Press

Bibliography

Bastide, R. (1972) 'Les Études et les recherches inter-ethniques en France de 1945 a 1968', unpublished paper

Bean, F. D., Vernez G. and Keely C. B. (1989) *Opening and Closing the Doors. Evaluating Immigration Reform and Control*, California and Washington DC, The Rand Corporation and the Urban Institute

Becker, H. A. and Beekes, A. M. G. (1991) *Loopbanen van mannelijke en vrouwelijke academici aan de Utrechtse universiteit*, Utrecht, University of Utrecht

Ben Jelloun, T. (1991) *Dove lo stato non c'è*, Einaudi

Bentivogli, F. (1990) 'Gli immigrati e l'assistenza sanitaria in Italia: problemi giuridici', *Studi Emigrazione*, 99, (September): 437–43

Bergmann, W. (1990) 'Der Anti-semitismuus in der Bundesrepublik Deutschland', in H. A. Strauss, W. Bergmann, Chr. Hoffmann (eds), *Der Anti-semitismus der Gegenwart*, Frankfurt Campus

Bessaignet, P. (1972) 'L'Organisation des études inter-ethniques en France', *Ethnies*, Paris, Mouton

Bhavnani, K. K. and Coulson, M. (1986) 'Transforming Socialist Feminism: The Challenge of Racism', *Feminist Review*, 23: 81–92

Billig, M. (1978) *Fascists: A Social Psychological View of the National Front*, London, Harcourt Brace Jovanovich

Billig, M., Condor, S., Edwards, D., Gane, M., Middleton, D. and Radley, A. (1988) *Ideological Dilemmas: A Social Psychology of Everyday Thinking*, London, Routledge

Bischoff, D. and Teubner, W. (1990) *Zwischen Einbürgerung und Rückkehr. Ausländerpolitik und Ausländerrecht der Bundesrepublik Deutschland*, Berlin, Hitit Verlag

Blaschke, J. (1990) *Foreigners' Work in Germany: Demographic Patterns, Trends and Consequences*, unpublished manuscript

Blaschke, J. and Greussing, K. (1980) '*Dritte' Welt in Europa: Probleme der Arbeitsmigration*, Frankfurt, Syndikat

Blumer, H. (1965) 'Industrialisation and Race Relations', in G. Hunter, (ed.) *Industrialisation and Race Relations: A Symposium*, London, Oxford University Press

Bodemann, Y. M. (1991) 'The State in the Construction of Ethnicity. Jews in Nazi Germany and the Federal Republic', in R. Ostow and J. Fijalkowski (eds), *Ethnicity, Structures, Inequality, and the State in Canada and the Federal Republic of Germany*. Frankfurt, Lang

Bourne, J. (1983) 'Towards an Anti-racist Feminism', *Race and Class*, 25, 1: 1–22

Bourseiller, C. (1991) *Extrême-droite*, Paris, François Bourin

Bouw, C. and Nelissen, C. (1986) *Werken en zorgen. Een vergelijkend onderzoek naar de arbeidservaringen van Turkse, Marokkaanse en Nederlandse vrouwen*, Ministerie voor sociale Zaken, The Hague

Bovenkerk, F. (1986) *Een eerlijke kans*, The Hague, ACOM

Bovenkerk, F. and Breuning-van Leeuwen, E. (1978) 'Ras-diskriminatie en

Bibliography

rasvooroordeel op de Amsterdamse arbeidsmarkt', in F. Bovenkerk (ed), *Omdat ze anders zijn*, Meppel

Bovenkerk, F., Brok, B. d. and Ruland, L. (1991) Meer, minder of gelijk, *Sociologische gids*, 38, 3: 174–86

Bovenkerk, F., Miles, R. and Verbunt, G. (1990) 'Racism, Migration and the State in Western Europe. A Case for Comparative Analysis', *International Sociology*, 5, 4: 475–90

———(1991) 'Comparative Studies of Migration and Racism in Western Europe. A Critical Appraisal', *International Migration Review*, 25, 2: 375–91

Brah, A. (1987) 'Women of South Asian Origin in Britain: Issues and Concerns', *South Asia Research* 7, 1: 39–55

———(1988) 'A Journey to Nairobi', in S. Grewal et al. (eds) *Charting the Journey*, London, Sheba

Brah, A. and Deem, R. (1986) 'Towards Anti-Sexist and Anti-Racist Schooling', *Critical Social Policy*, 16: 65–79

Brah, A. and Minhas, R. (1985) 'Structural Racism or Cultural Difference: Schooling for Asian Girls', in G. Weiner (ed), *Just A Bunch of Girls*, Milton Keynes, Open University Press

Brixton Black Women's Group (1984) 'Black Women Organising Autonomously', *Feminist Review*, 17: 84–9

Brock, C. (ed) (1986) *The Caribbean in Europe. Aspects of the West Indian Experience in Britain, France and The Netherlands*, London, Frank Cass

Brown, C. (1984) *Black and White Britain: The Third PSI Survey*, London, Heinemann

———(1992) 'Same Difference: the Persistence of Racial Disadvantage in the British Employment Market' in P. Braham, A. Rattansi and R. Skellington (eds) *Racism and Antiracism: Inequalities, Opportunities and Policies*, London, Sage

Brown, P. and Levinson, S. C. (1987) *Politeness: Some Universals in Language Use*, Cambridge, Cambridge University Press

Brubaker, W. R. (1990a) 'Immigration, Citizenship, and the Nation-State in France and Germany: A Comparative Historical Analysis', *International Sociology*, 5, 4: 461–74

(1990b) *Citizenship and Nationhood in France and Germany*, Columbia University, PhD thesis

Brubaker, W. R. (ed.) (1989) *Immigration and the Politics of Citizenship in Europe and North America*, Lanham, University Press of America

Bruni, M., Pinto, P. and Sciortino, G. (1991) 'Tra carenza di offerta e pregiudizio razziale: i lavoratori extracomunitari a Bologna', *Politica ed Economia*, 11, November, 33–40

Bryan, B., Dadzie, S. and Scafe, S. (1985) *Heart of the Race*, London, Virago Press

Bundesministerium für Arbeit und Sozialordnung, (1990) *Ausländerfeindlichkeit in der ehemaligen DDR*, Bonn

Burleigh, M. and Wippermann, W. (1991) *The Racial State: Germany*

Bibliography

1933–1945, Cambridge, Cambridge University Press

Cain, H. and Yuval-Davis, N. (1990) 'The "Equal Opportunities Community" and the Anti-racist Struggle' *Critical Social Policy*, 29: 5–26

Campani, G. (1989) 'Donne immigrate in Italia', in G. Cocchi (ed.), *Stranieri in Italia*, Bologna, Istituto di Ricerche Carlo Cattaneo, 3–16

Campioli, G. (1975) 'De la sociologie des Immigrés à la Sociologie de l'immigration, l'evolution des travaux belges', *L'Annee Sociologique*, vol. 26

Campus, A. and Perrone, L. (1990) 'Senegalesi e marocchini: inserimento nel mercato del lavoro e progetti migratori a confronto', *Studi Emigrazione*, 98, (June), 191–220

Carby, H. (1982) 'White Women Listen! Black Feminism and Boundaries of Sisterhood', in CCCS, *The Empire Strikes Back*, London, Hutchinson

Castles, S., Booth, H. and Wallace, T. (1984) *Here for Good: Western Europe's New Ethnic Minorities*, London and Sidney, Pluto Press

Castles, S., Cope, B., Kalantzis, M. and Morrissey, M. (1990) *Mistaken Identity – Multiculturalism and the Demise of Nationalism in Australia* (2nd ed.) Sydney, Pluto Press

Castles, S. and Kosack, G. (1973 and 1985) *Immigrant Workers and Class Structure in Western Europe*, London, Oxford University Press

CBS (Centraal Bureau voor de Statistic) (1989) *Minderheden in Nederland*, The Hague, Stichting Vademecum

CCCS: see under *Centre*

CEDEFOP (1986) *The Vocational Training of Young Migrants in Belgium, Denmark, France, Luxemburg and the United Kingdom*, Luxembourg, Office for Official Publications of the European Communities

Centre for Contemporary Cultural Studies (CCCS) (1982) *The Empire Strikes Back: Race and Racism in 70s Britain*, London, Hutchinson

Cheles, L., Ferguson, R. and Vaughan, M. (1991) *Neo-fascism in Europe*, London, Longman

Chevalier, L. (1973) *Laboring Classes and Dangerous Classes in Paris during the First Half of the Nineteenth Century*, Princeton, Princeton University Press

Chiarello, F. (1990) 'Teorie dell'emigrazione e flussi migratori: applicazioni e implicazioni' in G. Ancona (ed.), *Migrazioni mediterranee e mercato del lavoro*, Bari, Caccuci

Choenni, C. and Cain, A. C. (1991) 'The Intensification of Racism on the Dutch Labour Market'. Unpublished paper given at the conference: *Racism and the Labour Market in the Historical Perspective*, International Institute for Social History, Amsterdam, September

Choenni, C. and van der Zwan, T. (1987) 'Meer arbeidsplaatsen voor allochtonen', *LBR Bulletin*, 3, 2: 4–9

Choenni, C. and van der Zwan, T. (1989) 'Allochtonen en de arbeidsmarkt' *LBR bulletin*, 5, 1: 3–10

Cinanni, P. (1968) *Emigrazione e imperialismo*, Rome, Editori Riuniti

Cody, M. J. and McLaughlin, M. L. (1988) 'Accounts on Trial: Oral Arguments in Traffic Court', in C. Antaki (ed.), *Analysing Everyday Explanation: A Casebook of Methods*, London, Sage

Cohen, P. (1988) 'The Perversions of Inheritance: Studies in the Making of Multi-racist Britain', in P. Cohen and H. S. Bains (eds), *Multi-racist Britain*, London, Macmillan

Cohen, P. and Bains, H. S. (eds), (1988) *Multi-Racist Britain*, Basingstoke and London, Macmillan

Cohen, R. (1987) *The New Helots: Migrants in the International Division of Labour*, Aldershot, Avebury

Cohen, R. (1991) 'East-West and European migration in a global context', *New Community*, 18, 1: 9–26

Commission for Racial Equality (1991) *Sorry it's Gone*, London, CRE

Commission Nationale Consultative des Droits de l'Homme (1991) *1990 la lutte contre le racisme et la xénophobie*, Paris, La Documentation Française

Connolly, C. (1990) 'Splintered Sisterhood: Antiracism in a Young Woman's Project', *Feminist Review*, 36: 52–64

Contemporary European Affairs, no. 3, vol. 3, 1990.

Conversi, D. (1990) 'Language or Race?: the Choice of Core Values in the Development of Catalan and Basque Nationalisms', *Ethnic and Racial Studies*, 13, 1: 50–70

COST (1991) 'Report of the COST Workshop: Migration, Europe's Integration and the Labour Force', Leuven, Belgium, 14–15 October

Council of Europe (1991) *Community and Ethnic Relations in Europe*, Strasburg, Council of Europe

Couper, K. (1990) 'Petit lexique britannique en matière d'hommes et de migrations', *Hommes et Migrations*, no. 1137 (November)

Cross, M. and Entzinger, H. (1988) *Lost Illusions. Caribbean Minorities in Britain and the Netherlands*, London, Routledge

Cross, M., Wrench, J. and Barnett, S. (1990) *Ethnic Minorities and the Careers Service: An Investigation into Processes of Assessment and Placement*, London, Department of Employment Research Paper no.73

Current Sociology (1984) Special Number, 'Migration in Europe: Trends in Research and Sociological Approaches: Perspectives from the Countries of Origin and Destination 1960–1983', vol. 32, Nos. 2 and 3, Summer

Dalal, F. (1988) 'The Racism of Jung', *Race and Class*, 29, 3: 1–23

Daniel, W. W. (1968) *Racial Discrimination in England*, Harmondsworth, Penguin

Darras, L. (1986) *La Double Nationalité*, PhD thesis, Paris

Davis, A. (1981) *Women, Race and Class*, New York and London, Women's Press

De Rudder, V. (1992) 'Rassismus und interethnische Beziehungen', in *Rassismus und Migration in Europa*, Berlin, Argument-Sonderband

Delacampagne, C. (1983) *L'Invention du racisme*, Paris, Fayard.

Den Uyl, R., Choenni. C. and Bovenkerk, F. (1986) *Mag het ook een buitenlander wezen?*, Utrecht, LBR-reeks

Bibliography

Dench, G. (1986) *Minorities in the Open Society: Prisoners of Ambivalence*, London and New York, Routledge

Der Spiegel, (1992) 'Jede achte Deutsche ein Antisemite' 4: 41–50

Donald, J. and Rattansi, A. (eds), (1992) *'Race', Culture and Difference*, London, Sage

Doorne-Huiskes, J. v. (1979) *Vrouwen en beroepsparticipatie. Een onderzoek onder gehuwde vrouwelijke academici*. Dissertation, Utrecht, RUU

Dovidio, J. F. and Gaertner, S. L. (eds), (1986) *Prejudice, Discrimination and Racism*, New York, Academic Press

Dubet, F. (1987) *La Galère: jeunes en survie*, Paris, Fayard

_____(1989) *Immigrations: qu'en savons-nous? Un bilan des connaissances*, Paris, Documentation Française

Duffield, M. (1984) 'New Racism ... New Realism. Two Sides of the Same Coin', *Radical Philosophy*, 37: 29–34

_____(1988) *Black Radicalism and the Politics of De-industrialisation: The Hidden History of Indian Foundry Workers*, Aldershot, Avebury

Dummett, A. (1991) 'Europe? Which Europe?' *New Community* 18, 1: 167–75

_____(1992) 'Problems of Translation', *The Runnymede Bulletin*, (February)

Duval-Smith, A. (1991) 'What about Some Workers?', *Guardian* 16 August 1991

Edman, S. (1990) 'Sverige måste in i EG', *Dagens Nyheter*, 3 September, p. A4

Edwards, P. (1983) 'The Political Economy of Industrial Conflict: Britain and the United States', *Economic and Industrial Democracy*, 4: 461–500

Ehn, B. (1990) 'The Organisation of Diversity: Youth Experience in Multi-ethnic Sweden', paper for the conference *Organisation of Diversity*, Botkyrka, Sweden

Elias, N. (1978) *The Civilising Process: The History of Manners*, Oxford, Basil Blackwell

Elich, J. and Maso, B. (1984) *Discriminatie, vooroordeel en racisme in Nederland*, The Hague, Ministerie van Binnenlandse Zaken

Essed, P. (1984) *Alledaags Racisme*, Amsterdam, (English translation: *Everyday Racism*, Claremont, Hunter House, 1990)

_____(1987) 'Academic Racism Common Sense in the Social Sciences', Working Paper no. 5, Amsterdam, Centre for Race and Ethnic Studies

_____(1991) *Understanding Everyday Racism*, Newbury Park, CA, Sage

Essed, P. and Helwig, L. (1992) *Bij voorbeeld: multicultureel beleid in de praktijk*, Amsterdam, University of Amsterdam

Essed, P. and Reinsch, P. (1991a) 'Etnische verhoudingen binnen het Gemeentevervoerbedrijf Amsterdam', Deel I: Interimrapport, unpublished research report, University of Amsterdam

_____(1991b) 'Interculturalisering: over oude en nieuwe routes bij het GVB', unpublished research report, University of Amsterdam

Etzioni, A. (ed.) (1969) *The Semi-professions and their Organisation: Teachers, Nurses, Social Workers*, New York, The Free Press

European Journal of Political Research (1991) vol.19, no.1 (January)

Bibliography

European Parliament (1985) *Committee of Inquiry into the Rise of Fascism and Racism in Europe: Report on the Findings of the Inquiry*, Strasburg, European Parliament

Evrigenis, G. (1986) *Report on the Findings of the Committee of Inquiry into Racism and Fascism in Europe*, Strasburg, European Parliament

Farley, R. and Allen, W. R. (1988) *The Color Line and the Quality of Life in America*, New York and Oxford, Oxford University Press

Fekete, L. (1990) 'Europe for the Europeans: East End for the East Enders', *Race and Class* 32, 1: 66–76

Feminist Review (1984) 'Many Voices, One Chant: Black Feminist Perspectives', *Feminist Review*, 17, Special Issue

_____(1986) 'Feedback: Feminism and Racism' *Feminist Review*, 22: 82–105

Fenton, S. (1987) 'Ethnicity beyond compare', *The British Journal of Sociology*, 38, 2: 277–82

Fenton, S., Davies, T., Means, R. and Burton, P. (1984) *Ethnic Minorities and the Youth Training Scheme*, Sheffield, MSC Research and Development Paper, no.20

Fernandez, J. P. (1981) *Racism and Sexism in Corporate Life*, Lexington, Lexington Books

Feuchtwang, S. (1990) 'Racism: territoriality and ethnocentricity', in A. X. Cambridge and S. Feuchtwang (eds), *Antiracist Strategies*, Research in Ethnic Relations Series, Aldershot, Avebury

Forbes, I. and Mead, G. (1992) *Measure for Measure: A Comparative Analysis of Measures to Combat Racial Discrimination in the Member Countries of the European Community*, London, Department of Employment

Ford, G. (1990) *Report on the Findings of the Committee of Inquiry into the Rise of Racism and Xenophobia*, Strasburg, European Parliament

Foster, C. R. (1980) *Nations without a State: Ethnic Minorities in Western Europe*, New York, Praeger

Friedrich, W., Netzker, and W. Schubarth, W. (1991) 'Ostdeutsche Jugend, ihr Verhältnis zu Ausländern und zu einigen aktuellen politischen Problemen', MS, Leipzig

Funke, H. (1991) *'Jetzt sind wir dran'– Nationalismus im geeinten Deutschland*, Berlin, Aktion Sühnezeichen Freidensdienste e. V.

Fuss, D. (1989) *Essentially Speaking*, London, Routledge

Gallini, C. (1991) 'Le barriere culturali', *Politica ed Economia*, 9, (September), 7–16

Gallissot, R. (1985) *La Misère de l'anti-racisme*, Paris, Arcantère

Gaserow, V. (1991) '... von Deutschen beleidigt und geschlagen', *Die Tageszeitung*, 12 March

Gaspard, F. (1990) *Une petite ville en France*, Paris, Gallimard

Gates, H. L. (1990) 'Critical Remarks', in D. T. Goldberg (ed.) *Anatomy of Racism*, Minneapolis, University of Minnesota Press

Gaunt, D. and Olsson, E. (1990) 'Ett folkhem för alla?' Invandrare och Minoriteter, no. 5–6, pp. 38–44

Bibliography

Geiss, I. (1988) *Geschichte des Rassismus*, Frankfurt, Suhrkamp

Gemeente Rotterdam (1978) *Nota Migranten in Rotterdam*, Rotterdam

———(1981) *Moskeeën*, Rotterdam

———(1983) *Moskeegroepen als zelforganisaties*, Rotterdam

———(1984) *Beleid t.a.v. moskeeën – april 1984*, Rotterdam

———(1991) *De nieuwe Rotterdammers. Facetbeleid culturele minderheden in de jaren '90*, Nota van B & W aan Gemeenteraad, Rotterdam

Gheverghese, J. G., Reddy, V. and Searle-Chatterjee, M. (1990) 'Eurocentrism in the Social Sciences', *Race and Class*, 31, 4: 1–27

Gilroy, P. (1987) *There Ain't No Black in the Union Jack*, London, Hutchinson

———(1990) 'One Nation under a Groove: The Cultural Politics of "Race" and Racism in Britain', in D. T. Goldberg (ed.), *Anatomy of Racism*, Minneapolis, University of Minnesota Press

Goffman, E. (1967) *The Presentation of Self in Everyday Life*, Harmondsworth, Penguin

Goldberg, D. T. (1990a) 'The Social Formation of Racist Discourse', in D. T. Goldberg (ed) *Anatomy of Racism*, Minneapolis, University of Minnesota Press

Goldberg, D. T. (ed) (1990b) *Anatomy of Racism*, Minneapolis, University of Minnesota Press

Goldsmith, M. (1989) 'Social, Economic, and Political Trends and the Impact on British Cities, in M. Parkinson, B. Foley and D. Judd (eds), *Regenerating the Cities: The UK Crisis and the US Experience*, Illinois, Scott Foresman

Golini, A. (1988) 'L'Italia nel sistema delle migrazione internazionale', *Studi Emigrazione*, 91–2, (September–December), 544–65

Golini, A., Gesano, B. and Heins, F. (1990) 'South–North Migration with Special Reference to Europe', paper presented at the IOM (International Organisation for Migration) Seminar on Migration, Geneva

Gordon, P. (1989) *Fortress Europe? The Meaning of 1992*, London, Runnymede Trust

———(1990) 'A Dirty War: The New Right and Local Authority Anti-racism,' in W. Ball and J. Solomos (eds), *Race and Local Politics*, London, Macmillan

Gould, M. (1991) 'The Reproduction of Labour Market Discrimination in Competitive Capitalism', in A. Zegeye, L. Harris and J. Maxted (eds), *Exploitation and Exclusion: Race and Class in Contemporary United States Society*, Oxford, Hans Zell

Gowricharn, R. (1989) *Verschillen in werkloosheid en etnische afkomst*, Onderzoeksrapport, Gemeentelijke Sociale Dienst, Rotterdam

Grahl-Madsen, A. (1985) *Norsk fremmedret i stöpeskjeen*, Oslo, Universitetsforlaget

Gramsci, A. (1971) *Selections from the Prison Notebooks*, New York, International Publishers

Green, M. and Carter, B. (1988) '"Races and Race-Makers": The Politics of Racialization', *Sage Race Relations Abstracts* 13, 2: 4–30

Bibliography

Grewal, S., Kay, J., Landor, L., Lewis, G. and Parmar, P (1988) *Charting The Journey*, London, Sheba

Guillaumin, C. (1980) 'The Idea of Race and its Elevation to Autonomous Scientific and Legal Status', in UNESCO, *Sociological Theories: Race and Colonialism*, Paris, UNESCO

Hall, S. (1980) 'Race, Articulation and Societies Structured in Dominance', in UNESCO, *Sociological Theories: Race and Colonialism*, Paris, UNESCO

_____(1981) 'The Whites of their Eyes. Racist Ideologies and the Media', in G. Bridges and R. Brunt (eds), *Silver Linings. Some Strategies for the Eighties*, London, Lawrence and Wishart

_____(1988) 'New Ethnicities', in *ICA Documents: Black Film British Cinema*, London, ICA

_____(1989) 'Rassismus als ideologischer Diskurs', *Das Argument*, 31, 6: 913–21

Hammar, T. (1990) *Democracy and the Nation State, Aliens, Denizens and Citizens in a World of International Migration*, Aldershot, Avebury

Hammar, T. (ed), (1985) *European Immigration Policy: A Comparative Study*, Cambridge, Cambridge University Press

Hampsink, R. (1992) *Steunverlening aan islamitische gebedsruimten*, Reeks Recht en Samenleving, Nijmegen

Hannerz, U. (1987) 'Cosmopolitans and Locals in World Culture', paper for the First International Conference on the Olympics and East/West and South/North Cultural Exchanges in the World System, Seoul

_____(1990) 'Stockholm: Double Creolizing', paper for the International Conference on the Organization of Diversity, Botkyrka, Sweden

Haut Conseil à l'Intégration (1991) *Premier Rapport*, (February), Paris

Hazareesingh, S. (1986) 'Racism and Cultural Identity: An Indian Perspective', *Dragons Teeth*, Issue 24

Hechter, M. 1975, *Internal Colonialism: The Celtic Fringe in British National Development*, London

Heisler, B. S. (1991) 'A Comparative Perspective on the Underclass: Questions of Urban Poverty, Race and Citizenship', *Theory and Society*, 20, 4: 455–83

Henry, J. (ed.) (1991) *Creative Management*, London, Routledge

Hirdman, Y. (1989) *Att Lägga Livet till Rätta*, Stockholm, Carlsson Bokförlag

Hobsbawm, E. (1990) *Nations and Nationalism since 1780: Programme, Myth, Reality*, Cambridge, Cambridge University Press

Holmes, C. (1979) *Anti-semitism in British Society 1876–1939*, London, Edward Arnold

_____(1988) *John Bull's Island: Immigration and British Society 1871–1971*, London, Macmillan

_____(1991) *A Tolerant Country? Immigrants, Refugees and Minorities in Britain*, London, Faber

Hubbuck, J. and Carter, S. (1980) *Half a Chance? A Report on Job Discrimination against Young Blacks in Nottingham*, London, Commission for Racial Equality

Bibliography

Humphry, J. and John, G. (1971) *Because They're Black*, Harmondsworth, Penguin Books

Husbands, C. (1991) 'The Mainstream Right and the Politics of Immigration in France: Major Developments in the 1980s', *Ethnic and Racial Studies*, 14, 2: 170–98

INSEE 'L'Horizon 2000' (1991) *Economie et Statistique* (July)

Institute for Research in History (1983) *Ethnic and Immigrant Groups: The United States, Canada, and England*, New York, Haworth Press

International Journal of Refugee Law (1990), 2, 2, 279–80

IOM (1990) 'Background Document' presented at the IOM Seminar on Migration, Geneva

Ireland, P. (1991) 'True Fortress Europe: Immigration and Politics in the EC', in *Journal of Common Market Studies* 29, 5: 457–81

Jackson, P. (ed.) (1987) *Race and Racism. Essays in Social Geography*, London, Allen and Unwin

JCWI/CRER: See under *Joint Council*

Jenkins, R. (1986) *Racism and Recruitment*, Cambridge, Cambridge University Press

Jenkins, R. and Solomos, J. (eds), (1987) *Racism and Equal Opportunity Policies in the 1980s*, Cambridge, Cambridge University Press

Jerkert, B. (1990) 'Lång väntan på upprustning', *Dagens Nyheter*, 6 September, p. A18

Joint Council for the Welfare of Immigrants and Centre for Research in Ethnic Relations (1989) *Unequal Migrants: the European Community's Unequal Treatment of Migrants and Refugees*, University of Warwick, CRER

Jones, G. S. (1976) *Outcast London: A Study of the Relationship Between Classes in Victorian Society*, Harmondsworth, Peregrine Books

Jong, W. de and Verkuyten, M. (1990) *De smalle marges van Positieve Actie*, Zeist

Joshi S. Anf Carter, B. (1984) 'The Role of Labour in the Creation of a Racist Britain', *Race and Class*, 25, 2: 174–97

Kamman, K. (1984) *Probleme mehrfacher Staatsangehörigkeit*, Frankfurt, Lang

Karlsson, L. G. (1990) 'Samverkan – samordning – service. Om lokal och praktisk flyktingmottagning i omvandling', research report, Department of Sociology, University of Umeå

Kay, D. and Miles, R. (1992) *Refugees or Migrant Workers? The Recruitment of Displaced Persons for British Industry 1946–1951*, London, Routledge

Kazim, P. (1991) 'Racism is no Paradise!', *Race and Class*, 32, 3: 84–9

Kebrome, F. (1990) 'Objekten som subjekt: flyktingskap och flyktingmottagande, Den egna rösten – De egna villkoren. Om mänskligt liv i skuggan av samhällelig flyktingpolitik', report no. 1, Institute of Applied Psychology, University of Umeå

Kempadoo, K. (1986) 'Black and Migrant Women, and Positive Action in Amsterdam', unpublished MA Thesis, University of Amsterdam

_____(1990) *Construction of Black and Migrant Womanhood and the*

Bibliography

Women's and Minorities Policy in the Netherlands, paper presented at the conference 'The Social Construction of Minorities and their Cultural Rights in Western Europe', Leiden 12–14 September

Kerckhoff, A., Campbell, R. T. and Winfeld-Laird, I. (1985) 'Social Mobility in Great Britain and the United States', *American Journal of Sociology*, 91, 2: 281–308

Kloosterman, R. C. (1991) 'Racism and the Labour Market. Some Theoretical and Historiographical Observations', in: D. v. Arkel and R. C. Kloosterman *Racism and the Labour Market*, IISG, Amsterdam

KMAN, Horecabond FNV, KGCG (1985) *Uklachtenboek buitenlandse arbeiders in de horeka*, Amsterdam

Knowles, C. and Mercer, S. (1990) 'Feminism and Anti-racism', in A. X. Cambridge and S. Feuchtwang (eds), *Anti-racist Strategies*, Aldershot, Avebury

Koch, L. (1988) 'Impact of the Reversal of the Migration Situation on the Social Structures of Certain Countries – The Case of Italy', *International Migration*, 27, 2: 191–201

König, L. (1989) 'Aussiedler und Übersiedler. Ihre Rechtsstellung', In *Das Parlament*, 25, 6: 9

Lapeyronnie, D. (1991a) *Les politiques locales d'intégration des Minorités immigrés en Europe et aux Etats Unis*, Paris, ADRI

_____(1991b) 'La France et la Grande-Bretagne face à leurs minorités Immigrées', *Les Temps Modernes*, no. 540–1 July/August, 10–45

Lapeyronnie, D., Frybes, M., Couper, K. and Joly, D. (1990) *L'intégration des minorités immigrés: Étude comparative France-Grande Bretagne*, Paris, ADRI

Lash, S. and Urry, J. (1987) *The End of Organized Capitalism*, Cambridge, Polity Press

Lawrence, E. (1982) 'In the Abundance of Water the Fool is Thirsty: Sociology and Black "Pathology"' in Centre for Contemporary Cultural Studies, *The Empire Strikes Back*, London, Hutchinson

Layton-Henry, Z. (ed.) (1990) *The Political Rights of Migrant Workers in Western Europe*, London, Sage

Lee, G. and Wrench, J. (1983) *Skill Seekers – Black Youth, Apprenticeships and Disadvantage*, Leicester, National Youth Bureau

Les Temps Modernes, 1991, no. 540–1

Leveu, R and Kastoryano, R. (1992) 'Nations Europeens et leurs Minorites Ethniques d'Origine Immigres: Rapport au CNRS', Paris, CNRS

Lewis, G (1990) 'Audre Lorde: Vignettes and Mental Conversations', *Feminist Review*, 34: 100–15

Lieberson, S. (1980) *A Piece of the Pie: Blacks and White Immigrants since 1800*, Berkeley, University of California Press

Lieberson, S. and Waters, M. C. (1988) *From Many Strands: Ethnic and Racial Groups in Contemporary America*, New York, Russell Sage Foundation

Light, I. and Bonacich, E. (1988) *Immigrant Entrepreneurs*, Los Angeles, University of California Press

Bibliography

Livi Bacci, M. (1990) 'Introduzione', in M. Livi Bacci and F. M. Veronese (eds), *Le risorse umane del Mediterraneo*, Bologna, Il Mulino, 11–40

Livi Bacci, M. and Veronese, F. M. (eds), (1990) *Le risorse umane del Mediterraneo*, Bologna, Il Mulino

Lloyd, C. (1991) 'Concepts, Models and Anti-racist Strategies in Britain and France', *New Community*, 18, 1: 63–73

_____(1992a) 'Race Relations in Britain and France; Problems of Interpretation', in Special Seminar Series on 1992, Research Paper in Ethnic Relations no. 17, CRER, University of Warwick, Coventry

_____(1992b) 'National Approaches to Immigration and Minority Policy', paper to CRER Annual Conference, Mobilisation of Ethnic Minorities and Ethnic Social Movements in Europe, CRER Annual Conference 3–5 April

Lloyd, C. and Waters, H. (1991) 'France: One Culture, One Nation?', *Race and Class*, 32, 3: 49–65

Löblich, E. (1992) 'Ausländer-Gefährliches Pflaster-Sachsen-anhalt', 5 March 1992

Lutz, H. (1991a) *Welten verbinden. Türkische Sozialarbeiterinnen in den Niederlanden und der Bundesrepublik Deutschland*, Frankfurt, IKO-Verlag

_____(1991b) 'The Myth of the "Other" Western Representation and Images of Women of So-called Islamic Background', *International Review of Sociology*, 2: 121–37

_____(1992) 'In Between or Bridging Cultural Gaps? Turkish Women as Mediators in the Netherlands and West-Germany', paper for the International Seminar on Migrant Women in the 1990's. Cross-cultural Perspectives on New Trends and Issues, Barcelona, January

Magen, R.-P. (1990) 'Erfahrungen und Uberlegungen aus Sicht der Berliner Einbürgerungsbehörde', in *Doppelte Staatsbürgerschaft – ein europäischer Normalfall?* Berlin

Malzahn, C. C. (1992) 'Der adrette Rechtsradikale von nebenan', *Die Tageszeitung*, 8 April

Mama, A. (1989) 'Violence against Black Women: Gender, Race, and State Responses', *Feminist Review*, 32: 30–48

_____(1992) 'Black women and the British State: Race, Class and Gender Analysis for the 1990s', in P. Braham, A. Rattansi and R. Skellington (eds), *Racism and Antiracism. Inequalities, Opportunities and Policies*, London and Newbury Park, California, Sage Publications

Martiniello, M. (1990) *Elites, leadership et pouvoir dans les communautés ethniques d'origine immigrée. Le cas des Italiens en Belgique francophone*, PhD thesis, Institut Universitaire Européen, Florence

_____(1991) 'Racism in Paradise?', *Race and Class*, 32, 3: 79–84

Mayer, N. and Perrineau, P. (1989) *Le Front National à découvert*, Paris, FNSP

McArthur, M. (1976) 'The "Saxon" Germans: Political Fate of an Ethnic Identity', in *Dialectical Anthropology* 1, 4: 349–64

McDonald, M. (1989) *'We are not French!': Language, Culture and Identity in Brittany*, London, Routledge

Bibliography

McIntosh, N. and Smith, D. J. (1974) *The Extent of Racial Discrimination*, London, Political and Economic Planning

Memmi, A. (1982) *Le Racisme*, Paris, Gallimard

_____ (1983) *Racisme hoezo? Ontmaskering van een onderdrukkingsmechanisme*, Nijmegen

_____ (1990) *The Colonizer and the Colonized*, London, Earthscan Publications

Mendes, T. (1990) '"Et ruttet system" – Socialdemokratisk invandrarpolitik förvandlar flyktingar till hjälplösa bidragstagare', *Dagens Nyheter*, 2 June, p. A4

Merckx, F. and Fekete, L. (1991) 'Belgium: The Racist Cocktail,' *Race and Class*, 32, 3: 67–78

Michel, A. (1962) 'Tendances nouvelles de la sociologie des relations raciales', *Revue Francaise de Sociologie*, 3, 2: 181–90

Migration (1991) 'Perspectives de la recherche sur les migrations', Berlin, 29 November – 2 December (September)

Miles, R. (1982) *Racism and Migrant Labour*, London, Routledge and Kegan Paul

_____ (1984) 'Marxism versus the Sociology of Race Relations', in *Ethnic and Racial Studies*, 7, 2: 217–37

_____ (1987a) 'Racism and Nationalism in Britain', in C. Husband (ed), 'Race' in Britain: Continuity and Change, London, Hutchinson

_____ (1987b) 'Recent Marxist Theories of Nationalism and the Issue of Racism', *British Journal of Sociology*, 38, 1: 24–43

_____ (1987c) *Capitalism and Unfree Labour: Anomaly or Necessity?* London, Tavistock

_____ (1989) *Racism*, London and New York, Routledge

_____ (1990) 'Whatever Happened to the Sociology of Migration?' (review article), *Work, Employment and Society*, 4, 2: 281–98

_____ (1991) 'Die Idee der "Rasse" und Theorien über Rassismus: Überlegungen zur britischen Diskussion', in U. Bielefeld (ed), *Das Eigene und das Fremde: Neuer Rassismus in der Alten Welt*, Hamburg, Junius Verlag

_____ (1992) 'Migration, Racism and the Nation State in Contemporary Europe', in V. Satzewich (ed.), *Deconstructing the Nation: Immigration, Multiculturalism and Racism in 90s Canada*, Toronto, Garamond Press

_____ (1993) *After 'Race Relations'*, London, Routledge

Miles, R. and Phizacklea, A. (1984) *White Man's Country: Racism in British Politics*, London, Pluto Press

Miles, R. and Rathzel, N. (n. d.) 'Migration and the Articulation of Racism in Western Europe', unpublished paper

Miller, M. J. (1981) *Foreign Workers in Western Europe, An Emerging Political Force*, New York, Praeger

Minh-ha, T. (1989) *Women, Native, Other: Writing Post Coloniality and Feminism*, Bloomington, Indiana University Press

Ministerie voor Binnelandse Zaken (1983) *Minderhedennota*, The Hague

Ministero dell'Interno (1991) *Dati*, Rome, 30 November

Ministry of Labour, Sweden (1990) 'The Pre-requisites for and the Direction of a Comprehensive Refugee and Immigration Policy', paper presented at the IOM Seminar on Migration, Geneva

Minsky, R. (1990) '"The Trouble is It's Ahistorical": The Problem of the Unconscious in Modern Feminist Theory', *Feminist Review*, 36: 4–15

Modood, T. (1988) '"Black" Racial Equality and Asian Identity', *New Community*, 14, 3: 397–404

————(1990a) 'Colour, Class and Culture. The Three Cs of Race', *EOR*, no. 30 March/April: 31–3

————(1990b) *Muslims, Race and Equality in Britain. Some Post-Rushdie Affair Reflections*, CSIS Papers no.1, Birmingham

Mohanty, C. T. (1988) 'Under Western Eyes: Feminist Scholarship and Colonial Discourses', *Feminist Review*, 30: 61–89

Montagu, A. (1972) *Statement on Race*, London, Oxford University Press

Moore, R. (1977) 'Migrants and the Class Structure of Western Europe', in R. Scase (ed), *Industrial Society. Class, Cleavage and Control*, London, Allen and Unwin

————(1989) 'Ethnic Divisions and Class in Western Europe', in R. Scase (ed), *Industrial Societies. Crisis and Division in Western Captalism and State Socialism*, London, Unwin Hyman

Morokvasic, M. (1984) 'Birds of Passage are also Women', *International Migration Review*, 18, 4: 886–907

————(1991) 'Fortress Europe and Migrant Women', in *Feminist Review*, 39: 69–85

Mosse, G. L. (1978) *Toward the Final Solution: A History of European Racism*, London, Dent

MRAP (1984) *Chronique du flagrant racisme*, Paris, La Découverte

Mullard, C., Nimako, K. and Willemsen, G. (1990) *Ude plurale kubus: een vertoog over emancipatiemodellen en minderhedenbeleid*, The Hague

Murray, N. (1986). '"Anti-racists" and Other Demons: The Press and ideology in Thatcher's Britain', *Race and Class*, 27, 3: 1–20

Myrdal, G. (1962) *Challenge to Affluence*, New York, Pantheon Books

Nairn, T. (1981) *The Break-up of Britain*, London, Verso

————(1988) *The Enchanted Glass: Britain and its Monarchy*, London, Radius

Nascimbene, B. (1991) 'Lo straniero in Italia: profili giuridici alla luce della l.n. 39/90', *Studi Emigrazione*, 101, (June): 119–123

Naumann, C. (1989) 'Utlänningar ofta gärningsmän', *Dagens Nyheter*, 2 October, p. 6

New York Times (1991) 16 June, p. E2

Newnham, A. (1986) *Employment, Unemployment and Black People*, London, Runnymede Trust

Nobel, P. (1990) 'Mycket har gått snett', *Dagens Nyheter*, 8 September, p. A4

Noiriel, G. (1988) *Le Creuset français*, Paris, Seuil

————(1990) *Workers in French Society in the 19th and 20th Centuries*, Oxford, Berg

Bibliography

_____(1991) *La Tyrannie du national: le droit d'asile en Europe 1793–1993*, Paris, Calmann-Lévy

Nonis, M. (1989) 'Le condizioni socio-sanitarie degli immigrati dal Terzo Mondo a Roma', *Studi Emigrazione*, 95, (September): 338–67

Oberndörfer, D. (1987) 'Die offene Republik', *Die Zeit*, no. 47, 13 November: 80

Oberndorfer, D. (1990) 'Wert der Staatsbürgerschaft in Geschichte und Gegenwart, Entwicklung der Nationalstaaten', *Doppelte Staatsbürgerschaft*, Berlin

Oeting, J. (1992) 'Im Norden bekam der programmierte Jubel einen Fämpfer', *Die Tageszeitung*, 6 April

Olsson, E. (1989) *VakuumfÖrpackat: Flyntingfamiljer I Stockholm*, Socialltjänten, Stockholm

Omi, M. and Winant, H. (1986) *Racial Formation in the United States. From the 1960s to the 1980s*, London and New York, Routledge

Oosterhuis, G. and Glebbeek, A. (1988) 'Ras en geslacht bij de personeelsselectie', in *Mens en Maatschappij*, 63, 3: 237–59

Orfali, B. (1990) *L'adhésion au Front National. De la minorité active au mouvement social*, Paris, KIME

Ostow, R. (1991) 'The Political, Cultural and Institutional Matrices of Jewish Identity in the German Democratic Republic', in R. Ostow and J. Fiajkowski (eds), *Ethnicity, Structures, Inequality, and the State in Canada and the Federal Republic of Germany*, Frankfurt, Lang

Özsunay, E. (1983) *The Participation of the Alien in Public Affairs*, Strasburg, Council of Europe

Panayi, P. (1991) *The Enemy in Our Midst: Germans in Britain during the First World War*, Oxford, Berg

Parmar, P. (1982) 'Gender, Race and Class: Asian Women in Resistance', in CCCS, *The Empire Strikes Back*, London, Hutchinson

Patterson, H. (1980) *Class Conflict and Sectarianism: The Protestant Working Class and the Belfast Labour Movement 1868–1920*, Belfast, Blackstaff Press

Penley, C. (1989) *The Future of an Illusion: Film, Feminism and Psychoanalysis*, London, Routledge

Penninx, R. (1988) *Minderheidsvorming en emancipatie*, Alphen aan de Rijn, Samson

Political and Economic Planning (1967) *Racial Discrimination in Britain*, London, PEP

Perduca, A. and Pinto, F. (1991) *L'Europa degli stranieri*, Milan, Franco Angeli

Pereda, C., de Prada M. A., Actis, W. (1992) *Libros y documentos sobre migraciones*, Colectivo Ioe, Madrid

Pettigrew, T. F. and Martin, J. (1989) 'Organizational Inclusion of Minority Groups: A Social Psychological Analysis', in J. P. van Oudenhoven and T. M. Willemsen (eds), *Ethnic Minorities*, Amsterdam, Swets and Zeitlinger

Pettigrew, T. F. and Meertens R. W. (1991) 'Subtle Racism: Its Components and Measurement', unpublished paper

Bibliography

Phizacklea, A. (1990) *Unpacking the Fashion Industry: Gender, Racism and Class in Production*, London, Routledge

Phizacklea, A. and Miles, R. (1980) *Labour and Racism*, London, Routledge (1987) 'The British Trade Union Movement and Racism', in G. Lee and R. Loveridge (eds.), *The Manufacture of Disadvantage*, Milton Keynes, Open University Press

Phoenix, A. (1987) 'Theories of Gender and Black Families', in G. Weiner and M. Arnot (eds), *Gender under Scrutiny*, London, Hutchinson

Pieterse, J. N. (1991) 'Fictions of Europe', *Race and Class*, 32, 3: 3–10.

Piliawsky, M. (1989) 'Racial Politics in the 1988 Presidential Election', *Black Scholar* (January/February): 30–37

Poggi, G. (1991) 'Lo stato sfidato', *Rivista Italiana di Scienza Politica*, 21, 2: 191–221

Policy Studies Institute (1992) *Understanding the Underclass*, London, PSI

Pollert, A. (1985) *Unequal Opportunities: Racial Discrimination and the Youth Training Scheme*, Birmingham, Birmingham Trade Union Resource Centre

Pomian, K. (1990) *L'Europe et ses nations*, Paris, Gallimard.

Portes, A. and Böröcz, J. (1989) 'Contemporary Immigration: Theoretical Perspectives on its Determinants and Modes of Incorporation', *International Migration Review*, 23, 87: 606–30

Power, J. (1979) *Migrant Workers in Western Europe and the United States*, Oxford, Pergamon

Praag, C. van (1984) *Evenredigheid en toegankelijkheid*, Rijswijk

Pugliese, E. (1990) 'Gli immigrati nel mercato del lavoro', *Polis*, 1: 71–93

Purcell, J. N. (1990) 'Statement by the Director General of the IOM' presented at the IOM Seminar on Migration, Geneva

Quinn, D. B. 1966, *The Elizabethans and the Irish*, Ithaca, Cornell University Press

Race and Class (1991) Special Issue: 'Europe: Variations on a Theme of Racism', vol. 32, no.3, (January –March)

Ramazanoglu, C. (1989) *Feminism and the Contradictions of Oppression*, London, Routledge

Rath, J. (1991) *Minorisering: de sociale constructie van 'etnische minderheden'*, Amsterdam, University of Amsterdam

Rath, J. Groenendijk K. and Penninx, R. (1991) 'The Recognition and Institutionalization of Islam in Belgium, Great Britain and the Netherlands', *New Community*, 18, 1: 101–14

Rath, J. and Saggar, S. (1992) 'Ethnicity as a Political Tool in Britain and the Netherlands', in A. M. Messina, L. R. Fraga, L. A. Rhodebeck and F. D. Wright (eds), *Ethnic and Racial Minorities in Advanced Industrial Democracies*, New York, Greenwood Press

Räthzel, N. (1991) 'Germany: One Race, One Nation?' *Race and Class*, 32, 3: 31–48

Raulet, G. (1990) 'Citizenship, Nationality and Internationality', *Contemporary European Affairs*, 3, 3: 150–70

Bibliography

Reeves, F. (1983) *British Racial Discourse*, Cambridge, Cambridge University Press

Regeringens Proposition 1989–90/86 (1990) *Om Åtgärder mot Etnisk Diskriminering m.m*, Stockholm, Riksdagen

Renaut, A. (1989) *L'Ere de l'individu*, Paris, Gallimard

Reubsaet, T. J. and Kropman, J. A. (1985) *Beeldvorming over etnische groepen bij de werving en selectie van personeel*, Nijmegen, ITS

Rex, J. (1986) *Race and Ethnicity*, Milton Keynes, Open University Press

_____(1970) *Race Relations in Sociological Theory*, London, Weidenfeld and Nicolson

_____(1988) *The Ghetto and the Underclass*, Aldershot, Avebury

_____(forthcoming) *Race and Ethnicity in Europe*, London, Longmans

Rex, J. and Mason, D. (eds), (1986) *Theories of Race and Ethnic Relations*, Cambridge, Cambridge University Press

Rex, J., Joly, D. and Wilpert, C. (1987) *Immigrant Associations in Europe*, Aldershot, Gower

Reyneri, E. (1991) 'L'immigrazione extra-comunitaria in Italia: prospettive, caratteristiche, politiche', *Polis*, 5, 1: 145–55

Rich, P. (1986) *Race and Empire in British Politics*, Cambridge, Cambridge University Press

Riggs, F. W. (1991) 'Ethnicity, Nationalism, Race, Minority. A Semantic/Onomatic Exercise (Part One)', *International Sociology*, 6/3: 281–305

Roberts, K., Connolly, M. and Parsell, G. (1992) 'Black Youth in the Liverpool Labour Market', *New Community*, 18, 2: 209–28

Rose, J. (1986) *Sexuality in the Field of Vision*, London, Verso

Rose, S., Kamin, J. and Lewontin, R. C. (1984) *Not In Our Genes*, Harmondsworth, Pelican

Rulf, D. (1992) 'Berlins Rechte im Wartestand', *Die Tageszeitung*, 14 April

Runnymede Trust (1987) 'Combating Racism in Europe. A Report to the European Communities', London

Rusconi, G. E. (1991) 'Se l'identità nazionale non è più motivo di solidarismo', Il *Mulino*, 333, (January–February): 37–46

Ruth, A. (1986) 'Myten om kulturell apartheid', *Dagens Nyheter*, 30 November, p. 4

Ryan, W. (1976) *Blaming the Victim*, revised ed., New York, Vintage Books

Saghal, G. and Yuval-Davis, N. (1991) 'Le Fondamentalisme, le multiculturalisme et les femmes', *Les Temps Modernes*, 540–1: 258–70

Said, E. (1978) *Orientalism*, New York, Random House

_____(1981) *Covering Islam: How the Media and the Experts Determine How We See the Rest of the World*, New York, Pantheon

Sassen, S. (1988) *The Mobility of Labor and Capital*, Cambridge, Cambridge University Press

Satzewich, V. (1989) 'Racisms: The Reactions to Chinese Migrants in Canada at the turn of the Century', *International Sociology*, 4, 3: 311–27

Scheidges, R. (1992) 'Fritz' – oder warum Eugen W. kein Deutscher sein darf',

Der Tagesspiegel, 2 February

Sciortino, G. (1991a) 'Immigration into Europe and Public Policy: Do Stops Really Work?' *New Community*, 18, 1: 89–99.

_____(1991b) 'Migrazioni internazionali e ricerca sociale: qualche riflessione', *Dimensioni dello Sviluppo*, 1, 2: 194–210.

Scoppola, P. (1991) 'Una incerta cittadinanza italiana', *Il Mulino*, 333 (January–February): 47–53

Scott, M. B. and Lyman, S. M. (1968) 'Accounts: Inquiries in the Social Construction of Reality', *American Sociological Review*, 33: 46–62

See, K. O. (1986) 'Ideology and Racial Stratification: a Theoretical Juxtaposition', *Ethnic and Racial Studies*, 6, 1: 75–89

Segal, L. (1987) *Is The Future Female?* London, Virago Press

_____(1990) *Slow Motion: Changing Masculinities, Changing Men*, London, Virago Press

Seidel-Pielen, E. (1991) 'Vieles war schon vorher hier', Interview with Bernd Wagner, *Der Tagesspiegel*, 18 July

Sekaran, U. and Leong, F. (eds), (1992) *Womanpower: Managing in Times of Demographic Turbulence*, Newbury Park, CA, Sage

Seksig, A. (1990) 'Schools and Cultures in France: Pitfalls and Prospects', *Contemporary European Affairs* 3, 3

Sideri S. and Sengupta, J. (eds.) (1992) *The 1992 Single European Market and the Third World*, Geneva, European Assoication of Development Research and Training Institutes

Siegler, B. (1992) 'Rechte wollen Wende zu ganz Deutschland', *Die Tageszeitung*, 7 April

_____(1992) '1991 über 2,000 rassistische Straftaten', *Die Tageszeitung*, 2 January

Sikking, E. and Brassé P. (1987) 'Waar liggen de grenzen?' *LBR-Reeks*, no.4

Silverman, M. (1992) *Immigration, Race and Nation in Modern France*, London, Routledge

Silverman, M. (ed.) (1991) *Race, Discourse and Power in France*, Aldershot, Avebury

Sivanandan, A. (1989) 'New Circuits of Imperialism', *Race and Class*, 30, 4: 1–21

_____(1982) *A Different Hunger: Writings on Black Resistance*, London, Pluto Press

_____(1985) 'Race and the Degradation of Black Struggle', *Race and Class*, 26, 4: 1–35

_____(1988) 'The New Racism', *New Statesman and Society*, 4 November: 8–9

_____(1991) 'Editorial', *Race and Class*, 32, 3: v–vi

Skellington, R. and Morris, P. (1992) *'Race' in Britain Today*, London, Sage

Skocpol, T. and Somers, M. (1980) 'The Uses of Comparative History in Macrosocial Inquiry' *Comparative Studies in Society and History*, 22, 2: 174–97

Small, S. (1989) 'Racial Differentiation in the Slave Era: A Comparative Analysis of People of "Mixed-Race" in Jamaica and Georgia', unpublished PhD dissertation, University of California, Berkeley

_____(1991a) 'Attaining Racial Parity in the United States and England; We Got to Go Where the Greener Grass Grows!' *Sage Race Relations Abstracts*, 16, 3: 3–55

_____(1991b) 'Racialised Relations in Liverpool: A Contemporary Anomaly', *New Community*, 11, 4: 511–37

Smith, D. J. (1977) *Racial Disadvantage in Britain*, Harmondsworth, Penguin

Smith, S. J. (1989) *The Politics of 'Race' and Residence: Citizenship, Segregation and White Supremacy in Britain*, Cambridge and London, Polity Press

Solomos, J. (1988) *Black Youth, Racism and the State: The Politics of Ideology and Policy*, Cambridge, Cambridge University Press

_____(1989) *Race and Racism in Contemporary Britain*, Basingstoke, Macmillan

_____(1990) 'Changing Forms of Racial Discourse', *Social Studies Review*, 6, 2: 74–8

_____(1991) 'The Politics of Racial Equality and the Local State', *Local Government Studies* 17, 2: 33–46

SOPEMI (1990) *OECD Continuous Reporting System on Migration Report 1989*, Paris, OECD

_____(1991) *OECD Continuous Reporting System on Migration Report 1990*, Paris, OECD

SOS Racismo (1992) *Guia Antin Racista* (Edicao SOS Racismo), Lisbon

Spellman, E. V. (1988) *Inessential Woman: Problems of Exclusion in Feminist Thought*, London, Women's Press

Spivak, G. (1987) *In Other Worlds: Essays in Cultural Politics*, London, Methuen

Suarez-Orozco, M. (1990) 'Migration and Education: United States-Europe Comparisons', in G. A. De Vos and M. Suarez-Orozco, *The Self In Culture*, Newbury Park, CA, London, New Delhi, Sage

_____(1991) 'Variability in Minority Schooling. U.S.-Europe Comparisons', *Anthropology and Education*, 22, 2: 99–120

Summers, A. (1981) 'The Character of Edwardian Nationalism', in P. Kennedy and A. Nicholls (eds), *Nationalist and Racialist Movements in Britain and Germany before 1914*, London, Macmillan

Sunier, T. (1991) 'Wie heeft er belang bij 300 publicaties per jaar?' in *Buitenlanders Bulletin*, 4

Tagesspiegel (1992) 'Junge Mäinner schlugen auf Passanten ein', 15 April

Taguieff, P.-A. (1988) *La Force du préjugé*, Paris, La Découverte

_____(1990) 'The New Cultural Racism in France', *Telos*, 83: 109–122

_____(ed) (1991) *Face au racisme*, Paris, La Découverte

Tang Nain, G (1990) 'Black Women, Sexism and Racism: Black or Anti-Racist?' *Feminist Review*, 37: 1–23

Tapinos, G. P. (1990) *Development Assistance Strategies and Emigration Pres-*

Bibliography

sure in Europe and Africa, Washington DC Commission for the Study of International Migration and Co-operative Economic Development

Tassello, G. (1990) 'La conferenza nazionale dell'immigrazione', *Studi Emigrazione*, 98: 146–50

Taylor, M. (1991) 'Community Development and the European Community', *Community Development Journal*, 26, 2: 81–4

Tedeschi, J. T. (ed.) (1981) *Impression Management. Theory and Social Psychological Research*, New York, Academic Press

Tedeschi, J. T. and Reiss, M. (1981) 'Identities, the Phenomenal Self, and Laboratory Research', in J. T. Tedeschi (ed), *Impression Management: Theory and Social Psychological Research*, New York, Academic Press

ter Wal, J. (1991) 'Linguaggio del pregiudizio etnico', *Politica ed Economia*, 4, (April): 33–48

Tilly, C. (1990) *Coercion, Capital, and European States, AD 990–1990*, Oxford, Basil Blackwell

Toren, N. (1969) 'Semi-professionalism', in A. Etzioni (ed), *The Semi-professions and their Organisations*, New York, The Free Press

Touraine, A. (1984) *Le Retour de l'acteur*, Paris, Fayard

Tristan, A. (1987) *Au front*, Paris, Gallimard

Trow, M. (1979) *Elite and Mass Higher Education: American Models and European Realities in National Boards of Universities and Colleges*, Stockholm, Research on Higher Education Program

_____ (1988) 'Comparative Perspectives on Higher Education Policy in the UK and the US', *Oxford Review of Education*, 14, 1: 81–96

Tunander, O. (1990) 'Vi bygger en ny mur', *Dagens Nyheter*, 30 August

UNESCO (1951) *Race and Science*, New York, Columbia University Press

_____ (1980) *Sociological Theories: Race and Colonialism*, Paris, UNESCO

UNHCR (United Nations High Commissioner for Refugees) (1989) *Assessment of Global Resettlement Needs and Priorities for Refugees in 1990*, Geneva, UNHCR Resettlement Service

Uyl, R. den, Choenni, C. and Bovenkerk, F. (1986) 'Mag het ook een buitenlander wezen', *LBR-reeks*, no.2

van Dijk, T. A. (1984) *Prejudice in Discourse*, Amsterdam, Benjamins

_____ (1987) *Communicating Racism*, Newbury Park, CA, Sage

_____ (1991) *Racism and the Press*, London, Routledge

_____ (1993) *Elite Discourse and Racism*, Newbury Park, CA, Sage

Veenman, J. (1990) *De arbeidsmarktpositie van allochtonen in Nederland, in het bijzonder van Molukkers*, Groningen, Wolters Noordhoff

Verdery, K. (1985) 'The Unmaking of an Ethnic Collectivity: Transylvania's Germans', *American Ethnologist*: 62–83

Vita Italiana (1990) 'Da immigrati a cittadini', no. 1 (January–February): 89–102

von Kreitor, N. K. (1980) *Minoritet, kultur, identitet. En antologi*, Borås, Invandrarförlaget

Walby, S. (1990) *Theorizing Patriarchy*, Oxford, Basil Blackwell

Bibliography

Waldinger, R., Aldrich, H. and Ward, R. (1990) *Ethnic Entrepreneurs: Immigrant Business in Industrial Societies*, Newbury Park, CA, London, New Delhi, Sage Publications

Wallerstein, I. (1990) 'Culture as the Ideological Battleground of the Modern World System', *Theory, Culture and Society*, 7, 2–3: 31–56

Wallman, S. (ed.) (1979) *Ethnicity at Work*, London, Macmillan

Waters, M. C. (1990) *Ethnic Options. Choosing Identities in America*, Berkeley and Los Angeles, University of California Press

Watson, M. (ed.) (1990) *Contemporary Minority Nationalism*, London, Routledge

Webber, F. (1991) 'From Ethnocentrism to Euro-racism', *Race and Class*, 32, 3: 11–18

Weber, E. (1977) *Peasants into Frenchmen: The Modernisation of Rural France 1870–1914*, London, Chatto and Windus

Weber-Kellermann I. (1978) *Zur Interethnik*, Frankfurt, Suhrkamp Verlag

Weedon, C. (1987) *Feminist Practice and Poststructuralist Theory*, Oxford, Basil Blackwell

Weil, P. (1991) *La France et ses étrangers*, Paris, Calmann-Lévy

Weiner, G. and Arnot, M. (eds), (1987) *Gender Under Scrutiny*, London, Hutchinson

Weir, M. (1993) 'From Equal Opportunity to '"The New Social Contract"': Race and the Politics of the American Underclass', in M. Cross and M. Keith (eds), *Racism, the City and the State*, London, Routledge

Weiss, L. (1988) 'Explaining the Underground Economy: State and Social Structure', *The British Journal of Sociology*, 38, 2: 216–34

Wellman, D. (1977) *Portraits of White Racism*, Cambridge, Cambridge University Press

Westin, C. (1987) *Den toleranta opinionen: inställningen till invandrare 1987*, report no. 8, Stockholm, DEIFO

(1990) *Encounters. The Uganda Asians in Sweden*, report no.14, Stockholm University, Centre for Research in International Migration and Ethnic Relations

Wieviorka, M. (1990) 'Les Bases du national-populisme', *Le Débat*, September: 35–41

    (1991) *L'Espace du racisme*, Paris, Seuil

    (1992) *La France raciste*, Paris, Seuil

Wihtol de Wenden, C. (1988) *Les Immigrés et la politique*, Paris, Presses de la Fondation Nationale des Sciences Politiques

Willemsen, G. (1988) 'Minderheden op de arbeidsmarkt: de gevolgen van een verkeerd geïnspireerde politiek', *Migrantenstudies*, 4, 1: 50–66

Williams, R. (1990) *Hierarchical Structures and Social Value. The Creation of Black and Irish Identities in the United States*, Cambridge, Cambridge University Press

Willier, D. (1992) 'Die Reps fühlen sich von der CDU 1992 um ihre Themen betrogen', *Die Tageszeitung*, 7 April

Bibliography

Willis, P. (1977) *Learning to Labour*, Aldershot, Saxon House

Wilpert, C. (1983) 'Minorities' Influence on the Majority: Reactions of the Majority in Political, Institutional, and Social Scienific Spheres', in C. Fried (ed), *Minorities: Community and Identity*, Berlin, Springer Verlag

———(1984) 'International Migration and Ethnic Minorities: New Fields for Post-war Sociology in the FDR', *Current Sociology*, 32, 3: 305–52

———(1990) 'Racism – the Blindspot of Migration Research in the Federal Republic of Germany', paper for Congress on Racism and Migration in Europe, Hamburg, 27–30 September 1990

———(1991) 'Migration and Ethnicity in a Non-immigration Country – Foreigners in a United Germany', *New Community*, 18, 1: 49–62

Wilson, W. J. (1978) *The Declining Significance of Race*, Chicago, University of Chicago Press

(1987) *The Truly Disadvantaged: The Inner City, the Underclass and Public Policy*, Chicago, University of Chicago Press

Womack, P. (1989) *Improvement and Romance: Constructing the Myth of the Highlands*, London, Macmillan

Wrench, J. (1987) 'The Unfinished Bridge: YTS and Black Youth', in B. Troyna (ed), *Racial Inequality in Education*, London, Tavistock

———(1990a) 'Employment and the Labour Market', *New Community*, 16, 2: 275–87

———(1990b) 'New Vocationalism, Old Racism and the Careers Service', *New Community*, 16, 3: 425–40

Wrench, J. and Reid, E. (1990) 'Race Relations Research in the 1990s: Mapping Out an Agenda', Occasional Paper in Ethnic Relations no. 5, CRER, University of Warwick

Wrench, J. and Phizacklea, A. (1991) *Report on Visit to Emilia Romagna 15 May–18 May, 1991*, University of Warwick (unpublished)

WRR (1979) *Ethnic Minorities*, The Hague

WRR (1977) *Over sociale ongelijkheid. Een beleidsgerichte probleemverkenning*, The Hague

WRR (1989) *Allochtonenbeleid*, The Hague

WRR (1990) *Een werkend perspectief*, The Hague

Zanchetta, P. L. (1991) *Essere stranieri in Italia*, Milan, Franco Angeli

Zegers de Beijl, R. (1990) *Discrimination of Migrant Workers in Western Europe*, Geneva, International Labour Office Working Paper

———(1991) *Although Equal before the Law: The Scope of Anti-discrimination Legislation and its Effect on Labour Market Discrimination against Migrant Workers in the United Kingdom, the Netherlands and Sweden*, Geneva, International Labour Office Working Paper

Zolberg, A. R. (1989) 'The Next Waves: Migration Theory for a Changing World', *International Migration Review*, 23, 3: 403–30

Notes on Contributors

Aleksandra Ålund teaches in the Department of Sociology at the University of Umea. She has researched and written widely on the politics of multiculturalism in Sweden. She has co-authored *Paradoxes of Multiculturalism: Essays on Swedish Society* (1991), among other books.

Avtar Brah is Senior Lecturer in Multicultural Studies in the Centre for Extra-Mural Studies at Birkbeck College, University of London. She has written widely on aspects of race, gender and ethnicity, and has recently published *Working Choices: South Asian Young Women and the Labour Market* (1992).

Stephen Castles is the Director of the Centre for Multicultural Studies at the University of Wollongong. He has researched and written widely on migrant labour in Western Europe and in Australia, including *Immigrant Workers and Class Structure in Western Europe* (1973) and *Here for Good: Western Europe's New Ethnic Minorities* (1984).

Philomena Essed works at the Institute for Development Research in the University of Amsterdam. She has researched and written widely on the relationship between racism and sexism, including *Everyday Racism* (1990) and *Understanding Everyday Racism* (1991).

Tomas Hammar works in the Centre for Research in International Migration and Ethnic Relations at Stockholm University. Among his numerous publications on aspects of immigration policy are *European Immigration Policy* (1985) and *Democracy and the Nation State* (1990).

Cathie Lloyd is a Research Fellow at the Centre for Research in Race and Ethnic Relations at the University of Warwick. She has researched and written widely on racism and politics in France, and is currently working on a study of the role of racism in a number of European societies.

Helma Lutz is a researcher at the University of Utrecht where she is conducting a research project on the position of Surinamese women in the labour market. She has researched and written widely on the experiences of migrant women in the labour market.

Robert Miles is a Reader in the Department of Politics and Sociology at the University of Glasgow. He has written widely on the changing forms of racism and migrant labour in contemporary societies, including *Racism and Migrant Labour* (1982), *Capitalism and Unfree Labour* (1987) and *Racism* (1989).

Jan Rath works in the Institute for the Sociology of Law at the Catholic University, Nijmegen. He has researched and written on the role of ethnicity and minority politics in Holland, including *Minorisering: de sociale constructie van 'etnische minderheden'* (1991).

Carl-Ulrik Schierup is Associate Professor in the Department of Sociology at the University of Umea. He has carried out research on multiculturalism in Sweden and on migration policy in Yugoslavia. Among his publications are *Migration, Socialism and the International Division of Labour* (1990) and *Paradoxes of Multiculturalism: Essays on Swedish Society* (1991).

Stephen Small is a Lecturer in the Department of Sociology, University of Leicester. He has previously worked in the Department of Sociology at the University of Massachusetts, Amherst. He has carried out research on aspects of racialisation in both the United States and Britain and is currently writing a book which seeks to compare the two societies.

John Solomos is Reader in Public Policy, Department of Politics and Sociology, Birkbeck College, University of London. He has researched and written widely on aspects of politics and social change in contemporary Britain, and is currently working on a study of the dynamics of racial politics in Birmingham. His books include *Race and Racism in Contemporary Britain* (1989) and *Race and Local Politics* (1990).

Teun A. van Dijk is Professor of Discourse Studies at the University of Amsterdam. Much of his research has focused on the analysis of news in the press, and especially the reproduction of racism in discourse and communication. Among his many books are *Communicating Racism* (1987), *News Analysis* (1988) and *Racism and the Press* (1991).

Ellie Vasta is a Lecturer in the Department of Sociology at the University of Wollongong. She has carried out research on Italian migration to Australia and is currently researching aspects of immigration and racism in Italy.

Michel Wieviorka is Director of Studies in the Centre d'Analyse et d'Intervention Sociologiques. He has carried out research in a number of areas and much of his recent work has focused on the issue of racism in France. Among his books are *L'Espace du racisme* (1991) and *La France raciste* (1992).

Czarina Wilpert works in the Institut für Soziologie, Technische Universität Berlin. She has researched and written on aspects of immigration and racism in Germany and on family and generational change among migrant communities. Among her books are *Immigrant Associations in Europe* (1987).

John Wrench is Senior Research Fellow in the Centre for Research in Ethnic Relations, University of Warwick. He has researched and written widely on a number of aspects of racism and the labour market, equal opportunity policies and racism and trade unions. Among his publications are *Ethnic Minorities and the Careers Service* (1990).

Index

Africa
  North, 4, 56
Africans, 79
African-Caribbean(s), 160, 161, 196–8
Albanian migrants, 26, 84–98 *passim*
Aldrich, H., 23
Algeria, 59
Allen, S., 255
Allen, W. R., 236
Ålund, A., 29, 83, 105–7, 109, 113–4, 154, 221
Anderson, B., 47
Anthias, F., 137, 140, 210, 218–20
Anti-discrimination legislation, 17–8, 151–2, 153
Antilleans, 145, 147, 155
Anti-racism, 8, 17, 100, 107, 108, 195
Anti-semitism, 39, 42–3, 48, 50, 80–1
Apartheid, 182
Arab, 29, 59, 80
Ascherson, N., 42
Asia,
  migration and, 22–8 *passim*
Asian, 196–7
Australia, 32
Austria, 4

Bacci, L., 98
Balibar, E., 3–4, 25, 27, 35–7, 43, 259
Banton, M., 158–9, 234, 245
Barker, M., 35–6, 41, 64, 108, 219
Barrera, M., 236–7
Barrett, M., 206–7, 211
Barzun, J., 47
Balbo, L., 89, 93, 98
Baldwin-Edwards, M., 255, 262
Belgium, 27, 64, 221
Bergmann, W., 81
Billig, M., 42
'Black', 195–200
Blaschke, J., 24, 104
Blumer, H., 247
Bovenkerk, F., 4, 50, 137, 145–6, 215–6, 238–9, 244, 251
Brah, A., 25, 200, 203, 206
Britain, 4, 14, 27, 35, 41, 44, 45, 184, 185, 218–21, 231–2

Brock, C., 247
Brown, C., 161
Brubaker, W. R., 6, 28, 50, 91, 252
Bryan, B., 205

Cain, H., 199
Campani, G., 86–7, 95
Canada, 19, 29, 32
Carby, H., 206, 208
Carter, B., 233, 238, 245
Castles, S., 4, 20, 25–6, 44, 90, 104, 108, 241, 247
CCCS Race and Politics Group, 41
Chevalier, L., 47
Citizens, 117–8
Citizenship
  dual, 127–8
  multiculturalism and, 11–14, 30, 70, 73, 91–2, 115–28 *passim*
Cohen, P., 25, 42
Cohen, R., 4–5, 30, 105, 247
Conversi, D., 51
Council of Europe, 116, 127
Couper, K., 259
Cross, M., 166, 244

Daily Mail, 184
Daily Telegraph, 183–6
Daniel, W. W., 145, 159, 246
Davis, A., 239
De Rudder, V., 260
Deem, R., 203
Dench, G., 113
Denizens, 117–28 *passim*
Denmark, 122–3, 125
Desir, H., 56
Difference, 195, 211–14
Donald, J., 8
Dubet, F., 260
Duffield, M., 108
Dummett, A., 259

Education, 137–41
Edwards, P., 244
Elias, N., 46
Employment
  racism in, 160–2, 163, 165, 167

Index

young people and, 162–72
'Enemies within', 6, 24
Essed, P., 42, 108, 145–6, 150–1, 154–5, 180, 221
Ethnic descent, 73–4
Ethnic absolutism, 113
Ethnic minorities, 17
Ethnic minorisation, 222
Ethnicity, 6, 110, 112, 139, 140, 218, 219
Europe
    Eastern, 3–4, 51
    racism in, 6, 7–8, 11, 15, 17, 35, 42, 48, 63, 65, 145, 157, 215–16
    Western, 3–4, 50
European Community, 25, 36, 78, 215, 245, 255–6
'European identity', 4, 6, 26, 43–4, 51
'European racism', 3, 36–41 passim
Evrigenis, G., 254

Farley, R., 236
Fascist groups, 35
Feminism
    black, 202, 203, 204–10 passim
    race and, 195–6, 201, 205
    white, 204–10
Fernandez, J. P., 154
Feuchtwang, S., 108, 110
Forbes, I., 172–3
Ford, G., 254
'Fortress Europe' 29, 83, 99, 101, 103
Foster, C. R., 48
France, 4, 15, 27, 28, 38, 43, 44, 45, 48, 55–65 passim, 91, 99, 123, 126, 162, 187, 188, 189, 237–8, 261–2
Front National, 8, 55–6, 62, 63, 189–92, 239

Gaspard, F., 55
Gates, H. L., 40
Genocide, 6
Germans
    ethnic, 70–2
Germany, 4, 15, 23–4, 27, 28, 38, 49, 65, 67–81 passim, 91, 116, 117, 138, 139, 187, 188, 237–8
    East, 67–8, 78, 81
    'guestworkers' in, 19, 24, 71, 75
    national identity in, 49–50, 71–2, 78–9
    racism in, 67, 69, 74, 75, 77, 81
Gilroy, P., 25, 35, 108, 113, 199, 218, 242
Goldberg, D. T., 8, 39, 41
Gordon, P., 238, 243, 256
Gramsci, A., 76
Grant, B., 235
Green, M., 233, 245

Grewal, S., 206
Guardian, The, 236, 245, 262
Gulf War, 182

Haiti, 56
Hall, S., 41, 213–4, 216–7, 218–9
Hammar, T., 3, 12, 99
Hannerz, U., 111
Hansard, 175
Hazareesingh, S., 197, 199–200
Hechter, M., 46
Heisler, B. S., 9
Hobsbawm, E., 45, 47
Holmes, C., 42, 50
Husbands, C., 4

Identity, 213–14
Immigration,
    controls on, 6, 31, 103
    politics of, 5–7, 71, 221–23
    social policy and, 12–3
Independent, The, 43
India, 160
International Labour Organisation, 158, 160
Institutional racism, 74–6, 81
Ireland, 48–9
Islam, 182, 223–31
Italy, 4, 15, 29, 45, 63–4, 83–98 passim
    Albanian migrants in, 84–7
    emigration from, 83–4
    racism in, 91–7
    types of migrants in, 86–7

Jackson, P., 245
Japan, 116
Jenkins, R., 148
Jones, G. S., 47
Joshi, S., 238

Karlsson, L. G., 103
Kempadoo, K., 136, 146
Knowles, C., 208–9
Koch, L., 94–5, 98
Korea, 22
Kosack, G., 20, 25–6, 90
Ku Klux Klan, 239

Labour market
    discrimination in the, 145–7, 149–50, 153–5
    migrants in the, 20–1, 92–3
Lapeyronnie, D., 254, 257
Lash, S., 101
Latin America, 127
Layton-Henry, Z., 3, 12, 252

Index

Lee, G., 164
Lega Lombarda, 63, 92
Leipzig, 68
Le Pen, 189
Lewis, G., 206
Lieberson, S., 236–7
Light, I., 23
Lloyd, C., 3, 233, 237–8, 246, 261
Los Angeles, 8
  1992 riots in, 8, 10
Lutz, H., 137, 139, 225, 232, 239
Mama, A., 206, 239
Martiniello, M., 95, 221
Maastricht Treaty, 158
McDonald, M., 48
Memmi, A., 43–4, 223
Mercer, S., 208–9
Migrant labour, 17–34 *passim*
Migration
  changing forms of, 18–9, 31–2
  economic policies and, 21–2
  population growth and, 19–20
Miles, R., 3–4, 7–8, 25, 35, 38, 42–3, 46–7,
  140, 217–23 *passim*, 231, 233–4, 237,
  240, 245
Minh-ha, T., 213
Minority rights, 29–30
Modood, T., 197, 199, 218–20, 223
Mohanty, C. T., 200
Moluccans, 144, 145
Moore, R., 235, 239–40
Moroccans, 130, 131, 155, 222
Morokvasic, M., 136
Mosse, G., 42, 47
Movimento Sociale Italiano, 63, 92
Mullard, C., 144
Multiculturalism, 17, 29–30, 33, 108, 109,
  112
Murray, N., 181
Muslim communities, 13–4, 27, 58–9, 104,
  223–31
Myrdal, G., 9

Nairn, T., 45, 48
National Front, 63
Nationalism
  ethnic, 70–2
  national identity and, 27–8, 47, 51,
  70–2
  racism and, 26, 35–6, 44–50 *passim*,
  216, 262, 263
Nationality, 116
Neo-nazis, 35, 79–80, 81
Netherlands, 10, 29, 38, 44, 64, 125,

129–42 *passim*, 143–56 *passim*, 187,
  221, 222, 223–31
  policy towards immigrants, 144
New racism, 36–41 *passim*, 64–5
Newnham, A., 161
Noiriel, G., 45, 260
Norway, 122–3, 125

Omi, M., 233, 238, 241, 245
'Other' The, 46, 50–2
Ostow, R., 80
Pakistanis, 79, 160
Panayi, P., 50
Parmar, P., 206
Patterson, H., 49
Pettigrew, T. F., 69, 78, 146
Phizacklea, A., 23, 89, 91, 136, 237, 240,
  246
Phoenix, A., 206
Pieterse, J. N., 238
Piliawsky, M., 243
Poggi, G., 93
Poland, 24, 80
Policy Studies Institute, 161
Political participation
  migrants and, 17, 76, 90, 91, 93, 94,
  115–28 *passim*
Positive action, 143–4, 155–6
Public policy
  immigration and, 16, 28–32 *passim*

Quinn, D. B., 49

Race
  as social category, 5, 30, 47, 195
Race relations
  research on, 58–9, 245–6
  sociology of, 5–6, 35–6
Race Relations Act 1976, 173, 185
Racial discrimination, 10–11, 158–9, 162,
  172–3, 174
Racial ideologies, 46–8
Racialisation, 46, 215–21, 233–4
Racism
  definition of, 41–44 *passim*, 69, 158–9,
  192–3, 208, 209
  denial of, 11, 143–4, 157, 179–80, 181,
  183, 184, 185
  elite discourse and, 179–93
  in Europe, 4–8 *passim*, 25–7, 174–5,
  215–6
  new, 36, 37, 39, 158
Racist ideologies, 8, 70–2, 216–18
Racist violence, 4–8, 50, 69, 79–80

Index

Ramazanoglu, C., 207–8
Rath, J., 29, 145, 216, 222–4
Räthzel, N., 49, 237–8
Rattansi, A., 8
Reeves, F., 245
Refugees, 17–20
Pepublican Party, 80
Rex, J., 9, 234, 253
Reyneri, E., 94
Rose, S., 201
Rotterdam, 225–9
Rusconi, G. E., 92–3
Rushdie, S., 13–4, 59, 182

Said, E., 182, 225
Salisbury Review, 238
Sassen, S., 21–2
Satzewich, V., 245
Scandinavia, 14, 115–28 *passim*
Schengen, 19
Schierup, C.-U., 28, 83, 105–7, 109, 113–4, 154, 221
Sciortino, G., 95–6
Scoppola, P., 93
Scotland, 48
Second Generation, 29, 162–4
See, K. O., 71
Segal, L., 201–2
Siegler, B., 79
Silverman, M., 221, 260
Sivanandan, A., 36, 199, 241
Skellington, R., 175
Skinheads, 69, 182
Skocpol, T., 244
Small, S., 8, 235, 240, 245
Smith, D., 145
Smith, S., 245
Solomos, J., 6, 108, 166, 218, 251
SOPEMI, 18, 31, 86, 88–9
Soviet Union, 4
Spellman, E. V., 202
Spivak, G., 214
Suarez-Orozco, M., 244
Surinamese, 145, 147, 155
Sweden 15, 29, 99–114 *passim*
    immigration to, 101–2
    multiculturalism in, 99–100, 221

Taguieff, P.-A., 40–1, 43
Third Reich, 71, 72–3
Tilly, C., 43
Trevi, 19
Tunander, O., 103–4
Turkey, 56, 137

Turkish women, 137–41, 253
Turks, 65, 75, 76, 79, 80, 81, 104, 130, 131, 155, 222–31 *passim*, 237–8

Underclass
    race and the, 8–11, 162
Ulster, 49
UNESCO, 40, 253
United Kingdom, 15, 41, 49, 64, 157–76 *passim*, 187
United Nations, 158
United States of America, 19, 22, 42, 162, 187, 188, 233–49 *passim*
    immigration to the, 32
    racism in, 8, 15
Urry, J., 101

van Dijk, T. A., 42, 179, 181–2, 187, 221
Vasta, 26
Vietnamese, 79

Walby, S., 206
Waldinger, R., 24
Wallerstein, I., 35, 110
Wallman, S., 141
Ward, R., 23
Waters, M. C., 236, 246
Watson, M., 48
Weber, E., 45, 47
Weedon, C., 202
Weil, P., 90
Weiss, L., 89, 95
Welfare state, 9–10, 22–4, 57, 77, 131
Wellman, D., 42
Westin, C., 100, 109
Wieviorka, M., 27, 57, 63, 260, 263
Williams, R., 245
Wilpert, C., 73, 221, 254
Wilson, W. J., 10, 240, 247
Winant, H., 233, 238, 241
Women
    migrant, 129–31, 135–7, 138, 140
    racism and, , 141, 195, 200–203
Wrench, J., 91, 164, 166, 172, 251, 261

Xenophobia, 67, 77–8, 158

Yugoslavia, 80, 81
Yuval-Davis, N., 199, 210

Zanchetta, P. L., 89–90, 94
Zegers de Beijl, R., 174–5
Zolberg, A., 20

.

Printed in the United States
34439LVS00002B/279

9 781859 730072